Florida's Dark Chapters

ALSO BY MICHAEL G. HALL
AND FROM MCFARLAND

*Small Cities Thinking Big:
Revitalization Lessons from Augusta,
Maine, and Other Communities* (2021)

Florida's Dark Chapters

The Violent, Unsavory and Sometimes Bizarre History of the Sunshine State

MICHAEL G. HALL

McFarland & Company, Inc., Publishers
Jefferson, North Carolina

ISBN (print) 978-1-4766-9121-3
ISBN (ebook) 978-1-4766-5178-1

LIBRARY OF CONGRESS AND BRITISH LIBRARY
CATALOGUING DATA ARE AVAILABLE

Library of Congress Control Number 2024028547

© 2024 Michael G. Hall. All rights reserved

No part of this book may be reproduced or transmitted in any form or by any means, electronic or mechanical, including photocopying or recording, or by any information storage and retrieval system, without permission in writing from the publisher.

Front cover: (top) Map of Florida (Shutterstock); (bottom, left to right) Detail from a hand-colored engraving by Theodore de Bry titled *Sacrifice of the First-Born*, 1591 (National Portrait Gallery); Ku Klux Klan demonstration in Tampa on January 30, 1939 (*Cleveland Plain Dealer*); GeoColor image of Hurricane Irma bearing down on the state in 2017 (NASA); 1990 mugshot of Manuel Noriega in Miami (U.S. Marshals Service)

Printed in the United States of America

McFarland & Company, Inc., Publishers
Box 611, Jefferson, North Carolina 28640
www.mcfarlandpub.com

To all the friends and family
who encouraged me along the way,
and to the insanely hot, humid, crazy state
whose history inspired me to write this book.

"Florida isn't so much a place where one goes to reinvent oneself, as it is a place where one goes if one no longer wished to be found."
—Douglas Coupland

Table of Contents

Preface 1

Introduction: Embracing the Darkness 3

1. Bounty, Belligerency and Bloodlust: Florida in the Age of Exploration 5
2. Dead Man's Chest: Florida's Flirtation with Pirates, Privateers and Pillagers 24
3. A Tale of Two Floridas: Spanish Twilight in the Era of American Expansion 37
4. Guerrillas in the Mist: Florida's Seminole Wars 53
5. In the Shadow of the Big House: Florida, Slavery and Race Relations During the Civil War 68
6. Florida Brews a Revolution 89
7. Boom! Goes the Landscape: Florida on the Brink 103
8. The Era of Blood and Retribution: Florida in the Days of Prohibition and Wise Guys 123
9. We Shall Overcome: Florida in the Dark Days of Xenophobia, Segregation and Purple Panic 139
10. Drugs, Disco and Decadence: Florida in the '70s and '80s 159
11. Blood and Riots: Serial Killers and Destruction in the Twilight of the Twentieth Century 172
12. Politics, Terror and Economic Ruin: Florida Leaves Its Mark on the World 186
13. Retirees of a Different Kind: Dictators and Death Leaders 198

14. Towns Like No Other: Florida's "New" Urbanism	212
15. Demagoguery, Disease and Division: Florida in the Age of DeSantis	225
Conclusion: A Trip Through the Darkness and Back	240
Chapter Notes	241
Bibliography	257
Index	273

Preface

At just over 21 million people, Florida is our third most populous state, but how much do we really know about it? While most people can recount the exploits of the Pilgrims, or list the Civil War battlefields of Virginia, few have any direct knowledge as to the outsized role the people in this peninsula played in shaping North American history. For example, did you know that rivalry over this state led to two different international wars? Or that it was home to more pirate activity than any other place outside the Caribbean? Or that it was the only state to have a direct impact on another country's independence? Even the fact that more ex-dictators have called Florida home than anywhere else in the world has largely escaped the attention of historians.

As a native of Jacksonville, I was steeped in Florida lore from the very get-go. A lover of everything historic, I spent a huge chunk of my childhood exploring the soggy marshlands of the wilds; digging for Timucua arrowheads in my friend's backyard; retracing the paths of Spanish conquistadors in St. Augustine; rummaging through a Civil War sutlery near the Battlefield of Olustee; camping out in an abandoned Spanish-American fort along the St. Johns River; and even driving past an Al Capone hideout on my way to school. Each of these experiences taught me a ton about my home state—things that were often overlooked in all the regular history books I had read. It was these very things that drove me to write this book!

Through a combination of personal knowledge and extensive research utilizing first, second- and third-party resources, I have put together this collection of dark, bizarre, and often overlooked aspects of Florida state history, aspects you're not likely to find in any other book on the market. In so doing, I even learned a few new things myself!

Researched and compiled over a period of ten years and arranged chronologically, this book was indeed a labor of love and one I feel more accurately reflects the true nature of Florida's past—one that goes well beyond the beaches of Miami and the theme parks of Orlando. Stretching back six centuries into the past, I've made sure to include everything from human sacrifices to colonial massacres, drug lords to pandemics, and even the rise of the culture wars, with still plenty to be written about in the future!

So join me on an adventure rarely taken as we delve into Florida's dark chapters and its violent, unsavory and sometimes bizarre history.

Introduction
Embracing the Darkness

When most people purchase a book on American history, chances are they already know what they're going to find before they even open it—Pilgrims landing at Plymouth Rock; George Washington crossing the Delaware; slavery and the American Civil War; Nazis and World War II; and maybe a little something after 9/11. All of this is standardized across most texts, and most of us just assume that's just the way things played out. But did they really?

There have always been groups of people along the way who have decided what to put in and what to leave out in comprehensive history books. Most of them pick these topics depending upon the standards and fashion of the times, placing greater emphasis upon certain things over others. This has especially been a common occurrence throughout American history, which is often whitewashed to support a sanitized narrative, particularly in that group of states in the South.

Enter Florida.

Anyone who has ever traveled to Florida immediately assumes they've got the state figured out. It usually involves the common tropes we see splashed across news and social media: Disney, Miami, alligators, heat, retirees and weird people. As a result, very few people try to dig any deeper.

Even when we do take into account Florida history, it's usually done as an afterthought, with places like Virginia and Massachusetts taking center stage in national prominence, and with Florida maybe garnering a word or two in the Space Race, if mentioned at all. What people fail to realize is that there's another side of Florida history, one with national and international significance.

In the following chapters, I invite you to explore *Florida's Dark Chapters*—the part of Florida's past relegated to the dark, some good and some bad. These events, presented in sequential order and organized by theme, contain everything that has come to make up the Sunshine State: from the surprising, to the weird, to the horrifying, and yes, in some cases, to the inspiring. For this is the history of real Florida, and while not all of it is pretty, it's certainly entertaining.

1

Bounty, Belligerency and Bloodlust

Florida in the Age of Exploration

Florida's bloody roots go all the way back to its initial discovery by the Spanish explorer Juan Ponce de León.

Ponce de León first sighted Florida on April 2, 1513, and he anchored somewhere off the coast of modern-day Melbourne Beach. Describing this new "island" from his ship he wrote that it was "very pretty to behold with many woodlands and was level and uniform."[1] His initial enthusiasm, however, soon faded into bitter disappointment upon further exploration—despite what you might have read in the fictionalized accounts of Spaniards wandering through forests of flowers, it simply didn't happen that way. On the contrary, what was found was a desolate, uninhabited swampland filled with pine trees, scrub palms and thistle bushes of all sorts—a far cry from Ponce de León's prized Island of Bimini, supposedly filled with cities of gold, silver and rubies.

Naming it "Pascua Florida," in honor of the Easter season, he forewent (*thank God*) the more literal name of the land given to him by his Taino guides, who called it "Cautio"—a word that roughly translates to "jockstrap."[2]

Sailing south along the coast, he eventually discovered the Gulf Stream, a swift-moving current that forced his ships to take shelter in Jupiter Inlet. It was here that he encountered the local natives for the first time, who rowed out to their ships attempting "to steal his launch boat and weapons. Two Spaniards were wounded by arrows tipped with bone and fish spines. Their continued assault caused Ponce de León to flee."[3]

This initial attack signaled the beginning of a long and bloody journey ahead, as Ponce de León fearlessly, yet stupidly, journeyed forward.

Rounding the Keys, Ponce de León and his men once again set anchor near Sanibel Island, where, in a fit of déjà vu, they encountered the same scenario as before. Only through the use of an armed longboat did the Spaniards manage to fight the local natives off, chasing them inland, but not before suffering casualties. In spite of this, he managed to make off with "four of the native women,"[4] in a possible attempt at insurance against further molestations.

Though this incident helped ensure an uneasy peace between the two groups for the next few days, it was not to last. Several days later, after anchoring in Charlotte Harbor, Ponce de León and his men were again under attack.

Fending off the natives once more, Ponce de León sailed back to Spain via Puerto Rico, this time in an attempt to get the king to recognize him as governor of Florida and provide him with an armada by which to subdue the native tribes.

Returning in 1521 with 200 men, including priests, soldiers, artisans, and domesticated animals, he came ashore at the vicinity of Charlotte Harbor for the purposes of constructing a settlement.

At this anchorage, the Spaniards were told not to depart by the Calusa people, who said that Carlos, their chief, was going to come by with an offering of gold. Though Carlos did, in fact, come as promised, it was not gold he bore but "a flotilla of 80 armed canoes."[5] The resulting battle forced a hasty retreat by the Spaniards, who now realized effective trade between their groups would be impossible. Ponce De León himself would be mortally wounded during this melee after being struck in the thigh by an arrow dipped in poisonous sap from the "highly toxic manchineel tree."[6]

Stopping off again at Sanibel Island for fresh water and firewood on the journey back to Puerto Rico, a bitter and now dying Ponce de León named the place "Matanca," a Spanish word for killing, "due to the rotting Spaniard and Indian corpses littering the shores."[7] It's highly likely he meant the name to apply to the whole cursed land, as well.

A Different Kind of Native

Given the volatile nature of Ponce de León's first native encounters in 1513, it's hardly a surprise that his attempt at colonization ended so gruesomely in 1521. What is surprising, however, is the "why" factor surrounding it.

As described by the historian Herrera, Ponce de León was hardly a typical conquistador like Hernán Cortés, who had so brutally quelled the Aztecs of Mexico. His second journey into Charlotte Harbor contained hardly any soldiers, and was "made up largely of farmers, artisans and priests."[8] So why on earth did the natives react so violently? Perhaps the answer can be found in the politics of pre–Columbian Florida.

The Politics of Pre-Columbian Bloodlust

If you think Florida is a violent place now, you should've seen it in the 1500s. As a matter of fact, it was downright brutal—and this was well before the arrival of any Europeans onto the scene. A simple glimpse at the native culture shows just how cutthroat it was.

At the time of Ponce de León's explorations, Florida was divided among three main tribes: the Calusa, who occupied the south, the Timucua of the north and the Apalachee of the west. Together, "these tribes accounted for roughly 350,000 people."[9]

Living side by side and often abutting each other's territories, these mostly hunting-gathering tribes competed against each other for arable land, as well as dominance, going so far as to fight open wars of conquest against each other. A prime example of this can be found in the Calusa tribe—the very same that ran off Ponce de León and his men so brutally.

The Calusa people, whose name means "fierce tribe,"[10] exhibited imperial tendencies early on. Conquering huge swaths of south Florida territory, these people warred against the gentler Tequesta tribe of Biscayne Bay, ultimately forcing them into submission. The Calusa king had the power "of life and death over his subjects and was thought by them to be able to intercede with the spirits that sustained the environment's bounty."[11]

Many commoners in the kingdom of the Calusa supported the king through tributes such as "food and material necessities,"[12] and eyewitnesses in later expeditions claimed that the king's chief entertainment space was so large it could accommodate more than 2000 people.[13] Much of this prestige was gained through warfare.

When Ponce de León arrived, he learned just how powerful a reach the king had by finding out that a Tequesta chieftain "was, in turn, a vassal of the more powerful Calusa chief."[14] The fact that the Calusa had a war flotilla, as described earlier by Ponce de León's accounts, is also a testament to just how expansive their territory and trade was, as many of their artifacts, "including their dugouts, came from Mexico."[15]

As fierce as this power struggle was in south Florida, however, it was ever more a part of the Timucua chiefdoms of the north and eastern parts of the peninsula. These tribes were in a constant state of war with frequently changing military alliances.

Warfare, perhaps raids by the Apalachee on the Yustaga/Uzachile or even warfare among Timucuan groups, could have led to the exercise of chieftaincy by war chiefs who sought to form inter-village and inter-group alliances. When the Spanish invaded northern Florida and the French occupied their colony at Fort Caroline, the presence of those Europeans also provided a greater need to exercise chieftaincy, to exercise more complex political entities.[16]

This consistent and almost continuous practice of bloodshed over territory was a far cry from the docile and peace-loving Taínos, whom the Spanish had encountered in the Caribbean. Unlike their island counterparts, these tribes took war seriously, going so far as to fortify some of their villages with "walls, guard shacks and spy holes, so hunters could watch or shoot at enemies."[17]

Further still, early European explorers were quick to describe the use of human sacrifice among some tribes, namely the Timucua. According to

The Timucua tribes populated the northeastern portion of Florida and were among the first natives to live side by side with Europeans in Florida. The Timucua were particularly warlike and were known to fortify their circular villages with palisades. In the mid-sixteenth century, Timucua chiefdoms near Fort Caroline allied themselves with the French in the hopes of employing their services against rival tribes (Architect of the Capitol).

early accounts from French explorers, the sun and moon were the principal objects of adoration among the tribe. This probably means that their beliefs were similar to those of the Creeks and Chickasaw who made regular contact with other Mississippian cultures. A cultish sidebar of this religion included child sacrifice, whereby the first-born son of a prominent tribal member was offered up to the chief. During this ceremony, the grieving mother would sit on her heels, surrounded by female relatives and other friends, who would offer the child to the chief before dancing in a circle. The following account of a ceremony was described by French colonist Jacques Le Moyne:

> She who holds the child goes and dances in the middle, singing some praises of the chief. Meanwhile, six Indians, chosen for the purpose, take their stand apart in a certain place in the open area; and midway among them the sacrificing officer, who is decorated with a sort of magnificence, and holds a club. The ceremonies being through, the sacrificer takes the child, and slays it in honor of the chief, before them all, upon the wooden stump. The offering was on one occasion performed in our presence.[18]

With such a culture of bloodshed in place, it is easy to see why Ponce de León and his men were greeted with such hostility and suspicion. As both outsiders and foreigners, these men appeared as just another threat, and as such were dealt with accordingly. The fact that these foreigners had new weapons only made their desire to attack that much more palpable, as it promised them a new means to overcome other native tribes in battle.

An even more telling explanation of the hostile reception given the Spaniards, however, likely stemmed from European contact well before Ponce de León had even crossed the Caribbean to lay claim to the new land. As it turned out, Florida was well known to slavers and raiding parties well before it was even officially "discovered."

John Cabot and the Discovery of Florida

Although he may get credit for bringing the existence of Florida to greater awareness, Ponce de León was hardly the first European explorer to map the peninsula. That credit goes to John Cabot, the Italian explorer who sailed for England and reached the Florida coast in 1497. Yes, 1497!

Although official logs of his voyages were lost when his boat capsized in 1498,[19] there are several factors that strongly support the fact that Cabot made it to Florida almost 20 years before Ponce de León. One of these is a listing of maps showing a clear outline of the coast of Florida drawn by a series of cartographers shortly after Columbus's Third Voyage.

This engraving was produced for an ambitious illustrated travel account, published in Frankfurt, Germany, in 1591. Here, the artist represents Utina, a Timucua chief, seated beside Laudonnière, explaining the ceremony that unfolds in the distance, whereby a ring of dancing women surrounds a grief-stricken mother, whose infant son is being offered as a human sacrifice to the chief (*Sacrifice of the First-Born*, Theodor de Bry, 1591, National Portrait Gallery, Smithsonian Institution).

Three maps in particular seem to jump from the pages of history: one dated 1500 by Juan de la Cosa and in manuscript form—hand drawn since maps were not yet printed—details British flags along a sprawling coastline north of Cuba. That's likely the northeast coast of the current United States.

But the third is considered the most singular historic prize and one of the key pieces of evidence.... Peter Martyr published it and it was sequestered by the crown. "They tried to get rid of it," says Mr. Schmitt. "They were concerned other folks would get it—the English, the Portuguese—so there are very few remaining copies in the world."[20]

To support these claims, Peter Martyr described a southerly land where "he had the island of Cuba on his left hand almost in the same longitude as himself."[21] He later stated that they had described a flowing westerly current abutting this land, likely the same Gulf Stream Ponce de León found in 1513.

So, if, in fact, this is true, why on earth didn't England take credit for its discovery? Well, in a simple word: politics. At the time of Cabot's discovery, the pope had already divided up all the New World possessions between Spain and Portugal in the Treaty of Tordesillas. Because of this, Henry VII tended to encourage discreet expeditions so as not to incur the wrath of Spain or the papacy. This of course didn't stop the strong-willed Cabot, however, and certainly didn't stop English braggarts from claiming that they, and not the Spanish, were the real discoverers of Florida.

Given the speed of communication at the time between sailors, it's not likely this discovery stayed secret for very long, leading to more nefarious instances of raiding parties coming ashore to take off with new native labor.

Narváez Takes a Shot

As the entire Spanish world wrung its hands in confusion at the disastrous Ponce de León voyage, one explorer stepped up, vowing to subdue "Matanca" once and for all. And given his credentials, it was doubtless that he wouldn't succeed.

When first offered the governorship of Florida by the king of Spain, Pánfilo de Narváez—"a red-haired, one-eyed, monomaniacal conquistador"[22]—had every reason to be assured in his new position. As one of the earliest conquistadors of the New World, Narváez had a ringside seat to the likes of some of the most brutal warriors Spain had ever produced. Narváez himself had played a direct role in the subjugation of the natives of Jamaica in 1509 and was well aware of the brutality employed by Hernán Cortés in Mexico. Thus, at the time of his arrival, Narváez was fully prepared to unleash hell.

Bringing the Terror to Shore

Almost from the start of his landing in Florida, Narváez was uncompromisingly violent. Arriving around the Tampa Bay area in April 1528, Narváez and his men immediately took to ransacking a deserted Indian village.

Like Ponce de León before him, Narváez was convinced that somewhere within Florida lay the famed cities of gold he had heard so often about. He thus made the fateful decision to march inland ransacking more villages along the way to feed his huge army of 400.[23] Thus, when he came upon Chief Hirrihigua's city, he was determined to get the answers he sought.

Through the element of surprise, Narváez and his men were able to catch the unsuspecting natives off guard, forcing them to gather outside their village for questioning. Singling out their chief, Narváez inflicted punishment upon him "with the greatest cruelty, giving his aged mother to be torn to pieces by dogs, for complaining of an outrage which had been committed by one of the Spaniards on the person of a young Indian woman"[24] and then "seized [him] and [and had him] scourged, by order of Narváez, [who then ordered] his nose cut off."[25]

The invaders were quickly told of a land called Apalachen, reputedly to be filled with gold and silver. The natives of the village hastily drew a map and sent them on their way.

The March of Death

For nearly two weeks, the soldiers continued their march north as the heat and humidity weighed them down while food supplies dwindled to nothing. Along the way, the Apalachee harassed the soldiers.

> "The Indians made war on us continually," remembered a survivor, "wounding the people and the horses when we were at the places where we went to get water, and doing this from the lagoons and so safely that we could do them no harm."[26]

Only after another two grueling months did Narváez finally relent and admit that he had been had. Limping feverishly into an Indian village called Aute,[27] in what is now St. Marks National Wildlife Refuge in the corner of the Florida Panhandle, Narváez's soldiers began to talk openly of mutiny, but no one knew exactly where they would go. The trip had disoriented them greatly and many were suffering from a mysterious disease they could not shake. It was ultimately the fear of further guerrilla attacks which caused them to stick together. At their bleakest moment, one of their crew proposed to construct makeshift boats by which they could sail west to the safety of Mexico.

The work to build boats took weeks, and more casualties mounted as the Apalachee cut the helpless men off from any potential sources of food. Only at the brink of a serious discussion of cannibalism did the Spaniards finally agree to slaughter their malnourished horses[28]—naming the estuary the Bay of Horses—in honor of the animals' sacrifice.

Finally sailing in their hastily constructed boats, the remaining 242 survivors[29] became split up by a ferocious hurricane which scattered them across the Gulf Coast, four of them landing on Galveston Beach in Texas. Eight years later, after numerous years in slavery to the various tribes of Texas, the four survivors[30] finally reached Mexico in 1536 and recounted their horrible story. No other members of the expedition had presumably survived.

Ulele and Ortiz: A True Pocahontas Story

While Narváez and his soldiers suffered considerably at the hands of the natives, there is one documented case of some stragglers being treated more kindly by the local tribes, albeit after much initial suffering. One such instance involved a curious case where an abandoned soldier was captured by a tribe and nearly put to death before being rescued by a chieftain's daughter. If this at all sounds familiar, it should; it's essentially the Pocahontas legend, as told nearly 80 years prior to Jamestown, and one that John Smith of historical fame was likely familiar with.

It all began shortly after Narváez left to find the fabled city of Apalachen. Juan Ortiz, a young, 18-year-old soldier, lost sight of his men during the early days of the expedition and was captured by Chief Hirrihigua—the same chief previously mutilated by Narváez. Still angered over his prior humiliation, the vengeful chief sentenced Ortiz to death. Before his execution could be carried out, however, Hirrihigua's daughter, Ulele, cried out and saved Ortiz's life. That, however, is where the Disney version of the story ends, and the real, gory part begins.

Unlike in the later Virginia fable, where Smith goes on to lead a life of fame as a bridge between two cultures, Ortiz suffered a far more complicated fate. Though he was spared the gruesome death of his other comrades, Ortiz was made a laborer.

> He was employed in the most slavish and laborious occupations, and at times compelled to run all day in the public square where Indians stood ready to shoot him if he should stop. After about nine months of such life the chief

consented to suspend execution of the death sentence for a year on condition that he be required to keep guard over the cemetery of the tribe, three miles from the village; where, according to custom, the bodies of their dead were exposed on biers or stages several feet above ground.[31]

Only through the constant pleading of Ulele was Ortiz able to sustain life.

Still, in spite of the suffering Hirrihigua inflicted on Ortiz, Hirrihigua could never quite get over the memory of his mother being eaten alive by hounds at Narváez's orders and, along with his priests, set a date for Ortiz's death. Luckily for Ortiz, he was forewarned by Ulele. Ortiz made a passionate plea for her to join him in asylum and "accompany him to the land of his birth,"[32] but Ulele was already betrothed and thus sent him to the tribe of her fiancé, presenting him "with a girdle, as a token that she had sent him, and furnished him with a faithful guide."[33] There, he was taken in and treated kindly by the tribe. It was within their protection Ortiz gladly remained for the next 10 years, until 1539 when Hernando de Soto arrived and reunited Ortiz once more with his countrymen.

There She Blows: A Colony Scatters to the Winds

After suffering a half century of failure, Spain was beginning to consider Florida as an ungovernable place. With every expedition prior being met with hostility, hardships and hurricanes, Spain attempted one last ditch settlement, unknowingly pitting its obscenely financed crew to suffer the fates of all three misfortunes.

The settlers began to make a home, establishing a colony on a bluff just up from Pensacola harbor in August 1559, a crossbow's shot from where the ships anchored. They unloaded household items and equipment and brought ashore some provisions. At first, it seemed like things were going according to plan, but then on September 19, disaster struck, as a hurricane came barreling towards the shore. Agustín Dávila Padilla wrote of the storm: "As if the cables were strands of thread, and the anchors were not made of iron, thus they surrendered to the force of the air. The ships came loose, and were broken into small pieces." The food, left aboard one of the ships for safekeeping until a storehouse could be built, was lost. All but three ships had been destroyed. "Afterward they walked on the beach," Padilla wrote, "hoping the waves would make them some restitution of the great amount that the sea had robbed them."[34]

After two years of near starvation following the hurricane, word finally reached Vera Cruz of the settlers' plight. Though four successive fleets were sent to replenish the colony over the following year, it was not enough to sustain them. Some colonists tried to forge alliance with local Native Americans, moving inland in an attempt to obtain food, but even those efforts failed. Facing mutiny from even his most loyal crew Tristán de Luna y Arellano, the Spanish nobleman responsible, for the success of the colony was forced into retirement in 1561 and returned to Spain in disgrace. "His successor, Ángel de Villafañe, and the last fifty or so soldiers abandoned the colony several months later."[35]

Murder in the Marshes: The French Presence in Florida

Florida and Louisiana have a lot in common.

Both are hot, humid, alligator-infested swamplands, with a distinct culture separate from other states. Did you also know that both originally started out as French colonies?

Despite its inconspicuous Spanish beginnings, Florida was in fact a French outpost and could've very well ended up looking a lot more like modern Louisiana than the state we recognize today.

The Tragedy of Fort Caroline

After the disastrous expeditions of Ponce de León and Narváez, the Spanish had a run of more bad luck. Their expedition under de Soto proved fruitless, and their attempt at colonizing Pensacola failed after only three weeks. By 1560, Spain had all but given up on this "uninhabitable" peninsula, viewing it a lost cause.

Enter the French.

Encouraged by ongoing religious strife between Protestants and Catholics, the French king Charles IX, under the guidance of his Protestant advisor Gaspard de Coligny, sought a means to both expand French territory and solve the religious crisis once and for all. His plan: place a settlement for French Protestants in the New World.

Settling on Florida as the place where he would establish his first North American colony, the king, along with his minister, financed a small expedition in early 1562 under the capable captain Jean Ribault. This small reconnaissance group reached the northeastern shores of the state later that May.

Docking along the banks of the St. Johns River at what is now Jacksonville, Ribault spent the next few days exploring the lands and interacting with the friendly Timucua natives. He then sailed north, leaving behind a small monument engraved with the national fleur-de-lis symbol to mark the newfound territory.

Two years later, in 1564, with the volatile situation in the countryside growing from bad to worse, the king decided it was finally time to act and colonize this new land. Organizing an expedition under René Goulaine de Laudonnière, a mix of 300 colonists,[36] including free Black men (a first for Florida), artisans, farmers and women, were recruited to help plant the seeds of dominance in Florida.

After a rough journey, the French arrived in the early summer of 1564, making camp next to a small riverside bluff. The friendly Timucua, in stark contrast to the aggressive Calusa, welcomed the newcomers, going so far as to help them construct a triangular fort and provide them with food. While the ulterior motives for doing such were later made clear, their initial help made the colony of Caroline a thriving settlement.

Eventually, with the onset of winter, the Timucua began to grow weary of the newcomers. It was perhaps lost in initial translation that the Timucua living along this side of the river expected the French to help vanquish their enemies on the opposite shore. When the settlers failed to deliver on this promise, the Timucua began to distance themselves from the colony. As a result, the steady supply of food afforded to the settlers slowed to a trickle. With the threat of starvation, it was not long before the French amounted to thievery, turning the jaded Timucua into open enemies.

As Timucua attacks began to increase at a heightened pace throughout the spring, and the gold and silver deposits desired by the soldiers never materialized, several of the colonists mutinied, fleeing the fort for the Caribbean. There, they pirated and plundered several Spanish treasure ships before being captured. It was then that the colony's previously secret whereabouts became known to the Spanish king.

His reaction was anything but calm. Viewing it a slap in the face to both his Kingdom and the pope, the angry King Philip II ordered the colony wiped off the map.

The seasoned conquistador Pedro Menéndez de Avilés was chosen for the deed, and it was widely stated that "such an expedition could not have been placed in better hands for its success, as Menéndez had shown before that he was fully capable of performing the acts with which he was charged."[37] Furthermore, the king was well aware that Menéndez had made his fortune through the command of the treasure fleets and that he hated the Lutherans (a catch-all name for any Protestant during that era) with an intensity that matched his own. Success, it seemed, would be a foregone conclusion.

The Carnage Ensues

Arriving with a large fleet in late summer of 1565, Menéndez established a small colony thirty miles south of La Caroline, called St. Augustine. After watching over its construction, he then proceeded to organize his soldiers and prepare for an attack. What he didn't know, however, was that Caroline was a far cry from the struggling colony it had been a year prior; after being resupplied by Ribault with both colonists and soldiers, it was now stronger than it had ever been. Had those soldiers remained, it is likely that Florida would've been a very different place than it is today. Alas, however, this was not to be.

Aware of Menéndez's presence, Ribault made a fateful decision to face the Spaniards head on; this would forever change the course of Florida history. Sailing south to St. Augustine with almost all of the fort's soldiers, he left the colony utterly defenseless. Unwittingly navigating into the eye of a hurricane, he wrecked his ships well south of the new Spanish colony. Menéndez witnessed the struggling ships firsthand as they attempted to fight the gales and navigate toward St. Augustine Harbor.

Realizing the momentous opportunity provided him, Menéndez decided it was now or never. With the hurricane still blowing, Menéndez set out with 500 soldiers,[38] hacking a machete path 40 miles to the north. Through wind, rain and much misery, the troops battled through the scrub of the thickets, wading through marsh and swamplands until they reached the vicinity of La Caroline. There, less than a mile from the unguarded settlement, they established camp, waiting for the storm to die down.

The following morning, on September 20 at dawn, the signal was given by Menéndez for attack. Rushing upon the fort they found its inhabitants almost entirely unaware of their presence. There they began their bloody rampage.

By the time Menéndez, who was on high ground nearby watching the carnage unfold from above, was made aware of their gruesome fates and intervened to stop it, it was too late. "One hundred and forty settlers, mostly women and children, were dead."[39] A few helpless survivors managed to escape, making their way toward the mouth of the river, but were slaughtered in similar fashion.

Bringing the Slaughter Home

The French colony now completely wiped out, Menéndez set his sights on Ribault's wrecked retinue. Not wanting the fate of La Caroline to befall St. Augustine, he marched back to his colony, where he learned from the local Timucua about the fate of these men. They were stranded on a small inlet and on the brink of starvation.

Appearing on the opposite side of the banks from the wrecked sailors, Menéndez approached them, offering them quarter and food if they surrendered. Defenseless and desperate for any kind of sustenance, they agreed.

Transporting them across the marshy inlet, Menéndez had them marched in pairs to a small patch of palmetto scrub. There, "he fiendishly put them to death, with ax, halberd or sword."[40] The place of death was henceforth named "Matanzas," a Spanish word for slaughter. The massacre took the better part of the afternoon, amounting to the death of nearly 350 soldiers and sailors,[41] Ribault not among them.

Several days later, on October 12, Menéndez came across another party of Frenchmen. This time, he found Ribault.

Using the same ruse as before, Menéndez repeated the massacre. Unaware of the cruel fate being inflicted upon his men, Ribault put his trust in the Spaniard as a fellow Christian before surrendering himself. When it finally came to be his turn, he, like all the others, was bound and marched to the palmetto scrub. It was there, surrounded by the massacred corpses of his comrades, that Ribault succumbed to the same fate.

Revenge Is a French Dish

After the slaughter of the defenseless colony and its shipwrecked crew, Spanish authorities anticipated an inevitable attack and heightened their defenses.

Fortifying their fledgling colony in St. Augustine, they re-garrisoned Fort Caroline, which they renamed San Mateo, and established a string of defensive fortifications along the St. Johns River. No attack came, however. France was once again embroiled in another religious civil war and the Catholic Court had little regard for the happenings of a largely Protestant colony in the Americas. Such blatant disregard by the king outraged the French population who viewed the slaughter of their countrymen as an affront to national pride. Many called for vengeance, but one man in particular set about making it happen.

The Revenge Unfolds

Although a Catholic noble who had fought against the Protestants during the Wars of Religion, Dominique de Gourgues harbored an intense hatred for the Spanish. A former Spanish prisoner who was treated very cruelly by his captors, de Gourgues had little regard for the Catholic Spanish whom he viewed as cold-blooded murderers.

Outraged by the court's nonchalance, de Gourgues took it upon himself to exact revenge and restore national honor. Selling off his possessions and taking the rest upon loan, de Gourgues outfitted a private navy and raised an army.

Keeping his mission a secret, his three ships set sail to Cuba in August 1567, where he ultimately called his soldiers together and revealed his plan: "We must avenge the insult to our country," he said. "I will always be at your head; I will bear the brunt of the danger; will you refuse to follow me?"[42] The enthusiastic crew agreed on a course of action and sailed on to Florida.

Slipping past Spanish fortifications, de Gourgues navigated his ships several miles north of San Mateo to the mouth of the St. Marys River, where he encountered a group of Timucua. All had not been well with the tribe since the Spanish massacre and they were now in open war against the Spaniards.

Describing to de Gourgues how the Spaniards had ransacked their food, deprived them of their religion and run them through with swords, they presented the French with "a French boy sixteen years of age, Pierre de Bre, who, after the massacre (at Caroline), had been found and cared for by the Indians. They had kept him with them and protected him, though the Spaniards had repeatedly demanded that he should be given up."[43]

After an exchange of gifts between the two parties it was agreed upon that a date should be set and the two would become allies in their fight against the Spanish. The council ended and the two sides prepared for war.

Carnage Part Deux

Coordinating the attack for the Sunday following Easter 1568, de Gourgues set off with his new Timucua allies, setting up attack positions by sea while the natives set up positions by land.

Realizing that several hundred Spaniards had set up position in the area, and that they were divided between three forts, he gave the signal to attack the most vulnerable ones first. At daybreak, he fired upon them by sea as the Timucua rained arrows down upon them by land. Much as before, confusion added to the chaos.

Discovering the location of San Mateo with the aid of a captured Spanish spy, de Gourgues blocked any escape route from the sea, while his native allies blocked the land routes. They then set upon the fort in much the same manner as the others, but unlike at the previous forts, these soldiers, realizing their doom, soon surrendered, choosing to surrender to the French rather than the Timucua whom they had so unfairly brutalized in the years prior.

The fort was then taken, with all goods, food and weapons seized and immediately set on fire.

> The rest of the Spaniards being led away prisoners with the others, after that the general had showed them the wrong which they had done, without occasion, to all the French nation, were all hanged on the boughs of the same trees whereon the Frenchmen hung—of which number five were hanged by one Spaniard; which, perceiving himself in like miserable estate, confessed his fault, and the just judgment which God had brought upon him. But, instead of the writing which Pedro Menendes had hanged over them, importing these words, in Spanish: "I do not this as unto Frenchmen, but as unto Lutherans" Gourgues caused to be imprinted, with a searing iron, in a table of firewood: "I do not this as unto Spaniards, nor as unto mariners, but as unto traitors, robbers, and murderers."[44]

Though he was in a powerful position, with weapons and allies in place, de Gourgues knew his position was untenable in the long run and set about returning to France. When he arrived, the French had already gotten wind of the happenings and de Gourgues was celebrated as a national hero. At court, however, de Gourgues was not embraced as enthusiastically since the king feared a war with Spain.

With a bounty being placed upon his head by the Spanish king, and Charles IX of France openly refusing to shelter him, de Gourgues went into hiding for a few years in the court of a minor noble before ultimately seeking out new adventures in battle. The Spanish for their part rebuilt San Mateo and the other forts but never occupied the territory with as much power as they had before the attack. The area of Jacksonville where the fort sat would thus remain a relative no man's land for much of the next two and a half centuries, fought over and occupied, but never effectively controlled. France, it seems, had the last word.

La Caroline and the First Thanksgiving

While La Caroline's role in Florida proved relatively short, there was one thing of consequence that happened during its existence. For it was here that the First Thanksgiving was celebrated in North America. That's right. In spite of everything we've been taught about the traditions we uphold on the last Thursday in November, the real Thanksgiving actually took place in a little-known settlement on the shores of Florida.

1. Bounty, Belligerency and Bloodlust

Dominique de Gourgues' attack on the Spanish Fort San Mateo with his Timucua allies represents one of the greatest revenge stories ever to unfold on the North American continent (Fort Caroline, Theodor de Bry, 1617, Wikimedia Commons).

Almost 60 years before the Pilgrims landed at Plymouth Rock, the French colonists at La Caroline gathered with their Timucua allies in early 1565 to give thanks and feast on the harvest of their hosts. Prior to this, the French, strangers in a new and inhospitable land, had nearly starved to death, throwing themselves on the mercy of the natives outside their colony.

As was the case with the Pilgrims, the Timucua proved to be willing helpers, saving the fledgling colonists from the brink of death, while teaching them how to cultivate crops and hunt game. To thank them for their generosity, the French would later reciprocate by inviting them to dinner where they thanked God and reaffirmed mutual alliances and respect for one another. Unlike in Massachusetts, however, very few records exist of this interaction due to the calamity that would befall the colony just a few months after the event. Considering that the meal probably consisted of barbecued manatee, corn fritters and palm berries—all staples for the Timucua natives—it's probably for the best as such items would be hard to supply the millions of Americans partaking annually.

The Guale Rebellion

With the French threat vanquished once and for all, the Spanish, as their forbears had done and repeated in their other colonies, sought to Christianize their new lands through the introduction of the mission system. Establishing a string of missions up the east coast and around the panhandle, they concentrated their largest grouping in the lands of the Guale tribe, fringes of the colony's northern frontier, in what later become Georgia. Experiencing early successes with the conversion of many members of the Guale Nation, the friars' largest mission at Tolomato catered to hundreds of tribesmen including chieftains.

These initial good relations changed in 1597, however, when a local chieftain named Juanillo approached the head Franciscan priest named Father Corpa about taking a second wife.[45] His request was denied, and he was humiliated in front of the entire Tolomato mission.

Gathering a group of malcontents, Juanillo went deep into the interior where he joined a group of like-minded rebels, concealing themselves in the church at Tolomato, before attacking Father Corpa. Killing him and tying his head to a post as a warning to all others,[46] Juanillo gave an impassioned plea encouraging his followers to abandon the new religious order and embrace their traditions.

> "Now the father is dead, but he would not have been if he had allowed us to live as we did before we became Christians. Let us return to our former customs, and prepare to defend ourselves against the punishment which the governor of Florida will try to inflict upon us, for if he succeeds in it, he will be as rigorous for this one father as though we had made an end of them all, for he will surely persecute us for the father we have killed the same as for all."[47]

From there, the rebels turned their concentration on the other missions, attacking with sticks and macanas (wooden knives edged with flint) any priest unfortunate enough to be caught in their sights. Though several priests were spared complete annihilation in death, with some like Father Auñon—whom the Guale respected for his physical prowess[48]—being granted a Christian burial, most of the bodies were cast into the swamps or left to rot were they lay.

Continuing southward, the Guale continued to attack missions at St. Simons Island, where they put to the sword any who resisted, before continuing to Jekyll Island, where they overran the chief mission at Ospo.

Although the Spanish, sent an expeditionary force to confront the rebelling Guale upon hearing of the brutality inflicted on the mission priests and their Indian allies, little to none of the offenders were captured and the Spanish were forced to return to St. Augustine. The rebellion effectively ended the missions in that area for almost a hundred years, with little to no retaliation coming from the Spaniards. In fact, the priests and those in the mission were later castigated for causing the fledgling colony another headache by being too rigid in their zeal.

A Most Bloody Beginning

In the 84 years between Ponce de León's first voyage and the subsequent massacre at the hands of the Guale, Florida witnessed well over one thousand recorded European deaths, more than Cortéz's and Pizarro's forces lost during their conquests of the Aztecs and Incas combined! In fact, during its first official year as a viable Spanish colony in 1565, almost half that number was accounted for. No other state can even come close to matching such a history of violence this early on! For many years after, the colony of Florida would largely remain an unconquered land, sparsely inhabited along the coasts, opening the gates for greater chaos and travesty to come.

2

Dead Man's Chest

Florida's Flirtation with Pirates, Privateers and Pillagers

In the powder keg that was sixteenth-century Europe, Florida was the match that lit the world on fire. At least that's how Spain saw it.

In the years after the Fort Caroline massacre and the subsequent vengeance by de Gourgues's army, the Spanish colony of Florida slowly came into its own.

Making peace with their Timucua counterparts and staving off a few minor raids by French privateers, the capital city at St. Augustine seemed assured of success. That all changed with the arrival of England to North America, however.

By the time the 1580s rolled around, England was a far cry from its more timid days under Henry VII. Back in those times, England refused to step on any toes for fear of upsetting the Pope or Spain. This changed dramatically under Henry VIII and more so under his daughter Elizabeth. For one, Spain, a former friend and ally of England, was now its greatest enemy. And secondly, the Pope's authority in religious matters was no longer of any concern to the English, who had since become a Protestant nation. As such, they were now, more than ever willing to expand their power by planting a colony of their own in the New World.

Settling on Roanoke Island in present day North Carolina, the English established a small fortification and colony. In so doing, they flagrantly violated the now ignored Treaty of Tordesillas and in effect usurped Spanish claims to the territory. In fulfillment of Spain's worst nightmare, this action soon led to terroristic pirate raids in the Spanish colonies. Spain, it seemed, was no longer the sole contender in North America.

The Coming of "the Dragon"

Shortly after the establishment of the English colony at Roanoke, in 1585, Sir Francis Drake began to target Spain's Atlantic colonies.

Referred to by many in the Spanish Court by his Latin name "the dragon,"[1] Drake had long been a thorn in the side of the Spanish. With full blessings from his sovereign Elizabeth I, he went on a rampage around the coasts of central and South America, pirating off tens of millions of dollars in gold and silver from Spanish treasure fleets. At one point during these raids, he had captured so much gold, he was forced to bury it onshore.

Such losses of gold proved staggering to Spain, that at this point was relying more than ever upon shipments from the New World to keep up funding for its army and navy. As if all of this wasn't bad enough, Drake soon began to target Spain's Atlantic possessions. This time, however, it was not gold that drove his mission, but utter conquest and eradication of the Spanish from the continent, entirely.

The Sacking of St. Augustine

It almost seems comical that a raid on the tiny colony of St. Augustine proved to be one of the tipping points for what ultimately ended up being one of the greatest battles in European history. But for Spain, it was certainly no laughing matter.

In 1585, England and Spain were still officially at peace—*at least on paper*. You wouldn't know it, however, if you were a colonist in the New World. For all across the Caribbean, the alarm bells were sounding off. Sir Francis Drake and his cronies were on the move.

Dispatched with explicit orders from Elizabeth to deprive the Spanish of any thriving settlements, Drake began attacking and plundering the large cities of Cartagena, Colombia, and Santo Domingo. These attacks resulted in the loss of hundreds of millions of dollars of revenue and devastated nearly a half-century of progress Spain had made in the New World. So completely staggering were these raids that Spain was forced to shell out "$500,000 pesos"[2] (a staggering sum!) just to buy back a then partially burned-out Cartagena from Drake, as well as start completely over from scratch on the island of Hispaniola.

It was on his way back from these plunders on June 6, 1586, that "Drake spotted the small watchtower guarding the city of St. Augustine."[3] Sailing into its harbor, he discovered a thriving settlement of little clay houses with palm-thatched roofs and a small wooden fort along the shores of the Matanzas River.

Upon making landfall, Drake found the city to be completely deserted. It seemed that Governor *Márquez*, aware of Drake's arrival, had emptied out the city's population for fear that Drake would murder its inhabitants and sell the large portion of free Africans living there into slavery. Fleeing into the surrounding woods, they watched as the Englishman scavenged their homes for goods and treasure.

Disappointed by what they found—the Timucua, taking advantage of the situation, had beaten them to the looting—the English made their way further out into the surrounding woods. There, a brief scuffle with "a straggler in the Spanish rearguard led to the shooting and death of one of Drake's crewmembers."[4] In fit of vengeance, Drake ordered the town and the fort burned to the ground, destroying all of the crops along with it.

Drake initially made plans to stay in the colony. Like many, he viewed Florida to be rightfully English by right of Cabot's discovery a century earlier. He also blamed the Spanish for sabotaging the Roanoke colony through small attacks. His plans changed, however, as supplies ran low and he was forced to sail away.

In the meantime, St. Augustine's colonists came back, rebuilding the fort and the city. With additional help from Cuba, they were able to increase the status of the city from a mere outpost to an official presidio of the Spanish Empire. Such a status allowed St. Augustine to play a more crucial role in the guarding of Spanish treasure fleets—a role which would lead to further problems in the future.

The Little City That Ignited an International War

News of the ransoming and destruction of Cartagena and Santo Domingo infuriated the Spanish. But it was the burning and capture of St. Augustine that proved a final straw. The Spanish colony of Florida was now a far cry from what it had been at the founding of St. Augustine, and the Spaniards were no longer willing to tolerate official excuses about pirates acting of their own accord. They decided to do something about it.

Over the next two years, Spain raised an armada to invade England. When they finally launched it in 1588, however, their ships were battered by gale force winds off the coast of the Netherlands and routed. This defeat would ultimately play a major turning point in European politics, as England grew ever bolder and began to eye the vast unsettled lands north of Florida.

Blood in the Water: Searle's Invasion of St. Augustine

Remember the pirate invasion scene from the movie *Pirates of the Caribbean: Dead Man's Chest*, where the town of Port Royal was invaded and sacked by nightfall? That's not just some bit of Hollywood lore. It actually played out in real time during the 1668 invasion of St. Augustine.

By the late seventeenth century, Spain was no longer the dominant power in the colonies. Waning as a dominant force due to constant warfare and debt, its influence took a decided backseat after England captured Jamaica in 1655. From that point on, no part of the Spanish Main, not even those on the mainland, remained safe from invasion. The heyday of Florida piracy had begun.

Searle and His Buccaneers

Robert Searle had already been a pain in Spain's proverbial behind well before he even touched the shores of Florida. A pirate through and through, Searle had successfully led expeditions and invasions of Spanish and Dutch coastal cities including a famed raid against Santiago de Cuba. Though he faced punitive actions for his crimes, he managed to avoid arrest in the early part of his career, and eventually was given sanctioned command over a small fleet he had stolen. This changed definitively in 1668.

Searle Comes Ashore

Under the cover of darkness on May 29, Searle launched his attack. It was 1:00 a.m. and the city of St. Augustine was sound asleep.

As Searle sailed into Matanzas Bay the previous evening on two confiscated ships, the people of St. Augustine, including the governor, seemed certain that nothing was out of the ordinary. The city had been expecting the arrival of these ships for several days, and the crafty pirates gave no indication that they were anything but Spanish sailors. With false assurances, the city, along with the soldiers garrisoned inside the small fort, went to sleep.

Then, slowly it happened. The pirates began to disembark. Rowing across the waters, they landed in secret, until a lone, insomniac corporal spotted them.

Out in the waters at the time of their disembarkation, Corporal Monzon raced his dugout to the shore to sound the alarm. The pirates, not wanting their presence alerted pursued him, "shooting him twice."[5] The wounded Monzon, shouted as he made his way to shore, but by that point it was too late, the pirate invasion had begun.

The city of St. Augustine awoke to a thud, as the freebooters began charging down St. George Street. Confused and panicked, they rushed out of their doors to spy the situation unfolding. There, they were met with gunfire and beatings as the pirates rampaged across the city.

The frightened populace, under the direction of the governor, made their way to the wooden fort at the edge of the bay and for over an hour and a half, the townspeople and soldiers fought them off with musket and canon fire.

> By daybreak, with the arrival of more soldiers, the pirates, now with 11 dead and 19 wounded retreated back to the city. There, they continued their plunder, making off with the king's treasury of 138 silver marks, along with everything in the royal storehouses and all of the jewels from the civilian houses. They even stripped the parish church of all valuable ornamentation.[6]

As the looting drew to a close, the pirates took on a consolation prize of hostages, nabbing about "70 men, women and children."[7] Among them was the royal treasurer, who refused to abandon his home. Boarding the hostages upon their ships, the pirates demanded a ransom of meat, water and wood. The governor relented, upon receiving a much-needed shipment of flour, and the pirates, under parley, set all of the hostages free and unharmed. After this, Searle lifted anchor and sailed away.

Surveying the Death

After Searle's departure, the frightened citizens of St. Augustine emerged from their fortress to survey the damage. The raid, which had lasted roughly twenty hours, had left them destitute. Nothing was left. In addition, 60 of their fellow friends and family members were dead. The dead "amounted to a quarter of their pre-raid population."[8]

Though the people of St. Augustine suffered greatly, it was they who would have the last laugh. For, in the immediate aftermath of the raid, Searles was said to have been "haunted by the ghost of a 5-year-old girl he killed until he went mad and committed suicide"[9] while the City of St. Augustine was granted—by the queen of Spain herself—special funding to construct a coquina stone fortress. Such a fortress would assure the city's longevity. It wouldn't, however, prevent further acts of piracy from taking place.

Aviles Street in St. Augustine's Spanish Quarter is the oldest street in the U.S. Many of the structures present today were also present during the height of English piracy in colonial Florida (photograph by Elena photography, April 15, 2017, CC BY-SA 4.0, Wikimedia Commons).

Pirate Malaise

By the time the end of the century had rolled around, piracy had become the new normal for the people of Florida.

From 1682 to 1684, Spanish troops confronted no fewer than three large-scale attempts at taking the colony along with countless raids. Each time, these attempts met increasingly stiff resistance, leading to their collapse and departure of the raiding parties. This was not only due to increased Spanish defenses, but also from increased pressure by the other European powers. For, by the end of the century, these powers had begun to turn a healthy profit in their colonies, and piracy became universally recognized as bad for business. Because of this, piracy became less and less of a state-sponsored weapon and more and more of a nation-less nuisance.

The Miraculous Recovery of Andrew Ranson

Not all English pirates during this time were unwelcome in Spanish Florida. Some, like Andrew Ranson, were actually able to assimilate and become productive citizens. Charged with a number of crimes, Ranson was implicated by the very crew he had commanded.

Facing tortures of various kinds, this crew described in mass detail how Ranson had taken part in the most recent attempt to raid St. Augustine for gold. They talked about how Ranson captured a Spanish ship, the *Platanera*, and tortured its crew to find out answers about Spanish settlements in Florida. One of the crew even testified how "Ranson had beaten him to the point of unconsciousness, threatening to cut off his head."[10] They then talked about how Ranson had led them into an ambush, believing that St. Augustine was weak and undefended.

Captured by the soldiers in the very city he sought to attack, he was marched to the gallows and a rope was strapped around his neck to begin the very painful process of garroting. This strangulation was a fairly common punishment for the colony of St. Augustine and was quite the public event to behold. Unfortunately this time, something went wrong. Placing the rope around Ranson's neck, the executioner slowly turned the handle while Ranson "clutched a rosary"[11] in his hand.

> After those six turns of the handle, Ranson twitched for a short while and then stopped moving. Thinking to make sure his task of pirate execution was complete, the executioner gave the rope one more good twist. Incredibly, the rope broke.
> And as soon as that happened, Father Perez de la Mota rushed to the body only to find Ranson still breathing. Against all odds, the pirate execution had failed.[12]

With church bells ringing all across the city at the time of his collapse, the friars present took it as a sign of God's mercy and credited the incident a miracle. Whisking him away to the nearest church house, the friars restored him back to health, putting a rosary in his hand for good measure. "Witnesses claimed Ranson embraced it with tears in his eyes."[13]

While the Spanish authority demanded Ranson's release, the friars refused. They said that the man had since embraced the Church and redeemed himself from past sins.

Eventually, the authorities stopped calling for his release and accepted him among the colony. There were other matters to attend to and by all of the friar's accounts Ranson was a changed man. Thus, Ranson lived out the rest of his days a free man, becoming one of the few pirates to be embraced by the locals.

The Unlikely Adventures of Francisco Menéndez

Though it was avidly anti-pirate on paper, the little colony of Florida certainly employed its fair share of defensive piracy. This was especially true during the mid–1700s when cash strapped Spain could no longer afford to send adequate military funding to defend its overseas possessions.

Enter Francisco *Menéndez*, Florida's most famous African American pirate.

Menéndez and the Pirate Soldiers of Fort Mose

Starting out as a West African slave on a South Carolina plantation, *Menéndez* spent much of his early days toiling under the sun at a British plantation. With the help of a Yamasee raiding party, however, he managed to escape, leaving the plantation far behind him.

Joining the tribe in their war against the British, *Menéndez* found comfort in wreaking havoc on the very people who had treated him so brutally. When military fortune began to turn on his newly adopted tribesman, however, he was forced to once again seek out a new home, this time setting his sights south to Florida.

In those days, freedom from slavery meant a life in Florida. For while the Spanish did in fact possess slaves, their humane treatment of laborers far exceeded that of any other colony, and in the vast majority of cases, freedom could be obtained after only a few years of service. In fact, so advanced was Spain's treatment that it established a colony for newly freed slaves two miles north of St. Augustine called Fort Mose.

Arriving in the colony amid much fanfare as a result of his former attacks against the British, *Menéndez* lived comfortably among his new neighbors, eventually catching the eye of the colonial governor.

The governor, in hearing of the tales of *Menéndez*'s past raids, charged *Menéndez*, along with a group of ex-slaves, with the mission of defending the city from British attack. Gaining complete freedom as a result, he and his crew came to be some of the colony's most ardent defenders, repulsing attack after attack for years to come. In their minds, they knew what

British victory would bring to them and they were determined never to let that happen.

When, in the 1740s, fighting between Spain and England suddenly intensified into all-out war, Menéndez and his squadron turned to preventative action through piracy. Capturing several British ships, *Menéndez* built up a fleet and gained notoriety through his unusual actions of "castrating captured sailors."[14]

Eventually captured by the British, "*Menéndez* was forced to suffer through two hundred lashes of the whip before being pickled alive."[15] This involved the rubbing of salt and vinegar into his wounds to increase pain and degradation. He and his pirate soldiers were then sold back into slavery.

Escaping as he had done once before, *Menéndez* made a daring dart back into Florida where he once more took over command of Fort Mose, building up another pirate army to fend off further English attacks. When at last Florida was ceded to the British in 1763 as part of the Peace of Paris, most of the inhabitants of Fort Mose, *Menéndez* among them, immigrated to Cuba with the evacuating Spanish. Once there, he "established a community called *San Agustín de la Nueva Florida* that was modeled on Fort Mose."[16]

A pirate through and through, *Menéndez* became one of the most important African American figures in early Florida history and a testament to the thirst for freedom.

Scavengers Off the Treasure Coast

Not all pirates were interested in making military raids. Some just wanted treasure. This was certainly the case when it came to the pirate raids of South Florida in 1715.

During that time, a strong hurricane wrecked a fleet of Spanish treasure ships off the coast of present-day Fort Pierce. Headed for Cuba:

> ten of the ships were lost: two disappeared beneath the open seas while the remaining eight crashed into shallow waters off the Florida coast. More than a thousand sailors lost their lives, including General Ubilla, the fleet's commander.[17]

With cargo scattered all across the beachfront, and most of the gold and silver lost to the sea, an assembly of survivors hastily alerted officials in St. Augustine. When the royal government officials heard the story, they went into immediate action to rescue the remaining survivors from peril.

Around the same time that Spain dispatched this mission, word of the wreck spread like wildfire across the Caribbean, reaching the likes of Henry Jennings in Jamaica. A longtime pirate hunter for England, Jennings was enthralled with the notion of recovering such a huge amount of treasure. As a result, he decided to pursue the *if you can't beat 'em join 'em* philosophy and forego a life of privilege for a life of piracy.

Taking his ship the *Bersheba*, a gift from the governor of Jamaica, with an additional ship and three sloops, Jennings, along with "a crew of 300,"[18] set course for Florida. There, in November, they sighted the unfortunate Spanish camp.

With only a few soldiers and a few Indian divers, the outnumbered Spanish soon became overrun by the marauding English pirates. Sparing their lives, in favor of collecting the recovered treasure, they set about loading as much as they could onto their ships. This amount equaled about "120,000 pieces of eight,"[19] a staggering sum of money in those days!

With more gold in his ship than he and his crew could ever spend, Jennings went looking for a friendlier location. He and his crew decided that the Island of New Providence in the Bahamas was a nice "fixer upper" and with that in mind, his crew landed in the small shanty town of Nassau. "When Jennings arrived in 1715, Nassau was already a pirate hot spot but was more like a sleepy little 'one whore' tavern than a booming metropolis. Apart from a decent port and fresh water, it was of little consequence to Great Britain. Jennings found it an ideal place to set up shop."[20] Pirates had been using the town as a stopover and portage but now with the gold and silver brought by Jennings and crew, the town began to grow into a city and pirate haven. Jennings practically ran the town as its "unofficial mayor" while extorting tribute from those looking for "safe harbor."[21] As Nassau began to take on the trappings of that other famous pirate haven, Port Royal, the British government began to take note, dispatching Woodes Rogers as Governor to sort it out. Rogers successfully convinced Jennings and his men to abandon piracy[22] in exchange for royal clemency, and since the crew was already wealthier than many of the richest planters in the Caribbean, they agreed to the offer and effectively retired.

The Legend of José Gaspar and His Sex-Slave Island

Some pirates, as in the case of José Gaspar, raided for love ... *or so the legend goes!*

No one knows exactly what drove Gaspar or his crew to a life of piracy (*or if he ever really existed*), but there are more than few stories about it. One of the most popular versions tells the tale of his love affairs at the Spanish Court.

Born into a privileged, aristocratic background, *José* Gaspar, through bravery and skill, established a quick name for himself in the royal navy and became a close addition at the royal court, rising to the rank of "councilor to King Charles III."[23] Although it was normal for men of Gaspar's rank and background to play the field at court, it was Gaspar's love affair with the king's daughter-in-law that would ultimately lead to his downfall. For, ever the womanizer, Gaspar not only bedded her, but also a lot of the other women at court as well. Once discovered, the scorned daughter-in-law hatched a plot straight out of a Shakespearean play to get her revenge.

Petitioning the king directly, the scorned daughter-in-law angrily denounced Gaspar, stating that he had humiliated her in public. Worse still, she, with the backing of the prime minister, claimed that Gaspar had stolen crown jewels. This last part was all the information the king needed to call for his arrest. Angry, bitter and certainly not ready to spend the rest of his life in jail, Gaspar commandeered the *Floridablanca* and made a daring escape for the high seas. With nothing left to lose, he set sail for Florida, beginning his long life as a pirate.

Establishing his base on Gasparilla Island off the coast of modern-day Fort Myers, Gaspar set about attacking anything and everything that crossed his path. By career's end, it was said that Gasper's crew had personally plundered over 400 ships![24]

Though Gasper had a soft spot for his friends, he was ruthless to a tee in battle. He routinely rounded up all the enemy men and had them killed via the sword or the plank. His only mercy, it seemed, was shown toward women. In this regard, he would either ransom them for money—if they were wealthy—or hold them captive on one of the neighboring islands.

> [C]aptured ladies were not raped and murdered, but instead had the option of marrying one of his crew members or being transferred to Captiva Island in Florida. If marriage was selected, there would be a ceremony, and the marriage promise would be strictly enforced.[25]

After years of outrunning the Spanish, Gaspar finally met his end in 1821, the same year he was set to retire, after erroneously attacking a United States naval ship passing by. The story goes that when the Americans boarded his sinking ship, he wrapped a chain around his waist and dove into the water, sword upturned, in one last gesture of defiance to the world that had spurned him. His ship, as well as his secret stash of $30,000,000,[26] are said to remain buried in a forgotten sand dune on Captiva Island.

While *José* Gaspar's exploits largely remained confined to the back pages of Florida history for much of the ensuing century, community leaders in Tampa would eventually revive his legend in 1904 in the form of the Gasparilla Pirate Festival.

Boasting a parade, along with over 130 units, 90 elaborate floats, 14 marching bands, and 50 distinct krewes, this hangover-inducing bash has become an annual favorite for the citizens of Tampa each January/February, drawing in hundreds of thousands of revelers. It also follows a formula with Ye Mystic Krewe, the oldest and most prestigious of the group,[27] invading downtown from Hillsborough Bay in the world's only fully-rigged pirate ship, *The José Gasparilla*—a spectacle that would no doubt put a smile on the infamous swashbuckler's face.

A Peninsula of Pirates, Pillagers and Privateers

Strategically positioned along one of Spain's primary treasure routes, Florida has played witness to more pirate activity than any other area

The Gasparilla Pirate Festival in Tampa is one of the largest and oldest pirate festivals in the world drawing in over 500,000 revelers each year. Named for famed pirate Jose Gaspar, who reportedly kept a harem of prostitutes on Captiva Island, and whose buried treasure in the dunes has yet to be found, this century-old festival features 110 boats invading Tampa Bay each January and, like Mardi Gras, features numerous krewes composed of Tampa's elite (photograph by Rob Bixby, February 16, 2016, CC BY-SA 2.0, Wikimedia Commons).

outside the Caribbean. Such activity has played a dramatic role in the shaping of Florida's development and eventually led to international intervention in the form of endless wars and raiding. This penchant for instability would play a major role in the ensuing decades leading to increasing conflicts with a newly independent United States.

3

A Tale of Two Floridas

Spanish Twilight in the Era of American Expansion

By the end of the eighteenth century, the writing was on the wall for Spanish Florida. Having already experienced a shift in demographics as a result of a power transfer to Great Britain after the French and Indian War, it remained in a state of flux for nearly 20 years, once again finding itself on the losing side of a conflict as it fought with the Loyalists in the American Revolution; it became the only North American colony outside of Canada not to rebel.

When the Spanish arrived to take Florida back following the conclusion of the war, they found a very different colony from the one they had traded. For one, the land was practically empty. All of the Spaniards who had departed after the original British takeover were unwilling to return, and the newer British colonists were unwilling to remain. Taking their place was a mix of renegade Creeks, called Seminoles, and a small group of runaway slaves and former American Loyalists. Still, in spite of these new realities, what the Spanish found the most shocking was that Florida was now divided into two separate colonies.

Given the size and vastness of the Florida peninsula, the British found it easier to simply divide it up and separate government functions entirely through an East-West division. East Florida, with its capital at St. Augustine, consisted of a few small estates around Jacksonville and the Georgia border, with a large, unpopulated central and southern section. West Florida, with its capital at Pensacola, consisted of everything in the Panhandle, extending westward to Mobile and parts of Louisiana.

As it turned out, the Spanish loved the new system and decided to keep it in place. Like the British, they began to govern the land as if it were two separate entities. While this would prove beneficial from an administrative standpoint, it would prove disastrous from a funding and military point of view, as Spain found itself in possession of two more colonies it couldn't afford.

Anarchy in the FL

In the world of nineteenth-century Florida, East Florida was Somalia, and Amelia Island was Mogadishu.

A place of utter and hopeless chaos, its entire population existed on the brink of anarchy. Added to this were pirates, wandering bands of revolutionaries, and illegal smugglers of all sorts crowding into its ports. Mix in a few disgruntled American colonists, used to doing things their own way, and a near bankrupt mother country and you had the perfect recipe for colonial failure. All the greedy politicians in D.C. had to do was sit back and watch the implosion take place.

The Revolution That Couldn't

Sitting astride Spanish Florida's most northern boundary, Amelia Island in the eighteenth century was a hotbed of piracy and revolutionary activity, with hundreds of square-rigged vessels anchored in its harbor at any given time. This led to the island and the port at Fernandina being viewed as a real problem spot for the Americans living along the border and they began to take matters into their own hands.

Under the pretext of maintaining order, a flotilla of nine war vessels[1] was organized under the leadership of John McIntosh and launched against the population in the spring of 1812. The large force, unofficially supported by the United States government, easily overran much of the city of Fernandina without as a much as a shot being fired. By March 17, it completely capitulated and was made an official part of the newly formed Republic of Florida. John McIntosh was established as its president and commander in chief and plans were soon made to bring the revolution to the south and further solidify the new nation's territories.

Wasting precious little time, the Patriots, as they called themselves, marched their troops southward for an attack on St. Augustine. Surmised that a group of a few hundred should be more than sufficient to accomplish such a feat, they set up camp after a march of several days, two miles outside the capital.

Unfortunately, Spain was well aware of their encampment and launched its own preemptive strike from a strategically placed schooner. They pounded the Americans with cannon and mortar fire until they retreated a mile northward. Instead of relenting, however, the Spaniards followed them, launching another attack of cannon fire.

With circumstances growing dimmer for success, and more and more of their forces succumbing to swamp sickness,[2] the Americans soon abandoned their plans and began to march back to Fernandina. There along the banks of the St. Johns in Jacksonville, they met increasingly stiff resistance from hostile Indians and former slaves. An excerpt highlighted from the account of Col. Daniel Newnan recorded one such incident:

> Accordingly a half hour before sunset, having obtained a considerable reinforcement of Negroes and Indians, from their towns, they commenced the most horrid yells imaginable, imitating the cries and noise of almost every animal of the forest, their chiefs advancing in front in a stooping, serpentine manner, and making the most wild and frantic gestures, until they approached within two hundred yards of us, when they halted to commence firing.[3]

The failed attack on St. Augustine, as well as the ensuing losses from death, disease and malnutrition during their retreat, cost the Patriots a lot more than mere numbers. It cost them their dreams of a lasting republic. For, within the year, the American government would officially withdraw support from McIntosh, resulting in the complete collapse of the revolutionary cause.

One Island, Two Nations

In the 1810s, Americans weren't the only ones interested in inciting a revolution in East Florida. Latin American adventurers had seemed to catch the bug, as well. While many people may jokingly refer to South Florida as a part of Cuba, Amelia Island in North Florida can in fact lay claim to have once been a part of both South America and Mexico. This was all due to the activities of a few Latin American freedom fighters.

The whole affair started shortly after the departure of the Patriots. Spain, at that time, was completely immersed in stamping out the various revolutions, stretching from Mexico to South America, and was more than ever at its weakest. Sensing this vulnerability firsthand, Gregor MacGregor, a Scottish pirate turned Latin American freedom fighter, went into action.

Organizing a ragtag group of pirates and revolutionaries, he attacked the island and, in a repeat of 1812 history, easily overran its outnumbered forces. On June 29, 1817, he was ready to make his declaration to his victorious crew:

> Soldiers and sailors! The 29th of June will be forever memorable in the annals of the independence of South America. On that day a body of brave men, animated by noble zeal for the happiness of mankind advanced within musket shot of the guns at Fernandina, and awed the enemy into complete capitulation, notwithstanding his very favorable position. This will be an everlasting proof of what the sons of freedom can achieve when fighting in a great and glorious cause.[4]

Though he would remain in power until September, MacGregor would eventually abandon his position in Florida for more intense fighting in the Caribbean. In his stead, he would leave the Frenchman and notorious pirate Louis-Michel Aury, who in taking over would annex the island to the new Republic of Mexico.

Aury's tenure would go one step further than MacGregor's as it would oversee the election of a legislature and the drafting of a constitution for such purposes. To help affirm devotion to its incorporation, he would have each of the islanders take a solemn oath of loyalty to "renounce all allegiance to any state not actually struggling for the emancipation of Spanish America."[5] In this way, he would continue to rule for the next three months, until, in December of that year, he would be forced out by the Americans, under the guise of "restoring" the island to Spain. In actuality, the Americans would stay, effectively marking the beginning of the end of Spanish rule in East Florida.

Don Juan McQueen, John McIntosh and the Great Florida-Georgia Rivalry

Since 1904, Florida and Georgia have been battling it out in what's been referred to as one of the longest-running interstate rivalries in college football history. Occurring each year on the last Saturday in October, the game draws record-breaking crowds from both campuses, creating a very tense, party-filled atmosphere for all involved. So where exactly does this annual event take place? Why the neutral city of Jacksonville, of course.

Unlike most college rivalries, where the games alternate between campuses, Florida and Georgia chose to duke it out in Jacksonville. As it turns out, they could not have picked a more appropriate spot as this part of Florida was a well-worn battleground between the forces in Florida and Georgia long before the emergence of the SEC.

Around the end of the eighteenth century, the Spaniards in Florida found themselves in an increasingly perilous situation. Immigration from Spain and Cuba had slowed to a trickle and there was no way to buffer the population near its northern border in Jacksonville. In order to fix this,

3. A Tale of Two Floridas

the Spanish developed a policy similar to one Mexico would later apply in Texas, where they would grant land to Americans on the condition that they farm and develop it. In addition, they required that these grantees take a loyalty oath to the Spanish king and convert to the Catholic faith. While many did so with gusto, others resented the notion. This led to famous confrontations between the likes of two Johns—John McIntosh and John McQueen, two of early Jacksonville's most prominent American landowners.

Although both were Georgians who had fought in the Revolutionary War and each had lived on the same plantation grounds (McIntosh having purchased land from McQueen), they harbored different feelings toward the Spanish. McIntosh, for his part, was deeply hateful towards them. He believed that a republic like that of the U.S. needed to be established and that the ruling regime was corrupt. McQueen, on the other hand, embraced the Spanish. Having fled Georgia, and his wife and children, on a string of bad debts, he adopted the name Don Juan, and entered into a friendship with the governor, as well as became a judge and a Captain of the East Florida Militia and Commander of the Banks of the St. Johns and St. Marys.

Becoming one of Florida's largest landowners overseeing the future Kingsley Plantation on Fort George Island, McQueen enjoyed the social life of St. Augustine, and his Irish friends there, including "Father Michael 'Miguel' O'Reilly, the worldly parish priest, and Colonel Charles 'Carlos' Howard, the commander of Spanish military forces in East Florida."[6]

These differences soon came to a head in battle.

In 1793, McIntosh was arrested on suspicion of complicity against the Spanish Crown.[7] Spending a year in a Havana jail, he was eventually released and allowed to return to America. Banned from his former lands in Florida, he settled back in Georgia where he gathered a group of volunteers for an attack.

Marching south with an "army" under the command of Richard Lang, they made their way to the St. Johns River and, upon reaching the vicinity of Jacksonville, attacked a lightly guarded fort called San Nicholas.

> At 3:00AM one of the gang who spoke Spanish approached Commander Ignacio Lopez at the gate with a false announcement that the men were militia reinforcements arriving to strengthen the battery. A brief exchange of fire took place that resulted in the immediate deaths of two Spanish guards. A third soldier later died from his wounds. The battery was quickly overrun and Lieutenant Lopez and twenty-eight members of the Catalan Light Infantry Company were captured.[8]

There they harassed other boats and "terrorized" settlers in the vicinity.[9]

Meeting them head on to prevent further destruction, McQueen, along with a combined force of Spanish and American settlers, attacked them, forcing him to retreat back to the Georgia line. Though no one died, many were captured and sent to the dungeons in St. Augustine.

> The prisoners were confined in the Castillo de San Marcos, their health suffering as a result of the damp and dark condition of their cells. Before the two-year trial ended, Daniel Hogans, Richard Malpas, Solomon King, and George Arons died in prison. Francis Goodwin went insane and had to be moved to the Royal Hospital.[10]

As a result of the failed rebellion, a bitter rivalry began between those Americans in the region who were pro–McQueen and therefore pro–Florida and those Americans who were pro–McIntosh and therefore pro–Georgia which would lead to infighting across much of modern-day Jacksonville.

These exploits in the twilight of Spanish power in Florida were eventually novelized in the Eugenia Price classic "Don Juan McQueen" published in 1974. The book became a national bestseller garnering reviews from *Publishers Weekly*, the *Chattanooga Times* and even the *New York Times* for its attention to early colonial detail.

The Not-so-Neutral Nature of Florida in the War of 1812

Officially, the War of 1812 was fought between Great Britain and the United States. Unofficially, its impact was far more reaching.

When news of the war first reached Spain, it seemed as though the Spanish could gain everything by doing nothing. Like a spider waiting for its prey to struggle itself out of energy, the Spanish Crown watched as Great Britain and the United States struggled themselves into a stalemate. What they didn't expect, however, was this struggle messing up their web in West Florida.

The Siege That Shaped a Revolution and Doomed a Revolution and an Empire

It might come as a surprise to some that Spain was not always at odds with their neighbors to the north. In fact, during the American Revolution, it was their alliance with America as well as their actions against Britain that actually helped turn the tide of the war in America's favor. This was most noted during the Siege of Pensacola in 1781.

3. A Tale of Two Floridas

Transferred to Great Britain in 1763 as part of the Treaty of Paris that ended the French and Indian War, Florida was divided into two colonies—East and West Florida and administered by two capitals, St. Augustine and Pensacola. While East Florida was the better populated of the two, West Florida was far more strategic given its position on the Gulf of Mexico. Thus, at the outbreak of the American Revolution, Spain eyed an opportunity to avenge Florida's loss by allying with the Americans and attacking West Florida. The attack began in Mobile Bay when, in 1781, General Don Bernardo de Galvez led a force of 40 ships and 3,500 men[11] west to lay siege to British Fort Charlotte, a stronghold in what is today's Mobile, Alabama. With a Spanish victory there, the fort was garrisoned with a second fort built across Mobile Bay.

Turning his attention to Pensacola, and the ultimate prize of his campaign, Galvez positioned himself on a battery within range of Pensacola's Fort George and relentlessly shelled it for four continuous days.[12] With casualties mounting and the Spanish able to secure artillery closer to the fort's walls, "British General John Campbell raised the white flag of surrender on May 8th, 1781."[13]

The subsequent surrender of Pensacola effectively gave Spain control over Florida, as well as the Mississippi River, cutting off British supply lines and shortening their ability to continue war against the Americans.

While such actions would be celebrated at the time by their grateful American allies, things would start to deteriorate relatively quickly over the next three decades. This would come to a head during the outbreak of the War of 1812, when Britain and the United States would once again go to war, forcing Spain into an impossible situation as it sought to stay neutral. Thus, it would become clear that Spain's victory in securing Florida during the Siege of Pensacola would ultimately seal its doom on the North American continent.

A Lingering Presence

Though Britain had officially been out of West Florida since their transfer of power, they never fully relegated themselves to the shadows, continuing in trade with the colony and its Indians. By the time the War of 1812 had begun, the city of Pensacola had become almost totally dependent on this economic and military assistance as a means of sustenance and protection. Such reliance caused a great amount of headaches for Spain after war broke out, as the British policy of arming the Seminoles to stage attacks across the border began to rouse the ire of the United States, particularly the likes of General Andrew Jackson. To make matters worse, the

The Seminole or "wild men" were a tribe that arrived in Florida sometime in the 18th century. Composed of rebellious Creeks, runaway slaves, and even some Europeans, their multiethnic nature was an affront to everything the White supremacist planters stood for and sparked a series of guerrilla wars in Florida. To this day, they remain the only tribe never to have surrendered or signed a treaty with the U.S., earning them the moniker "unconquered" (photograph by John K. Small, January 25, 1927, State Library and Archives of Florida).

British were openly using Pensacola's port to store their war vessels and build up their forces. In Jackson's mind, this was an act of war.

Marching "4000 of his troops across the international boundary between the United States and Spanish Territory, Jackson, without orders from Washington, entered the outskirts of Pensacola on November 6, 1814."[14] Citing the Monroe Doctrine as a pretext for invasion, he demanded that Spain order the withdrawal of all British ships, including merchants and traders. When the governor refused, he stormed the city.

Overrunning its two earthwork forts, Jackson's forces quickly overcame resistance from the number of paltry troops stationed in the city. He managed to accept its surrender the following day and occupy the governor's mansion.

Luckily for Spain, however, he didn't stay long. The British had since fled, and Pensacola was seen as too small and inconsequential to be of any use in future battles. By the time Spain had begun to muster a protest, Jackson was already gone, having abandoned the city to counter British buildups in the West. His departure would be celebrated, but not for long. For, with his victory in the Battle of New Orleans and the successful annihilation of Spain's British allies, the authorities in West Florida knew it was only a matter of time before he would return. This time, however, there would be bloodshed.

The Republic of West Florida

When most people think of the Lone Star Flag, they think of Texas. But when Louisianans think of it, they think of Florida—West Florida to be exact—for during this time, West Florida used to consist of a sizeable southern portion of Louisiana, Mississippi, and Alabama. This included Mobile, Biloxi, the parishes east of New Orleans, and even the future Louisiana capital at Baton Rouge. It was in this latter group of provinces where revolutionaries would succeed where the Patriots of East Florida had failed.

Like John McIntosh in Amelia Island, the extreme western fringes of West Florida had a sizeable American population within its borders. These Americans greatly resented the Spanish, and the monarchy, and staged a small rebellion.

Declaring their intentions to form a republic in September 1810, they fomented a quick attack against the Spanish at Baton Rouge and captured the city. Afterwards, they declared the entire territory to be a republic and drafted a constitution, modeled closely after that of the U.S. This was followed by the election of a president, Fulwar Skipwith, who established his new capital at St. Francisville, Louisiana. Skipwith, a cotton planter who lived just north of Baton Rouge, once served as U.S. Ambassador to France under Thomas Jefferson and was hardly shy about his American sympathies:

> [W]herever the voice of justice and humanity can be heard, our declaration and our just rights will be respected. But the blood which flows in our veins, like the tributary streams which form and sustain the father of rivers, encircling our delightful country, will return if not impeded, to the heart of our parent country. The genius of Washington, the immortal founder of the liberties of America, stimulates that return, and would frown upon our cause, should we attempt to change its course[15]

They even had their own marching song and pseudo national anthem, which contained verses like:

> West Floriday, that lovely nation,
> Free from king and tyranny.[16]

Like those settlers who later initiated revolution in Texas, this group chose a lone star for their national flag. Unlike in Texas, however, the Republic of West Florida wouldn't wait long for American authorities to act, as the United States would come to annex the Republic within 90 days.[17]

Though it initially appeared that Skipwith and the other rebels had gotten their way, the U.S.'s refusal to recognize it as a single entity, dividing it up instead into Alabama and Louisiana, irked many of the residents.

Today, West Florida's short-lived existence remains a unique part of Southern culture. In Louisiana, all parishes east of New Orleans are still collectively referred to as the Florida Parishes and in Jackson, Louisiana, there is even a Republic of West Florida museum.

Still, their greatest contribution is in history, as their success would inspire both the Patriots of East Florida in 1812 and the Texans in Mexico to pursue their own dreams of independence.

The Gloves Come Off

The First Seminole War, more than any other event, proved the death knell for Spanish Florida. For more than five years after the War of 1812, Seminoles raided against the Creek and American settlers across the border, creating a border fraught with violence and bloodshed. Such violence culminated in a very big way at Negro Fort.

Constructed by the British along Florida's Apalachicola River at the height of the War of 1812, Negro Fort initially served as a rallying point for Seminole Indians to stage raids against Americans and Creeks. Lying just 60 miles south of the U.S. border, the fort was well-equipped with cannons, guns and ammunition. It saw little action in the war, however, and was completely abandoned by the British in 1815. Taking up this loss of command was a large group of runaway slaves and Seminole allies, all of whom received military training from the British.

Led by a black man named Garcon and an unknown Choctaw chief, the inhabitants of the fort continued to stage raids into American territory well after the conclusion of conflicts. Most of these raids resulted in the capture and recruitment of several American slaves to their forces, in turn leading to an increased amount of runaways escaping across the border. By year's end, the fort boasted nearly one thousand fugitive slaves[18] living within its confines.

Referred to as "Negro Fort" by American settlers living along the border due to the number of escaped slaves who had taken refuge there, its existence began to be seen as a threat to the institution of Southern slavery, with many viewing it as "a center of hostility and above all a threat to the security of their slaves."[19] The Savannah Journal wrote:

> It was not to be expected, that an establishment so pernicious to the Southern States, holding out to a part of their population temptations to insubordination, would have been suffered to exist after the close of the war. In the course of last winter, several slaves from this neighborhood fled to that fort; others have lately gone from Tennessee and the Mississippi Territory. How long shall this evil, requiring immediate remedy, be permitted to exist?[20]

The Battle Begins

To prevent further raids from Negro Fort, American troops began to construct a rival fort along the Flint River in Georgia. Calling it Fort Scott, it was sold as a way to keep the Spanish-American border protected. Its real purpose however was to prevent the loss of any more slaves. While the fort itself had no problem in attracting and maintaining soldiers, it did have a problem with receiving supplies. At the time, supplying the fort involved taking the materials overland, involving difficult travel through unsettled wilderness.

To shorten this distance, Major General Andrew Jackson, now the military commander of the southern district came up with an idea to supply it by boat over the Apalachicola River by going through Spanish territory. He saw this not only as an easier route, but also one that would lead to an eventual attack by Negro Fort giving him the right to invade and destroy it. His ploy worked when on July 17, 1816, an American naval force was fired on by the Negro Fort, "resulting in the death of four U.S. soldiers."[21]

Under the direction of Col. Duncan Clinch, a retaliatory attack was launched when the well-trained expedition crossed into Spanish territory to engage the armed fort. All along the way, they suffered through several guerrilla attacks by those near Negro Fort. None of them caused any casualties, however.

When they finally reached the fort, the Americans found it to be occupied by just a few hundred defenders. Freedmen and Seminole warriors accounted for a large number of this force, but there was also a sizeable amount of women and children inside. Refusing to surrender to the better positioned Americans, Garcon, the fort's defender, raised a British flag, as well as a red flag of no quarter.

The attack was on, and the defenders exchanged open fire with Clinch's men. As the Americans rained down a barrage of cannon fire, a glowing cannonball referred to as a "hot shot," landed in the middle of the fort's magazine:

> "The explosion was awful, and the scene horrible beyond description. You cannot conceive, nor I describe the horrors of the scene. In an instant lifeless bodies were stretched upon the plain, buried in sand and rubbish, or suspended from the tops of the surrounding pines. Here lay an innocent babe, there a helpless mother; on the one side a sturdy warrior, on the other a bleeding squaw. Piles of bodies, large heaps of sand, broken guns, accoutrements, etc., covered the site of the fort."[22]

Almost all the inhabitants died instantly, their charred and bloodied body parts flying high into the air with the rest of the fort.

When the smoke cleared, the fort was gone, along with the 270 men, women and children residing inside.[23] In the ensuing aftermath, Creeks charged at the few survivors, finishing them off. Garcon and his Choctaw partner, among those surviving, were immediately fired upon, executed for their role in the earlier killing of four American soldiers. The rest were carried upriver, where, adding insult to injury, they were reposted as slaves for their former owners to come claim.

The Battle of Fowltown

Resentment over the killing of innocent women and children incensed the Seminoles, who began attacking American settlers without quarter. Joining them, were the Mikasukis, a tribe living in southern Georgia. Angered that the Americans had played such a devastating role in the attack on Negro Fort, the tribe began to rethink their alliance with the Americans and their use of land as a supply depot for nearby Fort Scott.

Attempting to block access to the eastern side of the Flint River, the Mikasuki chief, Neamathla argued that his tribe was sovereign and therefore not bound by the Creek-American alliance. He warned that he would not support encroachment upon these lands and that any such action would constitute an act of war. Ignoring these threats, the Americans called for his arrest, sending a force to capture him.

Launching a two-pronged attack on November 21 and 23, 1817, the Americans managed to push back the chief's forces and ransack his village, murdering several of the women stragglers left behind.

> Arbuckle estimated Indian losses at 6–8 killed, but also reported that his own force had lost 1 killed and 3 wounded. The U.S. soldier killed was Aaron Hughes, a fifer from the 7th Infantry. The unfortunate musician was the first U.S. soldier killed in the Seminole Wars. Many others would follow.
>
> As quickly as they could, the soldiers finished loading their wagon, rounded up a few head of cattle, and began their return march to the Flint River. There they halted on the bluff at the present site of Bainbridge and built Fort Hughes, a small blockhouse named for the slain soldier.[24]

The Scott Massacre

The retaliation staged by the spurned Mikasukis was swift and deadly. Ducking down to the Florida-Georgia border after the American raid, they lay in wait along the banks of the Apalachicola for the perfect moment to get their revenge.

When, on November 29, an open boat bearing "40 American soldiers, along with seven women and children veered near their direction, they knew that moment had come."[25]

Opening a volley of gunfire upon the unsuspecting passengers, the Indians managed to fell most of the men almost immediately. Unsatisfied with these kills, the Indians rushed the boat and soon overran its sides. Those who were not killed outright suffered a prolonged and torturous death.

> The children were taken by the heels and their brains dashed out against the sides of the boat. The men and women were scalped, all but one woman who was not wounded by the previous fire. Four men escaped by leaping overboard, of whom only two reached safety.... In twenty minutes after the first volley had been fired into the boat, every creature in it but five was killed and scalped, or bound and carried off.[26]

The massacre brought American traffic on the river to a virtual standstill. For nearly a week after, no American ships were able to make any progress upstream, as the Mikasukis, now allied with the Seminoles, staged more ambushes. Killing more soldiers and wounding others in a subsequent raid on another boat two days later, it was soon realized that no one was safe. "Not a man could show himself for an instant above the bulwark without being fired upon."[27]

Only after a rescue party was sent from Fort Scott did traffic once again resume its normal flow, allowing for Fort Scott to be resupplied. Still, the threat of future attacks loomed large.

As word of the massacres spread to D.C., it was soon realized that the border raids were no longer a mere nuisance to American settlers but were a threat to national security. The Seminoles in Spanish Florida had to be dealt with once and for all.

Prelude to a Fall

Though the U.S. Army had previously made brief excursions into West Florida, resulting in quick battles, this latest incident called for full-out war. Launching an invasion, Andrew Jackson was given orders by

Secretary of State Calhoun to deprive the Seminoles of any village or fort that could potentially be used as a staging point for further raids.

With a combination of militia and regulars from Georgia and Tennessee, along with a retinue of Lower Creek warriors who were traditional enemies of the Seminole, Jackson's Army entered Florida in March 1818. Upon crossing the border, they made their way to the old remains of Negro Fort to establish a new post. After this, they set out for the Mikasuki villages, so instrumental in the Scott Massacre. These villages were subsequently surrounded and burned. "The villages of Tallahassee and Miccosukee were both taken in March, resulting in the destruction of over 300 homes and many more lives."[28]

Satisfied that he had wiped out all of the major villages, he turned south marching against the Spanish fort at St. Marks. The Spanish at this garrison had previously tolerated the British policy of arming these Indians and were therefore guilty of abetting crimes against Americans in the eyes of Jackson.

Upon reaching the river just outside the garrison, Jackson, ever the trickster, raised the Union Jack off of one of the gunboats he had brought with him. In doing so, he lured two unsuspecting Indian chiefs out onto the boat, where he had them beaten and bound with rope. Coming ashore with his men, he then had them immediately hanged on the nearest tree, a warning to all those watching from inside the fort's gates.

Fearing that the same would happen to them if they resisted, the outmanned and outgunned defenders caved and surrendered, opening their gates to Jackson's army. There, among the few Spanish regulars and Seminole warriors, they found a Scottish trader by the name of Alexander Arbuthnot, who had previously been rumored to be involved in trading weapons to the Seminoles. As a result, he was bound, imprisoned and executed.

While Jackson's actions triggered short-lived protests from the British and Spanish governments resulting in an investigation by the United States Congress, Congress chose ultimately not to censure the popular general, providing a dangerous precedent for further egregious acts.

Pensacola: The Final Nail in Spain's Coffin

Jackson was no lover of the Seminole. He proved that time and again during his rampages against them along West Florida's rivers. Still, as much as he despised the Indians, he hated the Spanish even more.

The Spanish in his opinion were the ones primarily responsible for all of the bloodshed that had occurred during this war, as a result of their inept weakness. They therefore needed to be wiped out to ensure future stability. Although Jackson had originally written, upon his departure from St. Marks, that the Indian problem was solved and that all was peaceful, he soon changed his tune.

Trumpeting charges that the Seminole were building up a large retaliatory force in the capital at Pensacola, he called for action to move against them. While Spanish authorities time and again protested that these were merely refugees from Jackson's earlier campaigns of terror and composed of only women and children, Jackson refused to hear them out.

Not waiting for government permission, Jackson marched with his troops to the outskirts of Pensacola and once again demanded its surrender. The governor this time, "responded with gunfire, having retreated to the safety of Fort Barrancas, with 175 of his men."[29] The ensuing clash resulted in the complete capitulation of the Spanish five days later, leaving Jackson in full control of the city, and therefore all of West Florida.

For his part, the Spanish Governor of West Florida, Jose Callava, bereft of his Seminole allies and Spanish aid, was arrested and thrown in jail with his small retinue of officers. James Parton, in his *Life of Andrew Jackson*, offers an account of Callava's night in the Spanish jail:

> [T]he calaboose was as forlorn, dirty and uncomfortable an edifice as can be imagined. It contained two prisoners, Lieutenant Sousa and a young man from New Jersey, who had been arrested for shooting a snipe on the common, contrary to orders....
>
> Upon getting within the calaboose, Colonel Callava, who was really a good fellow, was seized with a sense of the ludicrousness of his situation, and communicated the same to his officers. Peals of laughter were heard within the calaboose. Clothes, chairs, cots, beds, were sent for and brought in, also a superabundant supply of provisions, including cigars, claret and champaigne. There was a popping of corks and a gurgling of wine. There were songs, jokes, imitations of the fiery Governor [Jackson], and great merriment. In short, Colonel Callava and his officers made a night of it.[30]

The End of an Era

Although some talk had been thrown around in the early 1800s regarding Florida's purchase by the United States, it did not become serious until 1818. By that time, all of East and West Florida had fallen under the effective control of the United States, with West Florida's main capital at Pensacola occupied under Jackson's forces. Because of crippling debt problems and a revolutionary problem in Central and South America, Spain found no other choice but to accept a forced treaty and cede both colonies to its northern neighbor. This was seen not only as necessary, but vital to the health of the United States. For, as Secretary of State Adams put it so eloquently, Florida was nothing more than "a derelict open to the occupancy of every enemy, civilized or savage, of the United States, and serving no other earthly purpose than as a post of annoyance to them."[31]

On February 22, 1821, the flag of Spain was raised and lowered for the very last time over the shores of Florida, as the much-anticipated Adams-Onis Treaty took effect. In exchange for their loss, Spain received $5,000,000 in debt forgiveness and a promise by the United States to respect the boundary of Texas as a part of Mexico. Jackson for his part took over the role of establishing a new government:

> Their authority included the powers to pass ordinances, levy taxes and fines, acquire public property and make regulations. Rachel Jackson, his wife, who had arrived in Pensacola while still a Spanish colony on June 28, had written to a friend to complain about the lack of observation of the Sabbath, drunkenness and the gambling houses. It is possible this influenced Jackson's decision to include in the proclamation his urging of the council to make regulations for the observance of the Sabbath, prohibition of gaming houses and public gaming (except for billiards) and forbidding the sale of liquor to any United States soldier.[32]

As the last of the Spanish officials sailed out of Pensacola to new posts in Havana, Governor Jose Callava among them, the remaining Spaniards readied themselves for an uncertain future.

As Howard Zinn stated:

> Jackson began raids into Florida, arguing it was a sanctuary for escaped slaves and for marauding Indians. Florida, he said, was essential to the defense of the United States. It was that classic modern preface to a war of conquest. Thus began the Seminole War of 1818, leading to the American acquisition of Florida. It appears on classroom maps politely as "Florida Purchase, 1819"—but it came from Andrew Jackson's military campaign across the Florida border, burning Seminole villages, seizing Spanish forts, until Spain was "persuaded" to sell. He acted, he said, by the "immutable laws of self-defense."[33]

4

Guerrillas in the Mist
Florida's Seminole Wars

For a tribe whose name literally translates to "wild people,"[1] the Seminoles definitely lived up to that moniker and more.

Having first arrived as a trickle in 1767, the Seminoles began to pour across the border into Florida following a series of disastrous wars with the Upper Creeks in 1814. There, among the Spanish, they found a place where they could roam freely and live in moderate protection from outside invasion. In addition, they found a tolerant government that was willing to trade with and arm them, as well as one that did not frown upon their incorporation of runaway slaves into their tribe. They did not, however, find lasting peace. Continuous border raids from the Creeks and the subsequent invasions from the Americans saw to that.

By the time Spain officially transferred power over to the United States, the Seminoles were still an established force in the panhandle. Though diminished in numbers, they still retained claim over their old hunting grounds, roaming about freely in the panhandle. This worried the Americans, who wished to plant cotton on these lands and greatly resented the benign treatment that Seminoles afforded runaway slaves. Taking action, the Americans called for negotiations to resettle the Seminoles in new lands.

The resultant conference, "held over 250 miles from the Seminole homeland,"[2] at Moultrie Creek, concluded with greatly diminished freedoms for the Seminoles. For one, all the Seminoles were to be relocated from West Florida to a reservation in central Florida. Comprised of over "four million acres,"[3] this reservation would include no coastal lands whatsoever so as to deprive the tribe of any attempts at foreign trade. As a compromise, they would be "provided with $6000 worth of farm equipment, $5000 a year to be doled out over a twenty year period, as well as meat, corn and salt for a year."[4]

Though on paper this seemed like a fair trade, in reality it amounted to nothing more than a way to control tribal movement. Evidence of this lay in the fact that the Americans stipulated the maintenance of a White agent, a subagent and an interpreter to live on the land with the Seminoles in order to monitor reservation activity. Further stipulations argued that "the reservation could not serve as a haven for runaway slaves."[5]

As a result of the treaty, the bulk of the tribe moved south. The more militant braves never complied with the Treaty of Moultrie Creek. They had already been forced from their traditional hunting grounds and had changed their farming habits to suit their new circumstances and they were not about to make another change. Neamathia, a Mikasukis from North Florida, thus challenged Governor William Duval openly: "I will tell you plainly if I had the power, I would tonight cut the throat of every white man in Florida."[6]

A Treaty of Intimidation

The Seminole had barely begun to wear out their welcome on the new lands when a call went up from Washington to resettle them once again. This time, they would be going west to Oklahoma.

Contrary to what the musical of the same name may say, Oklahoma was hardly a land of plenty. In fact, to the Seminole, it was about as different from the swamps and marshlands of subtropical Florida as you could get. This was confirmed after a delegation of chiefs went to examine the lands and came back with stories of its desolation. More so, three of them stated that upon reaching it, "they were intimidated and tricked into signing away their Florida lands, so that they would be forced into relocating."[7] Such intimidation maneuvers would later form the basis of what became known as the Treaty of Payne's Landing, the Seminole version of the much larger Indian Removal Act.

While some tribal leaders felt that they had no choice, but to leave, others like Chief Micanopy resisted. They stated that the original Treaty at Moultrie Creek had, at the very least, guaranteed them rights to central Florida "for a period of 20 years."[8]

When the Americans finally set a firm date for their removal, tensions began to rise, as Whites began to curtail a few more of the basic Seminole freedoms that were left. The biggest of these were racially motivated, essentially reducing the Seminole to the position of slaves and barring them from owning property or employing weapons.

Upon seeing the treaty, Osceola, a Seminole warrior of mixed

European ancestry, thrust his dagger through the heart of the treaty, and cried out:

> "Am I a Negro slave? My skin is dark, but not black! I am an Indian, a Seminole. The white man shall not make me black. I will make the white man red with blood, and then blacken him in the sun and rain, where the wolf shall gnaw his bones and the buzzard shall live on his flesh."[9]

It wouldn't be long before he would make good on his word.

A Different Kind of War

The Seminole never made an official declaration of war against the Americans. In fact, the Seminoles needed no excuse to start attacking. They just did. These attacks began to manifest in far deadlier ways, as the official deadline for departure loomed closer. Their initial target for attack was not soldiers, but innocent civilians.

Almost immediately, American settlers in 1835 found themselves under full-scale assault. The Matanzas, Tomoka and Mosquito areas were particularly vulnerable due to their relative isolation from American forts and cities. As these regions had a large amount of sugar plantations, the Seminoles found it beneficial to not only steal their cattle, but also their

Published in 1836, this colorful piece of propaganda was released in an attempt to rouse sympathy among Americans outside of Florida. However, like Vietnam in later years, as the war wound on, the more unpopular it became. The caption along the bottom reads: "The above is intended to represent the horrid Massacre of the Whites in Florida, in December 1835, and January, February, March and April 1836, when near Four Hundred (including women and children) fell victims to the barbarity of the Negroes and Indians." (Wikimedia Commons).

valuables. Later, these attacks began to grow more violent as some of the radical Seminoles found that killing off the owners and freeing their slaves helped kill two birds with one stone. First, it scared the Whites from wanting to resettle the land and second, it helped increase tribal membership with the incorporation of the newly freed slaves.

By December 1835, two dozen plantations had been dealt with in such a manner, with all those dwelling on the property—the owner, his wife, their children, their extended family, as well as all the hired workers—paying the price. Such attacks had the effect of scaring off Whites from settlement resulting in the complete abandonment of entire communities. As the New Year approached, the message had been received loud and clear: If you're White, stay out of rural Florida or risk death.

While these attacks were largely targeted at settlers, the Whites weren't the only ones who had to worry, however. Soon, moderate Seminoles, who favored emigration out of Florida, found themselves under attack, as well. This was most dramatized following the brutal death of Charley Emathla, one of the Seminole leaders in favor of removal, who found himself the subject of a murderous ambush on his way home from selling cattle to the Americans.

When his mutilated body was discovered some days later, they found money scattered all about him, a clear sign from Osceola that Seminole siding with the Americans would be treated no different than the Whites. As these attacks became more prevalent, the moderate chiefs began to abandon their lands en masse, resulting in the fleeing of hundreds for the safety of the American forts. Like the settlers, they had begun to fear the rise of Osceola and his radicals and were unprepared for the lengths these warriors were willing to go to prevent them from leaving.

It soon became clear to both sides, just how different this war would be.

The Dade Massacre

As panic spread across the territory, increased calls for protection began to go up from the settlers. To quell the rebellion, in December 1835 the government decided to relocate two companies of men under the command of Brevet Major Francis Langhorne Dade from Tampa's Fort Brooke to Fort King in central Florida, where most of the killing was taking place.

Throughout their five-day march, the soldiers faced attack after attack, as they were shadowed by a fierce and unseen band of Seminole warriors crouching behind the thickets. These attacks eventually cornered them into an ambush, where, on December 28, in an all too eerie sign of things to come, they were fired upon from all sides.

In the attack, only three managed to escape alive. One of these, Edmund De Courcey, was hunted down and killed the next day by a renegade warrior, who shadowed his tracks much the same way the larger band had done to Dade's company. "Only Ransom Clark and Joseph Sprague managed to make it to the fort still alive, and alert the troops of what was going on."[10] By that point, however, they were all too aware of the situation.

Trouble at Fort King

Around the same time that the Seminoles were attacking Dade's company, a similar attack had occurred at Fort King. Led by Osceola, a Seminole of mixed Scottish and Creek ancestry who was rapidly becoming the face of the rebellion, this attack came as a complete surprise to the Indian Removal Agent Wiley Thompson, who considered himself a personal friend of the warrior after he had worked to gain his release and restore his arms.

Osceola, rendezvousing with other warriors, made use of his restored weapons, attacking Thompson along with his lieutenant and several others who had ventured outside for a stroll. Caught completely off guard, these soldiers met a similar end to Dade's company. Due to the surprise double ambush, it wouldn't be until February of the following year that an exploratory party could be mustered up to examine the results of the Dade Massacre.

There, upon witnessing the littered, decomposing corpses of his former comrades, Major Ethan Allen Hitchcock, who headed the party, vented his frustration—not with the Indians, but rather with the war itself.

In his journal he captured the hopelessness he felt, stating: "The government is in the wrong, and this is the chief cause of the persevering opposition of the Indians, who have nobly defended their country against our attempt to enforce a fraudulent treaty. The natives used every means to avoid war, but were forced into it by the tyranny of our government."[11]

As the casualties and losses continued to mount in 1836, Hitchcock's opinion gradually became the norm, as the American public, unused to losing so badly, began to slowly turn away from the war effort.

A Real Ghost of a City

While the first stage of the Second Seminole War was mainly confined to the hinterlands of rural Florida, bloodshed eventually spilled into the more populous regions of the state—the most notorious being the attack on Indian Key, a boomtown just north of Key West.

While much of South Florida was still underpopulated, the Florida Keys had proven an exception to the rule, for at the beginning of the 1820s, Key West was on its way to becoming one of the wealthiest cities in the United States.

Due to the jagged coral reefs located off the southern coast, as well the hurricane-prone nature of the nearby Gulf, many treasure ships found themselves run aground near the Keys. These ships would lay vacant for many years with no one to claim the goods or cargo they carried. Soon, American settlers in Key West started doing so for themselves. Such claims made many of the island's earliest proprietors extremely wealthy, attracting a substantial amount of interest from those outside the region. This all changed when Jacob Housman arrived down from New York.

Like most speculators, Housman was originally interested in opening up his wreckage and salvaging station on Key West. Disputes with the locals on the island, however, led him to go northward, eventually forcing him to set up base on Indian Key.

At first, the small island offered almost none of the promise of its wealthy southern neighbor. With time and investment, however, Housman was able to transform the small island into a thriving settlement, with wharves, warehouses, a general store, an inn and several dwellings.

Within five years, people were no longer interested in Key West, as Indian Key was the new "It" town. In fact, so successful was Housman at attracting new settlers that the once barren island became the new capital of Monroe County. Several reasons accounted for this. For one, it was easier to get to, being just a short sail from the mainland, and secondly, it was unestablished, drawing in newcomers from all over the country. Things soon took a horrible, ghastly turn, however, during the Second Seminole War.

Being far removed from the mainland, Indian Key was lulled into a false sense of security. Like Key West, the settlers felt that a massacre of New River proportions could never happen to them. Even when all the other Keys were abandoned, the city operated on a "not me" attitude and continued much the same in its daily operations. This all changed on August 7, 1840. In the early morning hours, a band of Seminoles led by Chief Chekika landed on the island and attacked the settlers.

Housman had sent a letter to the federal government proposing a contract that would pay him "$200 a head to capture or kill Indians in South Florida,"[12] Having been at the receiving end of the actions of such letter, the Indians went straight for him. As they smashed in his front door, Housman and his wife Elizabeth raced out the back. "The couple ran barefoot across the sharp coral and plunged into the water." Housman found a boat and rowed safely to the schooner *Medium*, tied up near Tea Table Key. The Indians "looted his house, then set it afire."[13]

Housman and his wife escaped but others were killed during the burning and looting. Dr. Perrine, a physician who had established himself on the island shortly before the raid, attempted to negotiate a peace with the raiding party while his family escaped "hiding in a turtle crawl under the house,"[14] but was "hacked" to pieces. His loss was particularly shocking due to his high status as "American consul to the Mexican state of Campeche."[15] At the end of the day, over a dozen of the island residents lay dead and all of the city's structures were burned to the ground, effectively wiping out Housman's settlement.

Though some settlers returned to rebuild, the island's salvaging industry never quite recovered. Housman wanted no part of it anymore and died the following year. Not surprisingly, Indian Key's status as the capital of Monroe County was lost shortly afterward to Key West, where it has remained until this day.

By 1880, the small community was all but extinct with only one wrecker and a couple of full-time residents still living there. Today, it is a ghost town—it's burned-out brick and stone foundations a testament to what once was and what might have been.

Tragedy and Hunger at Camp Izard

Horse: it's what's for dinner was hardly the slogan General Gaines had in mind when marching out to face the Seminoles. That is exactly what ended up happening, however, after a disastrous expedition under his leadership failed in a monumental way.

Establishing himself at Fort Brooke and finding it practically empty of supplies, Gaines led a contingent of soldiers out to Fort King to retrieve what he had viewed as a simple shipping error by his superiors. Following roughly the same path that Dade's star-crossed companies had traveled, his soldiers came upon their decaying corpses, still left unburied after all this time.

Stopping to bury the bodies in three mass graves, Gaines continued on to Fort King, only to find that it too was short on supplies. Not knowing what to do, he received a week's worth of rations from Fort Drane and resumed his march back to Fort Brooke. Though he was willing to accept the bad intel delivered to him by his superiors, he was unwilling to leave completely empty-handed. He had come too far for that.

Deciding that some accomplishment was better than nothing, he veered his troops down a different path on the way back to post to engage the Seminole directly in their stronghold "along the Cove of the Withaloochee River."[16] Lacking direct knowledge of the Florida backcountry, Gaines' expedition failed to find the main ford across the river, inadvertently alerting the Seminoles across the way to their arrival.

With the element of surprise completely shattered, Gaines was forced to engage them in cross-stream gunfire for the next two days, while seeking out a place where he might attempt to cross. When this was at last discovered, Lt. Izard, leading the charge, was wounded, forcing the expedition to a grinding halt.

Stuck from forging across the water and now barred from backpedaling, Gaines made the decision to strike camp and set up a fortification. For the next eight days, Gaines' forces battled the Seminole as their supplies dwindled down to critical levels. With almost no rations left, Gaines made the fateful decision for his soldiers "to eat their horses, as well as their mules and a dog to keep from starving to death."[17]

Eventually, their suffering ended after Duncan Clinch took the initiative to leave Fort Drane on his own accord. Though the men were saved, the expedition proved a complete disaster, and they eventually returned to Fort Brooke more demoralized than ever.

A False and Deceptive Peace

For all the death, gloom and destruction wrought by the Dade and New River Massacres, the American military actually had reason to hope in the beginning of 1837.

Flush from a win at the Battle of Hatchee-Lustee, where they managed to make off with a sizeable number of Seminoles, including women and children, as well as cattle, they were able to pressure most of the resisting leaders into a truce. By March, a complete capitulation treaty had been signed by several chiefs, including Micanopy, who "agreed to go West with their families along with the accompaniment of their Black and non–Seminole allies."[18]

While many Seminoles were excited at the prospect of peace, two leaders in particular, Osceola and Sam Jones, continued to oppose any form of treaty that required their relocation out of Florida. They vowed to fight on, marching into a lightly guarded Fort Brooke "with 200 warriors, to 'liberate' 700 of their departing brethren from captivity."[19]

Furious over this deception, Thomas Sidney Jesup stewed over what do.

Convinced that peace had come at last, Jesup had previously released a large number of soldiers and volunteers from their duty, reducing their presence in Florida. He was thus left unprepared for the renewed attacks Osceola and Sam Jones started throwing his way. As the war ground on, Jesup decided to pursue a different strategy to bring about victory, utilizing the same elements of trickery he felt that the Seminole had employed against him.

Sending out small reconnaissance groups to harass the Seminoles, Jesup put the pressure on like never before, employing guerrilla-style tactics to force more peace talks. When one of these engagements ended up with the capturing of King Philip, one of the most important chiefs in all of Florida, Jesup felt that his now-or-never chance had finally arrived.

Instructing King Philip to write his son, Coacoochee, to arrange a meeting "under a banner of truce to negotiate a new treaty, he set a trap for his arrival, ambushing him as soon as he arrived."[20]

Later, he used the same tactic against Osceola and Coa Hadjo, as well as Micanopy and three other chiefs, who had similarly "showed up under a white flag under the auspices of peace."[21] Osceola would later be transferred to Fort Moultrie, where he was visited by various townspeople and artists.

> The portraitists George Catlin, W.M. Laning, and Robert John Curtis, the three artists known to have painted Osceola from life, persuaded the Seminole leader to allow his portrait to be painted despite the fact that he was gravely ill at this point. Osceola and Curtis developed a close friendship, conversing at length during the painting sessions, with Curtis painting two oil portraits of Osceola, one of which remains in the Charleston Museum. These paintings have inspired numerous widely distributed prints and engravings, and cigar store figures were also based on them.[22]

Though Jesup's tactics proved effective in dwindling down leadership in the resistance, it did not, by any means, lead to peace. If anything, it hardened the Seminole even more. Further, his blatant use of deception to achieve their capture angered many in the American public. This was especially expressed upon Osceola's arrest, who, at that point, had achieved a sort of Robin Hood-like status in the minds of many Americans.

Thus, with the onset of increased fighting and the opinion that all honor had been effectively sapped out of the war by Jesup's trickery, the conflict became increasingly unpopular, garnering a significant anti-war sentiment from both the public and the government.

Seminole Multi-Racialism

Given all the bloodshed and violence that accrued as a result of the Seminole Wars, it's often lost on contemporaries as to why exactly the wars were fought in the first place. After all, the Americans had the Seminole right where they wanted them after the conclusion of the First Seminole War—confined to a reservation on the worst land available.

George Catlin captured the likeness of Osceola while the leader was imprisoned in Fort Moultrie in 1838. His treacherous capture by General Jesup under a white flag of truce caused an uproar among the international public, including members of Congress. Although an enemy of the American government, Osceola's bravery would become widely respected earning him a burial with full military honors. His gravestone at Fort Moultrie is inscribed with the words "Patriot and Warrior" (George Catlin, *Os-ce-o-lá, The Black Drink, a Warrior of Great Distinction*, 1838, oil on canvas, 30⅞ × 25⅞ in., Smithsonian American Art Museum, Gift of Mrs. Joseph Harrison, Jr., 1985.66.301).

Blocked from the sea and totally dependent upon the American government for support, this tribe instigated no violence or attacks against the settlers, and lodged minimal protests at best, mostly regarding inadequate deliveries for cattle and other supplies. So why then were the Americans so threatened by their mere presence? Well, it all boils down to acceptance.

More than any other tribe, the Seminole represented a direct threat to the planter elite, not because of their history as enemies, but rather their traditional tribal values regarding racial tolerance and acceptance. For, while planters could tolerate the cultural distinction of the Seminoles, they could not stomach their inclusion of Blacks and renegade Whites into their ranks. This, to the average nineteenth-century planter, was anathema.

It was no secret that the Seminole were not one tribe, but rather a strange amalgam of many different tribes, including Lower Creeks, Choctaw, Yamasee and Yuchi. This odd mixture accounted for their reputation as "wild men"[23] among the Spanish, as they roamed about as wanderers in the vast untamed jungles of Florida, unified only through their refugee status. Still what irked Americans the most was their inclusion of other non–Indian races into the fold, most notably runaway Black slaves.

Finding kinship with the slaves, who, like themselves, were treated as less than human by their American counterparts, many Seminoles practiced a policy of tolerance, openly including them within their ranks. This was disturbing to plantation society, in general, who feared that widespread knowledge of this might lead to increased runaways and rebellions. As if all this weren't bad enough for planters to stomach, the Seminoles also practiced polygamy and race mixing. This was just too bizarre for any of them to fathom, even for other Indian tribes of the time, and would ultimately boil over into war.

Pyrrhic Victories

Osceola's capture and death hardly proved the end of the Second Seminole War. On the contrary, it hardened resistance even more.

By the time the war was well into its third year, Florida was literally flooded with volunteers from all around the country "including such far-away places as Pennsylvania and Missouri."[24] These forces were so overwhelming that General Jesup had trouble feeding and coordinating them all.

Assigning a contingent to Col. Zachary Taylor, Jesup cleared the way for him to lead a striking and devastating blow once and for all, ordering him to march south toward Lake Okeechobee.

Along the way things looked pretty rosy, with ninety Seminole warriors surrendering outright in the face of Taylor's thousand-man army.[25] With things going so well, Taylor stopped and rested his army just north of the lake. There, "he constructed a small fort to house his sick and guard the newly captured prisoners"[26] before resuming his march on Christmas Day.

Taylor was unprepared for the harsh conditions he found on the battlefield. The Seminoles, led by Alligator, Sam Jones and Coacoochee, were well aware of his advances and had positioned themselves strategically behind the hammock—a type of forested island in wetland habitats—with a thick wave of sawgrass blocking their exposure. To get to them, Taylor and his men were forced to charge across swaths of mud-caked soil, incurring infections along the way.

Sending his volunteers out first, Taylor watched as the Seminole warriors easily routed them, killing twenty before they even had a chance to retreat.[27] To counter this, he sent in a second wave of over two hundred men. They suffered even worse casualties, with nearly forty percent of their force cut down including four of their officers.

> Only after a final third charge, with 160 soldiers, made up mostly from remnants and survivors leftover from the first two waves, were they finally able to lodge the Seminoles from their position. Upon doing so, they chased them to the shore of the lake, where Taylor attempted to flank and capture them.[28]

The Seminoles managed to escape, however, making their way across the lake to the other side of the shore. While Taylor claimed victory for dislodging the warriors, his far superior forces, which were double that of the Seminoles at the beginning of the battle, "sustained 26 deaths and over a hundred wounded to the Seminoles' twelve casualties."[29]

Following up on his "victory," Taylor's forces were joined by Jesup's under the command of Lt. Levin Powell in January the following year. Their combined forces attempted to surround and attack the Seminoles in the heart of their camp. In a repeat of Okeechobee, their initial attempts failed, however, and they were repelled suffering "22 wounded and four dead."[30]

A later battle near the Loxahatchee River finally managed to dislodge them, but again, at the end of the day, the victory was pyrrhic resulting in devastating losses. The Americans were finding out just how difficult guerrilla warfare really was.

Cities of Refugees

It might seem pretty strange, but Florida actually owes a huge debt of thanks to the Second Seminole War for contributing to the growth of its cities.

When the war first broke out, Florida was largely unchanged from much of what it had been under Spanish rule. By 1835, the main industry in Florida was still agriculture, with sugar rather than cotton gaining traction due to the subtropical nature of the region. Such agricultural development stymied any real growth in its cities, making Florida one of the least populated territories in the United States. In fact, according to census maps at the time, there "were less than six people per square mile"[31]—*a figure not even outmatched in rural Mississippi.* After the outbreak of hostilities, these figures became even bleaker as settlers and homesteaders abandoned their lands altogether, collapsing Florida's burgeoning sugar industry and forcing the territory's rural settlers to exile in the peninsula's many forts.

These forts were well armed and received increasingly large amounts of funding from the government, which in turn helped ensure protection and food for the fleeing refugees. As the war dragged on, however, things soon changed as the public began to resent the ongoing war effort.

Recognizing the need to scale down the conflict and save more money, more resolutions were pushed through to help economize the war. One such measure called for "the reduction of goods and materials to be made available to shelter-seeking civilians."[32] These people and their families, it was argued, were consuming a large amount of the rations that would normally be going to support the military. Such reliance created a culture of dependence among their population, which was at the heart of most of the war's funding problems.

Depriving the refugees of further food and materials, the army in turn turned them out on their own. Rather than leave, however, many stayed, clearing and settling on the lands immediately surrounding these forts. As the fighting got worse, these communities became closer-knit, forming a second area of defense around the stockades.

By war's end, these defensive communities became towns in their own right, often absorbing and later dismantling the forts they relied upon for survival. Today, the cities of Tampa (Fort Brooke), Ocala (Fort King), Fort Lauderdale (Fort Lauderdale), Lake City (Fort Alligator), Fort Pierce (Fort Pierce), Jupiter (Fort Jupiter), Orlando (Fort Gatlin), Palatka (Fort Shannon/Palatka), Fort Myers (Fort Myers) and Miami (Fort Dallas) can all trace their roots back to the Second Seminole War and the original refugees who fled there for protection.

The War Winds Down

On August 14, 1842, William J. Worth, the new commander of the armed forces in Florida, declared an effective end to all hostilities with the Seminoles.

By that point, the regular Army serving in the territory had dwindled down to just 1,890 men,[33] and attacks were largely scattered and unorganized. To maintain this peace, Worth offered each Indian leader, still in resistance, the choice of "whether to move West with a rifle, money and one year's worth of rations, or stay on a reservation in the southwest of Florida."[34]

By spring the following year, only one regiment, the Eighth Infantry, was still in Florida. In November 1843 Worth reported that the only Indians left in Florida were "42 Seminole warriors, 33 Mikasukis, 10 Creeks and 10 Tallahassees, with women and children bringing the total to about 300."[35] He also stated that these Indians were all living on the reservation and were no longer a threat to the White population of Florida.

Fort Dallas was one of many forts constructed across the state of Florida during the Seminole Wars. These forts would ultimately lead to the development of cities as settlers clumped around them for safety. This fort proved the impetus for Miami's settlement in the nineteenth century (Fort Dallas, Miami, Florida, ca. 1930, State Archives of Florida, Florida Memory).

A Vietnam Quagmire in the Heart of the Florida Backcountry

Up until then, Americans had never experienced a war quite like Florida's Second Seminole War; all major American wars had had a start and finish. You couldn't say that for the Second Seminole War. It began, just as it ended, inauspiciously, with major losses, little gains, and a complete disintegration of American morale.

Never before in American history had an entire company of American soldiers been wiped out, let alone by a group many in America considered to be savages. Also, never before had a war cost so much money, "by some estimates ranging up to $40 million,"[36]—more than $784 million in modern-day money.

Other firsts never encountered in an Indian War were the inclusion of almost the entire American military in the action. In the first year of the war alone, for example, "there were only 7500 troops in the entire regular Army, yet over 10,169 armed forces served in the conflict."[37] Massive volunteer and militia groups, which boosted numbers, significantly added to these forces, yet total victory remained elusive against a much smaller force.

> For the Seminoles, the fight was not entirely in vain. Chastened by seven years of humiliating defeats, the United States surrendered many of its most

stringent demands, even if it would not allow a critical mass of Seminoles to remain in Florida under any circumstances. Yet, Coacoochee was right, the whites were too strong. Not too strong to defeat the Seminoles, but too weak to admit they could lose to them, which, at a cost of tens of millions of dollars and over 1500 lives, amounted to the same thing.[38]

As the realization of losing began to sink in, American support for the war effort rapidly declined. Many began to view it as a lost cause—a war—which, due to its guerrilla nature, was unwinnable, evoking Vietnam-like sentiments that wouldn't be mirrored for the next 130 years. The fact that it ended just as inconclusively as its future counterpart drives the comparison home even more.

5

In the Shadow of the Big House

*Florida, Slavery
and Race Relations
During the Civil War*

When Florida joined the Union in 1845, there was never any question over whether it was to enter as slave or free. That matter had already been decided many years prior.

Three centuries before the United States acquired Florida, the institution of slavery had been endorsed and established on the peninsula. Its practice, however, varied greatly from what the United States was to introduce upon annexation, with many Africans playing a prominent role in government and military affairs.

> Floridanos of African descent were present from the earliest Spanish expeditions to the peninsula....
>
> The first recorded slaves to reach La Florida arrived in late September 1526 as part of the Lucas Vázquez de Ayllón expedition. Ayllón brought as many as 100 slaves to support a new Spanish settlement, which he named San Miguel de Gualdape (near present-day Sapelo Island, Ga.). The short-lived colony endured for less than two months; many of the slaves rebelled and by November 1526 the settlement was abandoned.[1]

As the ruling power for the bulk of its early colonial days, Spain had a free hand in regulating and codifying the treatment and cultivation of slaves in early Florida. Under their rule, a three-tier system was promulgated resulting in the development of an interchangeable hierarchy.

Within this hierarchy there existed Whites, slaves and free persons of color. All of these groups abided by different stations, according to their status, but not all were restricted from joining the other ranks. In fact, a great amount of fluidity existed, resulting in slaves changing places with slave owners and free Blacks joining the ranks of free Whites in cities and towns. Such a fluid nature evolved over time, with slavery in Florida becoming almost a mirror image of what had developed in French Louisiana.

As Florida grew and developed, so too did its liberalism with regards to slaves and slavery. Using the "Siete Partidas," a group of Castilian laws established in the thirteenth century, as an overarching guide, the conditions of slavery, as established in Florida, were not based upon race but rather the need for cheap labor. In many cases, "White criminals and convicts were pushed into a position of servitude to atone for their crimes and served as slaves,"[2] as well.

Furthermore, the Siete Partidas viewed slavery as an unnatural condition, by which persons should be allowed to escape. Because of this, a slave living his or her entire life in servitude was almost unheard of and in many ways, discouraged. On the contrary, Spanish Floridian slave owners practiced a policy of regular manumission, so that no slave spent more than a few years in that condition. To speed this up, slaves were also encouraged "to serve the Crown for a period of time in military service to achieve their freedom."[3]

In addition to the Siete Partidas, slaves were also guaranteed rights by the Catholic Church. These rights included the ability to attend school and learn how to read and write for all male slaves, as well as respect for their rights to attend mass if they chose to convert to Catholicism.

> Slavery existed in Spain, but slaves had legal rights within the Spanish slave system, including the right to own property.... Black African slaves arrived in the Spanish colonies in the early 16th century, where they replaced the forced labor of the indigenous population. Enslaved Africans first set foot in St. Augustine at its founding in 1565 as members of Pedro Menéndez de Avilés's colonizing expedition. Despite slave rebellions in the Spanish American colonies, by the 18th century, Spanish Florida had a growing population of both free and enslaved black colonists.[4]

Yet another unique feature present in early Spanish slavery, nearly absent from every other American state at the time, was the slave's right to equal access in court. In some cases, slaves could even take their owners to court to seek remedy for physical abuse or to prevent the separation of a family member or loved one. "In certain instances, they could even sue their owners."[5]

As a result of such loose restrictions, Florida cultivated a thriving community of Free Blacks. These communities lived right alongside their White counterparts and, in many cases, mixed with them through marriage, an act sanctioned by both the government and the church.

Zephaniah Kingsley and Slavery

When the Americans annexed Florida in 1821, they had done so with one primary goal in mind: to change the conditions of Florida society to match more closely with those in the United States. This, more than any other, was the most pressing matter of the time, and they certainly didn't waste a second rectifying it.

Shocked at what they found in the capitals of St. Augustine and Pensacola, where they discovered mixed race couples inhabiting the same home with the same legal rights as Free Whites, they sought to learn more about these policies, invoking the aid of wealthy, English-speaking planters who lived under Spanish rule. One such man they called upon was Zephaniah Kingsley, a plantation owner near present-day Jacksonville.

Appointed to the territorial legislature in 1823, Kingsley, an Englishman by birth, sought to persuade the legislature of the value of retaining the Spanish system, arguing the societal benefits of the three-tiered hierarchy in place. Like the Spanish, he felt that race should not be a determining factor in slavery:

> Kingsley's arguments also extended to the waffling status of free Blacks in Florida, a group, which lived very differently than their "free" Black counterparts in the U.S.
>
> Addressing the council on this matter, Kingsley stated, "I consider that our personal safety as well as the permanent condition of our Slave property is intimately connected with and depends much on our good policy in making it the interest of our free colored population to be attached to good order and have a friendly feeling towards the white population."[6]

Such arguments proved anathema to the White legislators, however, and Kingsley soon resigned from his post.

In spite of his disillusion, Kingsley tried one last time to convince the Americans of the value of this system by publishing a treatise imploring Americans to respect free Black property and rights.

> Few, I think will deny that color and condition, if properly considered, are two very separate qualities. But the fact is, that in almost every instance, our legislators, for want of due consideration, have mistaken the shadow for the substance, and confounded together two very different things; thereby substantiating by law a dangerous and inconvenient antipathy, which can have no better foundation than prejudice. It is much to be regretted that those who enact laws to regulate slaves, and free people of color, are often obliged to consult popularity rather than policy and their own good sense.[7]

Like his earlier pleas, this treatise had little effect in swaying opinion and was actually perverted to be used as a defense for the existence of the American version of slavery.

New Rules

By the beginning of the second decade under American rule, Florida no longer resembled anything of its former Spanish existence either in society or institution. It, for all other purposes, had become as Southern as Georgia or Alabama, adopting from its westerly neighbor the following codifications word for word:

> Alabama, 1833, section 31—"Any person or persons who attempt to teach any free person of color, or slave, to spell, read, or write, shall, upon conviction thereof by indictment, be fined in a sum not less than two hundred and fifty dollars, nor more than five hundred dollars."
> Alabama, 1833, section 32—"Any free person of color who shall write for any slave a pass or free paper, on conviction thereof, shall receive for every such offense, thirty-nine lashes on the bare back, and leave the state of Alabama within thirty days thereafter...."
> Alabama, 1833, section 33—"Any slave who shall write for any other slave, any pass or free-paper, upon conviction, shall receive, on his or her back, fifty lashes for the first offence, and one hundred lashes for every offence thereafter...."[8]

Furthermore, interracial marriages were banned outright. Even those interracial marriages recognized as legitimate under the Spanish government were dissolved by the new legislature, resulting in the breaking up of entire families.

The changes brought on by the United States, with regards to free Black society, forever changed the Floridian landscape. No longer was it a place where a Black man, born into slavery, could eventually aspire to freedom through hard work or manumission. Slavery was now codified as a cradle-to-grave institution.

Anna Kingsley: Story of a Black Slave Owner

While the new state government sought to eradicate all vestiges of Spanish Florida's past, they couldn't wipe out everything. For, under the terms of the Adams-Onis Treaty, all former "Spanish" landowners swearing allegiance to the United States were to have their property rights secured and their status as citizens unmolested. So it was that the increasingly racist Florida legislature was forced to reckon with one of the former holdouts, Anna Kingsley—a free Black woman, who happened to be one of the largest property owners in the State.

Born in a tiny village in West Africa, Anna grew up with all the privileges of royalty, having been born the daughter of a ruling chief. This privilege was short-lived, however, when Anna was captured by a rival tribe and sold into slavery. Brought to a disembarkation point, Anna was processed and later sent to Cuba in chains. There, she was examined and put up for auction.

Catching the eye of Zephaniah Kingsley, a slave trader and merchant living in Spanish Florida, she was purchased and brought back to his home near present-day Orange Park. Though Kingsley was 30 years her senior, she arrived at his home pregnant, having "married him in a traditional African ceremony prior to their departure."[9]

Kingsley, an Englishman, was unique for his time in viewing Africans to be superior to Whites in looks and aesthetics. Sharing relations with her, he soon set up housekeeping where she went on to bear him three children, George, Martha and Mary.

"Upon the birth of their last child, she and all the children were granted legal emancipation by Kingsley."[10] This not only upped their status on the plantation, but it also guaranteed that they could inherit land and remain protected from being resold back into slavery upon his death. As a result of her newfound freedom, Anna was granted greater responsibility over the management of the plantation. Like Kingsley, she was very liberal with her treatment of slaves and was well liked as a result. Her role in this position soon increased exponentially after the outbreak of the Patriot Revolution in 1812, when Kingsley was kidnapped.

Abandoning the land with her slaves, Anna appealed to the Spanish for aid, going so far as to burn her dwellings down to prove her loyalty. For her actions, "she was granted 350 acres of her own by the Spanish"[11] and was rewarded with more land by Kingsley himself, upon his return from capture.

After the Patriots were expelled, Anna and Kingsley moved to Fort George Island, where they took up residence in the former Patriot leader's home. Taking over management of this new plantation, Anna had Kingsley construct her a separate residence "where she might live and carry on with her duties."[12] Meanwhile, Kingsley entered into "a polygamous marriage with three other slaves, spawning two more children from them."[13] While this was anything but a usual home environment, it was, nonetheless, idyllic for Anna, who felt at home on the land and genuinely liked her duties.

This all ended with the Americans, who curtailed her freedoms and dissolved her marriage, denying her the property and rights she had worked so hard to obtain.

After moving with Kingsley to the all–Black Republic of Haiti, she returned to Florida upon his death, "suing the government for her former property and slaves."[14] As a result of a past agreement between the U.S. and

5. In the Shadow of the Big House

Kingsley Plantation on Fort George Island was one of the more unique plantations in the American South as it was owned and operated by an African American woman named Anna Madgigine Jai Kingsley. Anna had spent her early years as a slave before capturing the eye of her owner Zephaniah. She would eventually marry him and bear several children. Referred to by friends as "the African princess," Anna was granted lands in her own right by the Spanish government, and upon her husband's death, she would prevail in court over Zephaniah's sister and come to own Kingsley Plantation, as well. At the time of the Civil War, she and her children were among the wealthiest residents of Florida and were staunch Union sympathizers (photograph by Shrickus, CC BY-SA 4.0, Wikimedia Commons).

Spain, which respected the property of free Blacks before the transfer of power, Anna won her suit and resumed her life as a slave owner.

When the Civil War divided the country, Anna and her daughters' families supported the Union. With Florida's secession and hostility from Confederates intensifying, Anna had to leave her home again. In 1862 she traveled with relatives to New York. They returned to Florida later that year but lived in Union-occupied Fernandina until the end of the conflict. In 1865 Anna Kingsley returned to the St. Johns River for the final time.

Anna Madgigine Jai Kingsley died in 1870. No intimate letters, diaries, or other personal reflections on her life are known to exist on Fort

George Island, near the mouth of the St. Johns River, where the house she lived for 23 years still stands.

A New Kind of Slaveowner

The annexation of Florida by the United States brought more than just a shift in governmental structure; it brought a whole new kind of

This picture of the slave quarters taken around the end of the Civil War (ca. 1865) shows the living conditions of slaves on Kingsley Plantation. The slave system practiced on this plantation was unique for employing the task system, whereby slaves who completed a task were free to do as they chose for the remainder of the day. Contemporaries often contrasted the permissive nature operated by Kingsley Plantation with the often-brutal nature endured by those on American plantations in the state (State Archives of Florida, Florida Memory).

slaveowner to the peninsula. This was especially pertinent following large waves of American immigration into Middle Florida.

While at the time of annexation, the majority of society, including plantation life, was concentrated around the two capitals of Pensacola and St. Augustine, Americans bypassed this in favor of settling the vast swath of land lying between the Apalachicola and Suwannee Rivers. Finding the red clay hills and large, empty acres ripe for cotton cultivation, these hardy pioneers began divvying up estates around the frontier capital of Tallahassee.

Like the rest of the American South, the wealthiest of these settlers brought with them a "moonlight and magnolias" way of thinking, replete with Scarlett O'Hara belles and Rhett Butler beaus. On their land they built gaudy, Greek Revival mansions that they named after deceased family members or mythical places in literature. They also took to hosting elaborate social gatherings, barbecues and cotillions for their neighbors. All was indeed well in the land of Camelot—unless, of course, you were a slave.

The Cracker Prince of Tallahassee

While today it's fairly common to hear about Spanish Royals vacationing off the sunny shores of South Beach, the whole semblance of royalty ever visiting the swampy, mosquito-infested backwater of Early Florida was laughable. Yet one royal—Achille Murat—not only did so, but made it his home, becoming so enamored with the culture that surrounded him that he adopted it as his own.

Born in Paris, Murat was the eldest son of the Marshal of France and the princess of Naples, making him heir to the throne of the Kingdom of Naples.

As a nephew of Napoleon himself, via his mother, and a natural successor to the Neapolitan Crown, Murat was afforded all the privileges of an outstanding aristocrat, complete with a world-class education and servants to wait on him hand and foot. This changed dramatically following his uncle's exile from Europe.

To avoid the trappings of a royal exile, Murat made his way to America.

Fascinated by America since youth, he set about exploring several places, before finally settling just south of St. Augustine. Almost from the start, Murat was looked upon as a loveable eccentric by the town's population. A lover of the beach, "Murat would conduct business on the shore, with waves rolling underneath the furniture he had set up there for negotiations."[15]

Eventually, as in Europe, Murat tired of St. Augustine society, and once again set out to make a fresh start. Setting out for Middle Florida, Murat purchased land just outside the frontier capital at Tallahassee he called Lipona, an anagram of his beloved Naples (Napoli). There he built a simple log cabin and took to rearing cattle.

Like the bulk of the settlers pouring in at the time, Murat donned buckskin and mimicked the habits of the other Florida pioneer "Crackers" in the region. "He even took to chewing tobacco, using a large shaggy dog as his own personal spittoon."[16]

Eventually, the "Cracker Prince," as he came to be called, grew so popular among the local populace that he was elected alderman, mayor and then postmaster of Tallahassee. He would later serve as a volunteer in the Florida militia, gaining the rank of colonel. It was in this capacity he came to meet his wife Catherine Gray, a descendant of George Washington.

Though Gray's family was completely turned off by Murat, "who had an aversion for bathing and refused to ever drink water," Gray was nonetheless enthralled by his eccentricities and "moved with him to Lipona."[17] With Gray's addition, Lipona became the toast of the town, courting high-ranking military men and even sitting governors.

To the amusement of these guests, "Murat would show them his Spanish moss mattress and serve them up dishes of cow's ear stew, alligator steaks and roasted crow."[18] He also put his quirkiness on full display:

> He never cleaned his boots and never changed them until they were worn out. A shaggy dog which he kept was used as his spittoon. He cooked and ate all kinds of animals and experimented on his slaves with a diet of cherry tree sawdust.... On one occasion his wife, upon arriving home, found him bending over a huge kettle, where he was experimenting with a dye, having thrust into the kettle everything he could lay hands on—sheets, tablecloths, pillowcases, and even some of his wife's dresses. Murat had a curious aversion to water, taken either internally or externally. He said that water was for the beasts of the field, and he never drank it without adding whiskey to it. On one occasion he fell into a syrup vat on the plantation he owned near Baton Rougue. Those who stood about were fearful that lest he should be scalded, but his only comment was, "Kate will make me wash."[19]

Murat even challenged Governor Long to a duel, stating beforehand "You know I expect nothing hereafter," before firing wide, with no fatal results befalling either person.[20]

Eventually, Murat would leave Tallahassee for New Orleans to work as a lawyer and then return to Europe in an attempt to regain his birthright. Upon failing, he returned to Lipona and passed away in 1847. His wife Catherine would travel back and forth from France over the ensuing years before dying and being laid to rest next to her husband in an Episcopal churchyard in Tallahassee.

Slave Codes in the Swamplands

In the short time between its transition from territory to state, Florida was already acquiring a special reputation for cruelty toward slaves. Such cruelty took many forms and governed over most aspects of a slave's life. So ingrained was this cruelty, in fact, that soon it became a common notion across much of the other states in the South to threaten rebellious slaves with ending them south to Florida.

In this new reality, gone forever were the days of the task system—a labor system cultivated under Kingsley and other early planters in Spanish Florida—where slaves were given a daily task, and when finished they were allowed to leave. Now, under the American system, slaves were expected to work from sunup to sundown. A typical day in this kind of environment was described by former slave, Mack Mullen:

> There was a slave known as a "caller." He came around to the slave cabins every morning at four o'clock and blew a "cow-horn," which was the signal for the slaves to get up and prepare themselves for work in the fields. All of them on hearing this horn would arise and prepare their meal; by six o'clock they were on their way to the fields. They would work all day, stopping only for a brief period at midday to eat.... About sundown, the "cow-horn" of the caller was blown and all hands stopped work, and made their way back to the cabins.[21]

Yet another victim of the new system was a slave's freedom to wander about. Because of the failed Nat Turner Slave Rebellion in Virginia which resulted in the deaths of over 50 Whites, slaves in Florida were no longer permitted to leave their premises without express permission from their masters. This permission was granted in the form of a special permit. If a slave dared to visit a loved one without said permit, they were targeted by patrolmen, a special police task force assigned to assure that no slaves wandered too far off their property. Whipping posts were erected to maintain such authority:

> "He was given the whip to whip his brother slave. Very often the lashes would bring blood very soon from the already lacerated skin, but this did not stop the lashing until one received their due numbers...."[22]

Even free Blacks were forced to abide by these permit rules. One such person, Florida Clayton, told stories of how her mother warned her to stay away from White men with bloodhounds that she said would rip any person to pieces who the Whites determined were runaways.

The Obliteration of the Self

Perhaps the most damning consequence of the introduction of American-style slavery into Florida was not what was happening on the outside of the plantation, but rather what was happening from within. For, with the onset of this system came the complete obliteration of the self. This involved the denial of any dignity afforded basic human life, such as the right to learn.

Although education suffered under the American slave system and was strictly prohibited by law, some slaves did in fact learn to read and write. This was often taught to some of the younger slaves by their White peers, who they were obliged to accompany to and from school. In rarer cases, it was taught to a select group of slaves by the owners themselves, who, in flagrant violation of the law, would then have them pass on bits of their knowledge to their families. Both cases were in the minority, however, as learning even the most rudimentary knowledge carried severe penalties, even for the Whites involved. One such instance was recounted by Douglas Dorsey, who had the task of carrying his master's children's books to school and was caught by the mistress of the plantation learning to read and write:

> … She then took a quill pen, the kind used at the time, and began writing the alphabet and numerals as far as ten. Holding the paper up to Douglas, she asked him if he knew what they were; he proudly answered in the affirmative, not suspecting anything … she struck him a heavy blow across the face, saying "If I ever catch you making another figure anywhere I'll cut off your right arm…."[23]

A further degradation of the slaves on the plantation was brought about by the complete dissolution of the individual self. In this sense, not only were slaves not allowed to learn, but they were also not allowed to be human. They were allowed no self-direction, no right to marriage and no family relations. Such a view is backed up by the accounts of Mack Mullen, who states that all that was necessary for a slave to be considered married was a license and that no marriage ceremony was ever performed.[24]

Because of the nature of slave marriage, slave offspring were rarely recognized as belonging to their parents. Rather, they were seen as wards of the master. For, how can a calf belong to its mother? Thus, outside of

Louisiana, every Southern state or territory, including Florida, held no law preventing the breakup of slave families. One such instance was recounted by Dorsey, where a slave child who may or may not have been fathered by the master of the plantation, was brutally sent away:

> It was taken from his mother's breasts at the age of eight months and auctioned off on the first day of January to the highest bidder.... Twenty years later he was located by his family, he was a grown man, married and farming.[25]

As a result of there being no marriage and no families, slaves were also prohibited sanction over their own souls. That, of course, was left up to the master who determined the course of their religion. Long gone were the days when slaves were protected and sanctioned by a church, to which they were invited, not forced to be a part. Now, under mainline Protestants such as Baptists, Methodists and Presbyterians, they were systematically ignored and left out of services entirely.

These conditions would be tested in a very big way in the outbreak of the Civil War.

Florida and the Civil War

By 1860, Florida was a transformed land.

Always a land of slavery even from the outset, its institution had changed from one of small farms supported by indigo, rice and tobacco to one of large, corporate-style plantations wholly reliant on cotton. Though the overall "numbers of slaves amounted to a mere 39,310 in the 1850 census,"[26] placing Florida roughly on par with Texas—*one of the least slave-populated states in the South*—its concentration of slavery within wealthy Middle Florida assured that its interests would be protected in Tallahassee. In fact, so paramount was this system, "that 34% of families in the state were counted as slave owners in the 1860 census."[27] Of that, 70 percent of them were concentrated across a contiguous five county region.[28]

While it's true that the number of individual slave owners was far less than the overall proportion of slave-owning families indicates (just over 14 percent), it does, in fact, explain a lot about Florida's later calls for secession. For, after all, slavery was big business, and it was seen as hypocritical by planters for Northerners to complain about its existence, when they stood to profit from its taxation and cultivation.

Changing Demographics

Prior to the outbreak of the Civil War, "Florida had about 10 cities of note, none of which were more than 3000 in population."[29] Of these, Key West was by far the state's largest city, with Tallahassee and Jacksonville not too far behind.

Like today, these three cities represented vastly different cultures, mirroring closely that of modern-day Florida, with cities in the panhandle accounting for a largely Southern mixture, cities in the south accounting for significant northern migrants and cities on the east coast comprising a mix of both Northerners and Southern transplants. This was especially highlighted by Jacksonville's 1850 Census, in which a significant minority of the White population was born outside of Florida, "hailing from such states as New York, Massachusetts, Connecticut, Pennsylvania, and Rhode Island."[30]

As a result of this heterogeneity, Florida was unique among other Southern states, in that it was not completely dominated by the Democratic Party. In fact, in many cities along the east and southern fringes of Florida, where slavery did not play as a big a role in the local economy, moderate parties such as the Whigs actually ran quite well. This was accounted for many times and was also anchored in the fact that cities like Jacksonville "had two newspapers, one Democratic and one Republican."[31] This was partially the reason why Florida communities were so divided over the notion of secession, as a strong minority from within these communities favored the Constitutional Union Party, which desired to maintain the status quo.

Nevertheless, when Florida did secede, and war was pushed upon them, the majority of those in the state eventually came around to the idea of secession. Still, even during the most intense of times, Florida was hardly uniform in its support. For, as the war continued and defeat loomed near, most in Florida would ultimately come to adopt the viewpoint of their East Florida brethren.

Loyalty is in the Eye of the Beholder

Outside the South, there is no other part of the United States that knows what it's like to meet defeat and destruction at the hands of an invading force. The effects of this defeat were long, and its devastation was total. In just four short years, the entire Southern way of life had been turned on its ear. Florida was no different.

Like the rest of the region, Floridians experienced all of the hardships and tragedies associated with a long and drawn-out war. These hardships changed lifestyles and also changed opinions.

When, in January 1861, Florida's Secession Convention took the state out of the Union, the final vote was 62–7,[32] a firm affirmation of the State's support for the Southern Cause. However, more Unionism existed in the state than this margin indicated, with a large minority of Floridians harboring pro–Union or anti–Confederate sentiments, a number that grew as the war progressed.

For, as the war was being fought, the Union was a near persistent force along the Florida coast, occupying Fernandina, Jacksonville, St. Augustine and Key West. As a result, many within these cities fled to the Union side, proclaiming loyalty, as in the case of the "Proclamation of the Loyal Citizens" in Jacksonville:

> We, the people of the city of Jacksonville and its vicinity, in the county of Duval, and State of Florida, embraced within the territory and jurisdiction of the United States of America, do hereby set forth our declaration of rights and our solemn protest against the abrogation of the same by any pretended State or other authority.[33]

While for some proclamations such as the above provided a chance to express repressed loyalty to the Union, for others it was simply a matter of exploiting the times. As the war wound on and shortages grew rampant, merchants on the East Coast saw dollar signs in maintaining friendly relations with the occupying Army. As the war wound on, the state became a haven for deserters and dissenters of all sorts who flocked to Occupied Florida for protection, decreasing morale even further.

Fort Barrancas and the First Real Shots of the Civil War

In almost every Civil War history text you'll find a segment in the beginning chapter entitled "The First Shots," followed by a brief synopsis of the Battle of Fort Sumter between the Confederacy and the Union. So consistent are these segments that it can almost be taken as fact. Too bad it *technically* isn't.

One thing people often forget when reading about the Civil War is that the Confederacy did not just start out as a united entity; it was in fact formed by seven sovereign republics. Florida was one of those republics. Before becoming so, however, sovereignty had to be tested to prove that it could defend itself. When the state convention was called to determine a vote on secession, Col. William Chase saw a golden opportunity to prove just that.

Not willing to let the prospect of secession slip from Florida's fingers, Chase and the Florida militia set out to Fort Barrancas on January 8, 1861, to demand its surrender. Like Fort Pickens, across Pensacola Bay, Fort Barrancas was a Federal garrison and was seen as vital to Florida's coastal defenses.

While initially lightly guarded, its commander, Lt. Adam J. Slemmer, was given orders from Washington not to allow the Florida militia to seize it in the event of secession. "Taking 46 men with him,"[34] Slemmer, like everyone else, waited around for the results of the secession vote. What he didn't count on, however, was Chase's impatience.

Accompanied by troops from Alabama, as well as a sizable number from within his own ranks, Chase demanded that the garrison surrender and open itself up to occupation. When Slemmer refused, a brief exchange of gunfire ensued before Slemmer "decided to spike the guns and head for the much larger Fort Pickens."[35]

Hoisting a secession flag above its ramparts, Chase and his men occupied the fort and declared it to be a part of the new Republic of Florida. The event was later memorialized in an 1865 letter from one of the soldiers, R. L Sweetman, to the widow of his friend who helped capture the fort.

> In his letter, Sweetman said something like "Your husband can claim that he commanded the post where the first shot was fired."...
> The letter sparked the local legend that continues to this day—and plays into Pensacolans' belief that their city has been cheated by history.[36]

While the victory was a hollow one, it nevertheless had the effect of swaying the Florida delegation to vote for secession, making Florida, not South Carolina, the true epicenter for the start of the Civil War.

The Desperate Plight of Florida's War-Ravaged Civilians

When the conflict first began, Florida's role was considered to be so minuscule as to have little impact whatsoever on the war effort. There was good reason to think this, as Florida had the smallest and poorest population in the Confederacy and had little to offer in terms of large cities.

Referred to by the *Philadelphia Inquirer* as "the smallest tadpole in the dirty pool of secession,"[37] after joining up with the Confederacy, Florida, seemed for a while to live up to that reputation. For, outside the coasts, much of the interior part of the state was spared invasion, leaving its capital and its agricultural base relatively intact. As a result, Florida gained the reputation as a supplier state.

5. In the Shadow of the Big House

While Florida was productive in many things, its two principal exports during the war were beef and salt. These two items became critical for the half-starved Confederate troops towards the end of the war, allowing them to continue fighting. This was especially true as more and more Confederate territory succumbed to invasion, disrupting supplies from elsewhere. Late in the war, however, things began to change.

As the Confederacy began to lose its grip and the reasonable path to victory fizzled out, desperate guerrillas began stealing shipments. These guerrillas, mostly deserters and draft dodgers seeking to make a quick buck, would take these supplies and sell them for wages to the Union Army in the east and south. By the end of the war, former farmers and evacuees began joining them in these ventures, not out of greed, but desperation.

Like the guerrillas, they resented the Confederate draft, which forced them to fight not for the protection of their own state, but rather for states like Virginia and Georgia. Not wanting to leave their families, they became fugitives from the law, eking out a living from the good nature of others.

Launching a campaign to rid Florida of these disruptions, the governor dispatched a contingent of Confederate cavalry under the command of John Dickison and Charles Munnerlyn. These two men took their jobs very seriously, hunting down deserters and guerrillas in the impoverished countryside. All who were caught were lynched, and all who got away were chased into enemy territory to be captured.

By March of 1864, this campaign took a nasty turn, as the cavalry began not only to target miscreants and guerrillas, but all those involved in the hijacking of supplies, including women and children.

Invading the wetlands and forests of Taylor and Lafayette County, the dispatched soldiers began burning out the makeshift homes of the poor farmers, arresting all whom they captured. An excerpt from the archives of Taylor County, Florida, recounted the following destruction wrought by one of their command:

> Major Charles H. Camfield apparently had charge of all house burnings and for many years after the war ended he was regarded as just about the meanest man that ever set his foot in Taylor county. He did not stop with burning deserters' homes, but acted as if his duty required him to burn anywhere there were one or two deserters in the family, although as many or more might be loyally serving the Confederacy. One J.H. Ellison had four sons in the Southern army and two who had deserted, yet his house was burned.[38]

Taking those captured to Camp Smith, a literal concentration camp six miles south of Tallahassee, the impoverished families were subjected to poor living conditions, crammed into six dilapidated shacks, where they survived on reduced rations and disease-infested water. Only after the fate of these poor people became known to the governor—via press and word of mouth—were they finally freed.

Quite embarrassed by the debacle, the governor was appalled that such measures had been taken against the innocent, let alone by his own order. As a result, he ordered a complete and immediate halt to the campaign. For many of the families, however, the order had come a little too late. Their husbands were dead, and with no homes to return to, their futures remained uncertain.

The Battle of Olustee

Unlike many parts of the South, Florida managed to avoid major battles like Vicksburg or Chattanooga. Instead, they had small skirmishes and gunboat exchanges. This changed as the Union Army began sweeping further south, and Florida's status as a beef exporter became increasingly vital to the Confederate cause.

In February 1864, Major General Quincy A. Gillmore, commander of the Union's Department of the South at Hilton Head, ordered an expedition into Florida to secure Union enclaves and disrupt supplies from making their way to Virginia. He hoped that through this invasion he might experience two-fold success by starving off the Confederacy and by gaining new Black recruits.

Correctly assessing the Union's motives, General P.G.T. Beauregard, hero of Fort Sumter, ordered a dispatch to meet Gillmore head-on so that he could prevent them from achieving their objectives.

> Following the Florida, Atlantic and Gulf Central Railroad, the Union led their 5,500 men in the direction of Lake City. At approximately 2:30 in the afternoon of February 20, the Union force approached the 5,000 Confederates entrenched near Olustee Station. While the initial plan was to send out an infantry brigade to halt the Union advance by luring them into Confederate entrenchments, the plan went awry. The opposing forces met and a raging battle went on in the pine forests at Ocean Pond.[39]

Making the mistake of thinking that he was engaging Florida militia instead of Confederate regulars, Gilmore sent in small detachments of troops instead of charging with full force. As a result, the hardened Confederates repulsed their attacks, forcing them into a disorderly rout back to Jacksonville by nightfall.

The aftermath of the Battle of Olustee resulted in a total Confederate victory, with Union losses of 40 percent. In fact, the ratio of Union casualties to the number of troops involved made it "the second bloodiest battle of the Civil War for the North."⁴⁰ It's what happened in the immediate aftermath of battle, however, which makes it particularly notorious.

Atrocities on the Battlefield

Following the Union rout, Confederate soldiers began examining the dead and wounded left behind. This soon took a nasty turn when eyewitnesses began to gossip about the plight of wounded Black soldiers, who were being fired upon, rather than treated.

Though word of these atrocities filtered in from some on the Northern side, it was the Southern reports that proved the most damning. William Penniman, of the 4th Georgia Cavalry, reportedly heard a series of gunshots following the battle, which he mistook for skirmishing.

> "What is the meaning of all this firing I hear going on.[*sic*]" His reply to me was, "Shooting niggers Sir. I have tried to make the boys desist but I can't control them." I made some answer in effect that it seemed horrible to kill the wounded devils, and he again answered, "That's so Sir, but one young fellow

Civil War reenactors engage in battle on the former site of Olustee. Victory during this battle prolonged the Confederacy's survival for over a year, but Confederate treatment of captured African American soldiers would forever mar any victory (photograph by Excel23, February 15, 2014, CC BY-SA 3.0, Wikimedia Commons).

over yonder told me the niggers killed his brother after being wounded, at Fort Pillow, and he was twenty three years old, that he had already killed nineteen and needed only four more to make the matter even, so I told him to go ahead and finish the job."[41]

One Confederate soldier later recounted:

> The wounded negroes they bayoneted without mercy. Close beside me was a fine-looking negro, who was wounded in the leg: his name was Brown, an orderly sergeant in one of the companies of the 8th United-States Regiment. A rebel officer happened to see him, and says, "Ah, you black rascal, you will not remain here long!" and, dismounting from his horse, placed his revolver close to the negro's head, and blew his brains out."[42]

Even Black men in the service of Southern ranks were not innocent in these murders as Winston Stephens of the 2nd Florida Cavalry wrote home about witnessing one Black man kill another wounded Black man from the North, "simply for offering to shake his hand."[43]

While these massacres continued for quite some time, there is considerable evidence that Confederate officers, upon hearing of this shameful episode, intervened to stop the violence. Eyewitnesses later described "how they were given express orders not to discriminate between Black and White wounded and provide them the same kind of equal care."[44] Still, the unfortunate murders would add yet another chapter of gruesomeness to a war that was rapidly spiraling out of control.

Teenagers Save Tallahassee from Invasion

By 1865, the Confederacy's days were already numbered. Defeat after defeat had led to Union occupation in almost every Southern state east of the Mississippi and only a few, small holdouts remained. Tallahassee, with its large swath of planters and cattle ranches just outside the city limits, was one of those areas.

In an attempt to speed up the Confederacy's demise and forever deprive the few fighting troops left of any available cattle or salt, Union General John Newton, a veteran of the Gettysburg and Atlanta campaigns, tried to once again invade Florida's interior. His main purpose, it was stated, was to prevent further raids against Fort Myers and gain an upper hand for the northern Gulf Coast. However, his true intention was to take Tallahassee and then invade the southern portion of Georgia through Thomasville.

Coming ashore near St. Marks Lighthouse on the chilly spring night of March 4, 1865, Newton's troops set sights on the small Florida capital, attempting to take it by surprise. Their plan failed, however.

5. In the Shadow of the Big House

As word spread like wildfire about the sudden Union presence, panicked telegrams began going out all across North Florida, calling for troops. Answering these calls were a broad mix of teenagers from the nearby Florida Military and Collegiate Institute and elderly gentlemen from the city of Tallahassee.

Marching inland with two companies of troops and a battery of two howitzers manned by U.S. sailors, Newton drove off the hastily assembled forces formed by Confederate Generals Samuel Jones and William Miller, but failed to dislodge them from the Newport Bridge over the St. Marks River.

Hearing of another bridge upstream near Woodsville, Newton turned his troops west and a race soon began between the two forces to reach it first. By the time the Union Army reached it, however, the volunteers from Tallahassee were already in place on the other side, waiting for them.

Launching attack after attack against them, the Confederate soldiers, now bolstered by the support of both the elderly and the teenagers, dug in.

> Over the course of the battle, active duty troops were joined by militia units from Gadsden, León, Jefferson and Madison counties—mostly consisting of aging veterans and militiamen—who arrived by train. Trains also brought other volunteers, Confederate soldiers home on leave and cadets from West Florida Seminary—the forerunner of FSU—as well as additional active duty Confederate troops.
>
> By mid-afternoon, when the heaviest fighting occurred, there were as many as 1,000 Confederate troops, or nearly twice the number of Union soldiers. Included in those Confederate ranks were two volunteers who would go on to be Florida governors: Abraham Allison and Francis Fleming.[45]

By the end of the day, the Confederates had succeeded and the Union was in retreat.

The Battle of Natural Bridge on March 6 was one of the last major battles to be fought in Florida and was certainly one of the last to be fought in the dying Confederacy. Within a month, Robert E. Lee and his few half-starved troops would surrender at the tiny hamlet of Appomattox Courthouse in Virginia. Still, while the victory remained tactical and tactical only, it represented one of the few successes the Confederacy had in its last days of existence, protecting Florida's capital from certain doom.

Total Defeat in a Total War

Though small from the perspective of other states in the Confederacy like Virginia and Georgia, which saw massive invasions and a complete destruction of infrastructure, Florida did nevertheless suffer for its involvement. This suffering resulted in a hostile occupation, a grinding halt to its economy, and the complete destruction of Jacksonville, one of its largest cities. Not all were completely sorry with the results, however. As was recounted in the archives of Taylor County:

> The end of the war was not displeasing to the majority of Taylor county citizens. There were not many slave owners and these were not greatly hurt, as they, in general, had more wealth in cattle than in negroes; and during the years following the war they had little trouble in hiring the service of their former slaves at low cost.[46]

As a further positive, the war freed 140,400 slaves—nearly 40 percent of Florida's entire population at the time![47] One such former slave described the day he was told of his freedom when the plantation owner's son, a Confederate colonel, gathered up all 85 slaves and told them they were free:

> The slaves were happy at this news, as they had hardly been aware that there had been a war going on. None of them accepted the offer of the colonel to remain, as they were only too glad to leave the cruelties of the Matair plantation.[48]

6

Florida Brews a Revolution

To many people, it would seem Florida, due to its proximity to Cuba, a mere 90 miles from its shores, had war thrust upon her unduly. History tells a different story, however. For, given all of the events that preceded the outbreak of hostilities, and all of the events that occurred following it, it seems that most Floridians were not only involved in hosting a war, but actually went to great lengths to incite one.

Florida, Cuba and the Politics of Proximity

No other state outside of Texas has shared the kind of relationship with another foreign country that Florida has shared with Cuba. In many ways the two places are almost symbiotic.

> Floridians have always been peculiarly sensitive to events in Cuba. This derives from more than just the accident of geography that places them so near each other and from more than fear of invasion or economic rivalry. Added to these must be the long pull of historical association. In the more than two centuries of Spanish control, Havana was the source of all things Spanish—government and administration, money, goods and services, religious authority and guidance, and defense. Indeed Spanish Florida was little more than a military outpost of Havana. A few Spanish families remained in Florida to add to the flavor left by Spanish architecture and place names.[1]

Because of their proximity, Cuba and Florida have also shared a history of immigration. For centuries, immigrants have migrated to and from both areas, with people settling and resettling in each land. This was true at Florida's outset when Pedro Menéndez left his position as governor of Florida to become governor of Cuba, taking men and soldiers with him, and was also true during the transfer of power to the British when Floridanos left in droves for Cuba.

Memorialized most dramatically, however, was the departure of many of Florida's last remaining Spanish families upon annexation to the United States, symbolized through the departure of Jose Callava and his loyal followers.

Such a history of immigration from Florida to Cuba and vice versa did not disappear completely with the arrival of the Americans. On the contrary, it soon increased. This was especially pronounced in the years immediately following the Civil War, when Florida, desperate for cheap labor in its burgeoning cigar industry, began employing Cuban immigrants.

> Some 6000 Cuban cigar makers migrated to Key West and Tampa after 1868 to make cigars, for which much of the tobacco was imported from Cuba. Only New York received more Cuban tobacco. Political refugees from Cuba in the last decade of the nineteenth century operated principally in Key West, Tampa and New York.[2]

These Cubans not only brought with them their skills as workers, but also continued close ties to their homeland.

> Well-established transportation routes allowed Cubans in the US and Cubans on the island to remain in regular contact with each other. Some of these interactions were apolitical. The Cuban mutual aid societies in Tampa sent paid [sic] for members to travel and receive medical care in Havana, and individuals often returned to see family members. On the other hand, many of these interactions were expressly political. The daily newspapers of Havana were imported, and lectores read them to cigar workers every day. This practice kept them well informed about political developments back home. The free flow of information and people to and from Havana was a crucial element that allowed Cubans to act on their nationalism by aiding in the political and economic struggles of Cubans on the island.[3]

Soon, this nationalism would spill back over the Straits of Cuba in a very violent and bloody way.

David Yulee and the Issue of Cuban Statehood

Before we delve into Florida's role in the Cuban War for Independence, it's important to recognize that many within the state had Cuba on the brain long before any such conflict had broken out. This was most prominently displayed in America's not-so-subtle attempt to annex the island through the Ostend Manifeto.

Although we pointed out that there was much interest among certain circles for Cuban annexation, there was little serious discussion until the administration of Thomas Jefferson. During his administration, Secretary of State John Quincy Adams described Cuba as "an object of transcendent importance to the commercial and political interest of our Union" and a "natural appendage to the North American continent."[4] Still, their comments were made in private and were largely kept out of the public eye. This began to change after the Mexican-American War.

Following the U.S. victory over Mexico in 1845 and the Gadsden Purchase three years later, the U.S. found its land nearly doubled, a position it had not dealt with since the Louisiana Purchase. With tons of new land and no clear direction for settlement, the status of whether these territories would become slave or free came to the forefront, spurring a race between the slave-owning South and the free-soil North. Though this race could have likely gone on for years, it became instantly clear, given the harsh desert-like conditions of much of the new land, that the North was likely to win out in the end. Soon, the question of annexing new land suitable to sustain a plantation economy began to emerge, and as had been the case in the past, slave owners began to look south.

Although initial interest in Cuba had died down at this point as all eyes rested with expanding into Mexico, it was a Floridian senator by the name of David Levy Yulee who brought it back into the spotlight, introducing a Senate resolution concerning the purchasing of Cuba from Spain.

In his resolution, he espoused the proximity of Cuba to Florida, as well as its importance to the Gulf states. It was only natural after the U.S. secured Texas, the most western state on the Gulf, that it should also annex Cuba, the easternmost island, as well. It was simple Manifest Destiny. Besides, quick annexation would in one fell swoop provide the perfect solution to the delicate slave and free soil situation playing out West.

While he withdrew his resolution before debate even began, Yulee had successfully planted the tantalizing image of cheap Cuban land in the minds of thousands of slave owners. They would not soon forget this image, or the dream that Cuba could one day become a state.

In the years following Yulee's debate, Southerners began to take a keener interest in expansion and annexation. This included John C. Calhoun who concurred that

> "it is indispensable to the United States that this island should not be in certain hands." Even President James K. Polk got involved, offering $100 million to the Spanish in return for selling the island. Their response was anything but conciliatory, stating flatly that "sooner than see it transferred to any power, [Spanish officials] would prefer seeing it sunk in the ocean."[5]

By the time Franklin Pierce entered office, he was bound and determined to make Spain drink the Kool-Aid, making Cuba an integral part of his campaign platform. He stated bluntly, "The policy of my

Administration will not be controlled by any timid forebodings of evil from expansion."⁶ Thus, upon taking office, he went to work, organizing a meeting in Ostend, Belgium, between his ministers to France, Britain and Spain concerning what to do about the matter.

During this meeting, the three ministers concluded that Cuban annexation was not only necessary, but a matter of survival. From a national security standpoint, they warned against inaction on the matter:

> We should, be recreant to our duty, be unworthy of our gallant forefathers, and commit base treason against our posterity however permit Cuba to be Africanized and become a second Santo Domingo [Haiti], with all its attendant horrors to the white race, and suffer the flames to extend to our own neighboring shores, seriously to endanger our actually to consume the fair fabric of our Union.⁷

Furthermore, they declared Cuba to be "as necessary to the North American republic as any of its present members, and that it belongs naturally to that great family of states which the Union is the Provincial Nursery" and that the U.S. would be "justified in wresting the island from Spanish hands."⁸ It was this last part that landed them in the most trouble.

To the chagrin of the Pierce administration, the Ostend Manifesto leaked out to the press, likely from the blabbing of the U.S. Minister to France. The incident caused outrage among Northerners and even more outrage in Europe. As a result, the matter of Cuban statehood was forever dropped.

Planting the Seeds of Revolt

If there was ever a man that gave credence to the old adage "if at first you don't succeed, then try, try again," General Narciso López was that man. For, in his attempts to free Cuba from the heel of Spain, that's exactly what he did.

It seemed López was born a bit too early for his own good. Caught in between two great periods of revolt in Latin America, he was too young to fight for the freedom of his own native Venezuela and operated twenty years too early in his attempt to free Cuba. Nevertheless, he is immortalized for his attempts, particularly in the United States.

Importing a Fight

Ever since it achieved independence, there had been interest among those in the United States to take over Cuba. As far back as 1809, Thomas

Jefferson went on record as having stated that Cuba's annexation would be a "blessing," stating in a letter to President James Monroe in 1823:

> But we have first to ask ourselves a question. Do we wish to acquire to our own confederacy any one or more of the Spanish provinces? I cordially confess that I have ever looked upon Cuba as the most interesting addition that could ever be made to our system of States. The control which, with Florida point, this island would give us over the Gulf of Mexico and the countries and the isthmus bordering on it, as well as those whose waters would flow into it, would fill up the measure of our political well being. Yet, as I am sensible that this can never be obtained, even with her own consent, but by war, and its own independence....[9]

When the charismatic López arrived in the U.S. in 1848, after narrowly escaping arrest for anti–Spanish activities on the island, it seemed that the U.S. had finally found a person who could give them their chance. A former assistant to the governor-general, López was well connected to the independence movement and, like those in the U.S., saw Cuba's future tied with the Americans as a state. These views combined with his past connections as an aristocrat excited American interests almost from the start and he soon began to make plans for an expedition.

If at First You Don't Succeed

One of the first connections López made was with John L. O'Sullivan, an expansionist and coiner of the phrase "Manifest Destiny." In him, López found support and the financial backing to launch a first expedition with recruits from New York's burgeoning Cuban population. Set to launch simultaneously from New York and New Orleans, his expeditions never got off the ground, however, having been blocked by President Taylor, who had both ships seized before they could ever leave port.

Though López had failed to get a revolution launched, his attempt provided a huge PR opportunity in the press and in less than a year, he had once again achieved the finances and recruits necessary to try again.

Unlike his first expedition, his second one comprised filibusters "mainly from the South."[10] With their aid, he was able to mount a successful invasion of the island and capture the city of Cárdenas. This was short-lived, however, as they would be pushed out several days later and forced to make a hasty retreat back to Key West.

Trying Again from Florida

While López's forces were hailed as heroes upon their arrival in Key West, they were not so warmly treated by officials in the United States. It seems López's attempts to use American troops had caused an international incident, stirring Europeans to complain of American warmongering. As a result, he was indicted, but never convicted of violating international law by an American jury.

Not forgetting the warmness of the Floridians upon his return from Cárdenas, López decided to make another attempt at an expedition, organizing one to launch from the Sunshine State. He gathered over 450 men[11] to the island-city of Key West to joyous celebrations.

López's original idea was to depart from North Florida, via the mouth of the St. Johns River. He had a secret stash of artillery stored up there that he was set to pick up. He later changed his mind, however. It seemed the logistics of reaching the St. Johns from Key West posed too great a risk of capture by the Americans and López had never forgotten how his first expedition was foiled. At the same time, López had begun to hear rumors about a fragile three-city revolt happening on the island. To López, it was now or never.

Foregoing the necessary artillery, López launched in haste from Key West, landing at Bahía Honda, a mere 40 miles from Havana. To his surprise, the Cubans did not join him and actually joined the ranks of the Spanish to fight against him.

Facing overwhelming odds and very heavy casualties, López's force was captured and defeated two days later. Within a week, the surviving 51 members of the expedition were executed by firing squad and nearly two weeks later, López, himself, was put to death. His last words before the assembled masses in Havana who came to witness his execution were, "My death will not change the destiny of Cuba."[12]

He died never knowing just how prophetic his words would be.

A Tampa Native Leads the Charge

Not more than 20 years after the failed López expeditions, Cuba lay entirely forgotten in the minds of most Floridians. Though some of the more prominent may have known about the longstanding conflict being fought between Cuban insurrectionaries and Spanish loyalists, most were vastly ignorant, and even if they were in the know, were unlikely to support a war of intervention. After all, this was just a mere ten years after Floridians had waged their own destructive war against the government,

6. Florida Brews a Revolution

resulting in millions of dollars in economic and structural losses on their own home turf. Furthermore, they were still under occupation, having remained so since the end of the war. Getting rid of that once and for all was thus at the forefront of most of their minds— until the exploits of a local Tampa native captured their attention.

It might seem surprising that a gentleman from Tampa, with little to no connections to Cuba, would bring the U.S. to the brink of war with Spain and spread awareness of the deteriorating situation on the island. A closer look at Capt. Joseph Fry and his actions, however, helps explain everything.

An ex-officer who had captained ships for both the Federal and Confederate navies, Fry came under the employment of John Patterson, an agent of General Manuel Quesada and the Cuban Junta of New York.

Patterson, a rebel sympathizer, had purchased a Civil War–era ironclad for the purposes of running arms to the Cuban insurgents. For this mission, Patterson chose Fry, primarily due to his naval background during the Civil War. He hoped that Fry's past Confederate enlistment would make him sympathetic to the Cuban cause and would motivate him to work harder for the rebellion.

For his part, Fry knew what he was getting himself into, for: "...the nationality and ownership, character and occupation, of the *Virginius* were matters of newspaper notoriety when her command was offered to Captain Fry."[13]

Prior to taking over as captain, Fry took to recruiting a crew of British and American shipmates. Afterward, he began to formulate intricate plans to traffic illegal weapons and freedom fighters into Cuba.

Spain, having known about the *Virginius*, caught on to his scheme, however, and began to target it as a pirate ship. As such, the Spanish navy began to fortify their harbors on the chance that Fry and his crew would dare try to smuggle arms into that country.

On the Brink of War

Prior to Fry's takeover, Spain had already attempted to trap the crew once before during a routine docking in the city of Aspinwall, Panama. There, they found the vessel and attempted to block it from exiting the port. Luckily for the crew, an American vessel intervened prior to their capture after noticing the huge American flag that hung from the mast.

Though the *Virginius* managed to escape impoundment, it would not be so lucky under the captainship of Fry.

The first stop after leaving Kingston in late October was Haiti, where the VIRGINIUS' crew picked up 300 Remington rifles, 300,000 cartridges, 800 daggers, 800 machetes, shoes and gunpowder for the Cuban rebels. Flying the American flag, it then started for a beach where two large artillery guns were buried. Unfortunately for the crew, the Spanish corvette TORNADO intercepted them en route on October 30.... Within site of Guantánamo Bay, the TORNADO captured the infamous contraband vessel, and hauled it and its crew to internment at Santiago.[14]

Sailing for Cuba the following day, the vessel sprung a serious leak and had to slow its course. "The ship's sluggishness alerted the Spanish to their arrival and they were spotted six miles off the coast. There, with the mountains of Guantanamo in plain view, the warship *Tornado* intercepted them."[15]

In an attempt to avoid capture, Fry, despite the worsening leak, turned back toward Jamaica and in an eight-hour chase managed to elude the pursuing *Tornado*. Along the way, Fry had the crew dump hundreds of pounds of ammunition and equipment over the sides of the vessel to gain speed. It didn't work, however, as the ship's deteriorating condition forced them to stop a mere six miles from the Jamaica coastline.

Seeing no other choice, but to drown or turn himself over, Fry made the fateful decision to surrender to the Spanish. Towed back to Santiago de Cuba on November 1, "a total of 155 members on board, 102 of whom were Cuban, the crew, including Fry, were immediately put on trial."[16]

Without so much as a thought about the serious diplomatic consequences, Fry and "53 other members of the *Virginius*"[17] were put to death for crimes of piracy. This included several British sailors.

Almost immediately a firestorm erupted in both Britain and the United States. Britain, for one, argued that the vessel was technically captured off British territorial waters, Jamaica belonging to them at the time, and that Spain's actions constituted an act of war. Likewise, the Americans argued that the *Virginius* was flying an American flag and that Fry, being an American hero, deserved at the very least to be extradited back to the U.S. for trial. Cubans, particularly those in New York and Florida, began to call for war. Soon, an increasing amount of journalists and politicians began to get involved bringing the threat of war even closer.

Ultimately, a last-minute bargain offered by Spain averted direct U.S. and British involvement in Cuba, as Spain agreed to pay an indemnity to both powers and return the *Virginius*, intact, back to the United States.

While this incident failed to bring the U.S. and Spain to war, it showered attention upon the increasingly deteriorating situation in Cuba, garnering greater interest among journalists in the country. This would prove essential to the eventual outbreak of hostilities between the two nations

6. Florida Brews a Revolution

Tampa native Joseph Fry would succeed López in trying to wrest Cuba from Spanish control in 1873. Launching an invasion from his ship *Virginius*, Fry along with his crew were captured and promptly executed by the Spanish, igniting an international uproar (Manuel Fernández Sanahuja, *Capture of the North American Steamer Virginius by the Spanish Corvette Tornado, October 31, 1873*, 1877, Museo Naval de Madrid via Wikimedia Commons).

and can thus be laid at the feet of one man—Tampa's own, Capt. Joseph Fry.

The Man Who Built a Country

Even among some of Florida's brightest scholars, there is a shocking ignorance with regard to the role that Floridians played in Cuba's independence movement. These people tend to ignore the fact that it was right here along the state's sandy shores that an entire revolution was bankrolled, drafted and launched. This was of course in no small effort due to the peninsula's large émigré community, but was made possible even more so by the presence of José Martí.

Call him the George Washington of Cuba or the Sam Adams of

immigrants, José Martí was anything but a passive patriot. A rebel through and through, he built a legacy going to the places Cubans in the U.S. socialized and worked in order to spread the vision of a new and different Cuba—one in which their homeland was free from Spanish oppression.

Arriving in New York in the winter of 1891, Martí was already an avid patriot. Twice he had been exiled from Cuba because of his anti–Spanish activities, even suffering punishment in a jail cell for sedition.

A diehard believer in Cuba's right to self-governance, he published "Nuestra America." In it, he argued that man is often so preoccupied with the minor things in life that he ignores the big picture. "He drew clear allusions to Cuba's domination by Spain and ... historical parallels to America's own Revolution against England."[18]

The work proved extremely popular in the Cuban émigré community, and because of its far-reaching implications, was even picked up by the Liberal Party of Mexico.

Almost overnight, Martí became the voice for Cuban independence.

José Martí's Versos Sencillos

While Martí is remembered as being a great soldier and speaker, he was also an excellent poet. One of his most famous works, entitled "Versos Sencillos," or Simple Verses, combined all of his experiences in a Spanish prison, in addition to his life's work toward independence. As in his former work, he also highlighted the suffering of the Cuban population. One such poem within these works is entitled "A Sincere Man Am I":

> A sincere man am I
> From the land where palm trees grow,
> And I want before I die
> My soul's verses to bestow.
>
> I'm a traveller to all parts,
> And a newcomer to none:
> I am art among the arts,
> With the mountains I am one....[19]

Bringing the Cause to Florida

Martí came to Florida for two primary reasons: to build a revolution and to woo the population of Cubans living there. In this way, he separated himself from Narciso López and Joseph Fry, both of whom dealt entirely with the Cuban immigrants living in New York. Martí knew better, however.

6. Florida Brews a Revolution

In the two decades that passed between Fry's *Virginius* Affair and Martí's arrival in the United States, serious demographic changes took place that effectively displaced the center of Cuban culture. These changes were a direct result of the Ten Years' War, the conflict which Fry had helped arm through his illegal trafficking. Like Fry's trafficking adventures, the war did not go very well for the Cubans and many suffered from the backlash of the victorious Spanish. Thus, they chose to immigrate and immigrate they did—in droves, coming not to the cold of New York, but rather the subtropical warmth of Florida.

The father of Cuban independence Jose Martí is best remembered for bankrolling the revolution against Spain from Tampa. His impassioned pleas would ignite a war that would eventually lead to America entering the Spanish-American War (Wikimedia Commons).

Attracted by both the proximity and the burgeoning cigar industry blowing up in the state, these exiles formed strong communities in the cities of Tampa and Key West. By the 1890s, these communities were surpassing in vitality the community that existed in New York, effectively bringing the resistance movement to the sunny shores of Florida's Gulf Coast.

When Martí arrived in Florida in November 1891, he found a community that was firmly rooted, yet hadn't completely severed ties to its homeland. Many of these people were first-generation immigrants and as such had strongly-rooted connections with the anti–Spaniard political scene on the island. This proved to be exactly the kind of audience Martí needed to preach his movement.

Funding and Drafting a Revolution

When Martí arrived in the working-class enclave of Ybor City in Tampa, a community of primarily Cuban cigar rollers, he arrived as a celebrity.

Already famous for his previously published works, he was invited to the Club Ignacio Agramonte to give a speech. There, in what might as well be considered the Independence Hall of Cuban liberty, he gave two pro-independence lectures, which were quickly picked up and reprinted in English and Spanish across the United States. The receptions from these speeches effectively bankrolled the Cuban Independence Movement, and their sensational nature catapulted Martí to further stardom, earning him a coveted invite to Florida's most established Cuban community.

Traveling to Cayo Heuso, a heavily Cuban community in Key West, in January 1892, Martí met with a group of emigration representatives and took the steps of forming a solid political party.

By March, Martí had managed to collect enough money for a newspaper called the *Patria*, dedicated to the mission of the Cuban Revolutionary Party. His dedication to this party led him to be chosen by the Cayo Hueso Club to be the official spokesperson for the movement, a role which sent him to all of the far-flung communities of Cuban exiles located in the United States and the Caribbean.

Eventually making his way back to Florida in 1894, he made his most famous and daring attempt to bring about revolution—a move which placed Florida at the forefront of defining Cuban history.

The Fernandina Plan

"Loose lips sink ships" is more than an expression. It is actually grounded in real life incidents. This is something Martí found out all too painfully when launching his first attempt at revolution.

Satisfied with the funding he collected during his North American and Caribbean travels, Martí went back to Florida to work on organizing a war expedition. Settling on the small port city of Fernandina, Martí put into place the aptly named "Fernandina Plan." For this purpose, he chose three yachts, the *Amadis*, *Lagonda* and *Baracoa*.[20] Their speed was superior to most of the boats used by the Spaniards and they were large enough to accommodate a small army. According to the plan:

> the destination was to be Central America, with stops as follows: at a certain point in Florida to take on board Carlos Roloff and Serafín Sánchez with 800 men; in Costa Rica for (Antonio) Maceo, Flor Crombet, and 200 men; and in

6. Florida Brews a Revolution

Santo Domingo for Maximo Gomez's group. All members of this group would go as agricultural workers with suitable tools, which would actually be implements of war.[21]

Once the ships were at sea, Martí would then and only then, make the fateful announcement that the ship was headed to Cuba rather than to Central America. If any objections were made, he would give the order to have the dissidents imprisoned below until they reached the island.

By late December of 1894, everything was in place to get the expeditions going. Sending messengers to report about the progress, Martí informed the revolutionary leaders in Cuba of his imminent arrival, prepping them to defend his invaders at all costs. Then, a terrible blow happened.

A crewmember on board what was to be Serafín Sánchez's yacht spilled the beans to one of the unknowing captains who, in turn, passed the information along to the ship's owner. Overhearing the plan by way of the owner's rants, a Spanish official "lodged a protest to Washington, and on January 14, 1895, the federal government detained the three yachts, confiscating all their war materials."[22]

The blunder was a terrible loss for Martí. In an instant, three years of work and preparation went up in smoke, with $58,000[23] being lost. Still, despite the loss of money and preparation, it was the loss of morale that worried Martí the most. He calculated that the failed expedition would effectively end the resistance movement and halt the revolution in its tracks.

It didn't.

Rather than become demoralized, the Cuban revolutionaries actually became invigorated. It startled them that Martí could have organized such a detailed plot, especially considering the limited resources at his disposal, and they were amazed at the high levels of secrecy that went into it. As such, the various military chieftains assured Martí that they were ready to try again. As was the sentiment, the Fernandina Plan "showed that he could organize and execute a plan privately, without official support from another nation, in the pursuit of Cuban independence, even if it ultimately failed. It provided some hope for the Cuban independence movement."[24]

In due time, Martí did make his famous invasion, this time from outside of the United States. There, with General Máximo Gómez, he fought the battle-hardened Spaniards, losing his life in the ensuing melee as he charged from the front to meet them head on.

With his death, Martí proved a self-fulfilling prophecy he had previously written, which stated that his death would be attributed to his revolutionary zeal.

Like most heroes, Martí never lived to see the day on May 20, 1902, when Cuba really did win its freedom from Spain, with military assistance from the United States. Still, he is honored for launching what later became known as the second war of independence for Cuba—a war he inspired, initiated and funded all from the coasts of Florida.

Florida: The Mother of Cuban Independence

No other state in U.S. history has played such a direct role in the formation of another independent country's existence. This, above all else, is the single greatest factor in Florida history and one that sets it apart from all others. For while Texas and California can properly claim to have been birthed from Mexico, Florida is the only state that can say with utmost certainty that it birthed a free and independent Cuba.

In many ways, Florida's role in this matter was a complete reversal from its earlier reliance on Cuban wealth and immigration and served as poetic justice for a state that had taken so much.

While some people might argue, and rightly so, that Cuba, without Florida's aid, would have become independent of its own accord, they fail to recognize the integral role that the state's citizens played in speeding up its independence. For without Florida being used as both a way to fund and launch a second attempt at revolution, it's unlikely that the rebels would have been able to pull off a successful independence movement. Furthermore, without Florida's use as a base for American soldiers during the Spanish-American War, it's highly doubtful the war would have ended as quickly and bloodlessly as it did in 1898.

Because of Florida's stalwart contributions to the cause of independence, the state might very well be called the mother of Cuban independence. Still, in spite of this, the contributions of the state go largely unnoticed, even among historians well versed in the subject. Most shocking of all, however, is the state government's blatant silence on the matter. For, in a state with both the highest percentage of Cuban-Americans in the country and the largest recipient of Cuban exiles, there has been little formally done in the way of recognizing the state's integral role or in making Cuban Independence Day a state holiday.

7

Boom! Goes the Landscape
Florida on the Brink

The Spanish-American War in 1898 changed more than just Florida's relationship with Cuba. It also changed its relationship with its fellow Americans.

For the third time in a century, Florida was overrun by hordes of American soldiers, this time in an attempt to protect Florida from foreign invasion. The soldiers were stationed largely in cities like Tampa, Jacksonville and Miami, exposing an entire new generation to the state.

Once the war ended, many of these soldiers stayed, writing to their relatives up North about the abundance of cheap land available and giving rise to a second population boom. As with all booms, however, with more people came more problems.

Murder in the Marshes

In many ways, Guy Bradley was a martyr to modern-day environmentalism. Assigned to the role of game warden following President Roosevelt's creation of the first wildlife refuge in 1903, Bradley was killed trying to protect the land and birds he loved so much.

At the time of his murder on July 8, 1905, Bradley had been active in conservation for a little over a year. During this stint, he faced stiff resistance and general vilification at the hands of South Florida residents. These people resented the new environmental restrictions and, even more so, the financial losses they were suffering as a result of no longer being able to kill plume birds for their valuable feathers.

Like so many others, they had profited from the deaths of many of these birds as plume feather hats became all the rage in high society. Often, they would make their kills while the plume birds nested over their young, as they were unwilling to abandon their nests for danger. This resulted in a virtual genocide of plume birds in the Florida wetlands and a general call to action from the Audubon societies to protect them.

Upon Bradley's appointment as warden, conservationist publications such as the *Auk*, wrote beaming articles about his role in saving the dying species:

> The natives are beginning to realize that the birds are to be protected and that the wardens are fearless men who are not to be trifled with. The Bradleys have the reputation of being the best rifle shots in the vicinity and they would not hesitate to shoot when necessary.[1]

Unfortunately for both Bradley and the Audubon societies he sought to serve, the restrictions only increased the slaughter of these fragile birds as prices for plume feathers continued to rise.

Although Bradley took the slaughter as a sign of the value increase attributed to these birds, he also took it as a warning sign that hunters were spying on his whereabouts and purposely targeting protected areas that were under his authority. Furthermore, both Bradley as well as his family found themselves the target of threats and violence at the hands of hunters. This all came to a head on July 8, 1905, when Guy Bradley failed to return home:

> Fronie called on her neighbor, Gene Roberts, and asked him to search for her husband.... Near the water's edge, he noticed an empty dinghy bobbing. Roberts immediately recognized it as Guy's.
> Splayed at the bottom of the boat was Bradley's body: A gaping red gunshot wound festered by his collarbone and a .32 caliber pistol lay near one hand. Roberts inspected the weapon and determined that it had not been fired.
> Around the time Roberts made this discovery, his neighbor, Walter Smith, was busy tying his schooner, *The Cleveland*, to a dock 70 miles south in Key West. There, he'd walk straight to the Monroe County Sheriff, Frank Knight, and deliver some unexpected news.
> "I've shot Guy Bradley," he said.
> The reason, he'd later explain, had something to do with bird feathers.[2]

Even in death, Bradley could not escape the hatred of the hunters as Smith, who turned himself in on the charge of murder, pleaded self-defense, was found not guilty and "only served five months in the county jail."[3]

While Bradley's death caused outrage across the country with such papers as the *New York Times*, the *New York Herald*, the *Philadelphia North American*, and *Forest and Stream* all carrying articles about it, the incident would hardly be the last in the Sunshine State.

Just three years after Bradley's infamous murder, another game

7. Boom! Goes the Landscape

Guy Bradley would literally become a victim to fashion after he was murdered trying to protect what remained of the plume birds in the Everglades. Here he is pictured shortly before his death (*Bird-Lore*, 1905, via Wikimedia Commons).

warden, Columbus G. McLeod, was murdered in DeSoto County in November 1908. Unlike Bradley, his body was never found; the only evidence recovered was his bloodstained hat, which was cut with long gashes into the crown, likely the work of multiple axe strikes. The perpetrators behind this attack were never caught "by way of sinking the victim's boat and remained elusive."[4]

Dying for Change

While the two murders represented growing resistance to federal encroachment they also symbolized something else—the death of Old Florida.

Right after Reconstruction—and especially after the Spanish-American War—Florida witnessed what was to be the first in an ongoing series of population booms. Starting first with tourists, who came in increasing numbers after the Civil War, they stuck mostly to the older developed areas of the state, such as Jacksonville, St. Augustine and Palatka. Later, with the arrival of the railroad barons, they started to drift further south, exploring more and more of the undeveloped western and southern fringes of the state.

Like before, these changes began to affect the settlement patterns of the state as tourists became regular winter visitors and then turned into permanent residents. As a result, the natural habitats, protected previously from large human encroachment, became increasingly disturbed, leading to the complete disruption of natural Florida wildlife.

By the beginning of the 1890s, there was a clear railroad line, owned and operated by Henry Flagler, that stretched all the way from Jacksonville to Palm Beach. This virtual caravan for tourists abutted areas next to the Everglades, resulting in plumes, aigrettes and all other forms of swamp life becoming threatened.

Soon, tourists joined in with the natives, hunting these exotic creatures for both money and sport. The resulting outcome was the decimation of entire species of wildlife. It was in their attempt to prevent this—to recapture and preserve that bit of Old Florida—for which Bradley and McLeod paid the ultimate price.

The Man Who Built Florida

He might not be as famous as Henry Flagler or Walt Disney, but Hamilton Disston did more than any other person to contribute to the rise of modern-day Florida, both for better and for worse. It might seem hard to believe, but Florida's development after the Civil War, and all its subsequent environmental problems, can pretty much be laid at the feet of Disston.

Born to a wealthy Philadelphia industrialist, Disston inherited his family's massive saw company following his father's death in 1878. That same year, he made his first venture down to Florida, accompanying a friend on a fishing excursion. It was during this trip, while viewing his friend's estates on the St. Johns River, that his interest in Florida land development piqued. His interest was particularly focused upon the several million acres of land the federal government had deeded in 1850 to the state of Florida for the administration of internal improvements, including railroads, canals and other construction projects. Much of the land lay under water, covered by swamps and bayous.

Organizing a meeting with Governor Bloxham, Disston and his associates signed a drainage agreement with the state, purchasing 4 million acres for roughly $1 million for the purposes "to drain and reclaim by draining all overflowed lands in the State of Florida practicable and lying south of Township 24 and east of Peace Creek." This included a large part of south and central Florida below Orlando. The *New York Times* reported at the time:

> What is claimed to be the largest purchase of land ever made by a single person in the world occurred today, when Hamilton Disston, a prominent manufacturer of this city, closed a contract by which he secured 4,000,000 acres of land from the State of Florida.... The land acquired, a tract nearly as large as the State of New Jersey, was a part of the public domain of the State of Florida under control of the Board of Internal Improvement of the State.... It is Mr. Disston's intention to at once begin an emigration scheme which will result in a very large addition to the population of Florida. To this end, he has already established agencies in several places in this country, and will at once organize bureaus in England, Scotland, France, Germany, Holland and Italy.[5]

His first drainage project joined the Caloosahatchee River to Lake Okeechobee, permitting Florida's largest lake to drain into the Gulf of Mexico. His second and most successful project concerned a canal connecting a series of lakes around the upper Kissimmee Valley, allowing the reclaimed lands to be converted to agricultural production. For his efforts, Disston was deeded additional acreage by the state.

Proudly proclaiming (and rightly so) that he owned two-thirds of the state, his efforts led to the direct growth of Fort Myers, Orlando, Sarasota and Naples. Furthermore, he became personally credited with the founding of Kissimmee, St. Cloud, Disston City (Gulfport) and Tarpon Springs. In spite of this, things quickly soured.

Not more than six years after Disston began his drainage ventures, a damning report was released showcasing the devastating environmental consequences of all of this quick growth. Within it, Disston was directly cited for creating drought-like conditions in the areas directly north of Lake Okeechobee, making this land virtually barren for agricultural output. Meanwhile, Lake Okeechobee, which typically rises and falls seasonally with the Florida climate, became inundated despite the presence of Disston's canals, resulting in the Caloosahatchee River spilling over its banks to destroy newly settled farmland.

As if all of this weren't bad enough, the structures by which he had meant to drain the Everglades had little intended effect on the wetlands resulting in a huge loss of investment capital. His faulty investments in the construction of hotels and wharves to drive up tourism and residency in Tarpon Springs, as well as his drive to make Disston City outshine nearby Tampa, never materialized, leaving an opening for St. Petersburg to lead the charge. Coupled with a series of devastating freezes, a financial panic and a less-than-friendly trade law passed by Congress, Disston was forced to mortgage the remainder of his Florida assets for $2 million.[6]

Falling into depression and believing that he had singlehandedly ruined the family fortune, Disston returned to Philadelphia, where, after having dinner, he crawled into his bathtub,[7] aimed a gun at his temple and killed himself. The official coroner's report stated that he died in bed from heart disease.

Upon his suicide, his family, having no further interest in Florida, refused to invest any more money in his lands, resulting in creditors foreclosing on all of his former properties just four years later. With that, Disston's dreams of becoming a great land developer like Henry Flagler and Henry B. Plant went down the toilet.

Jacksonville Becomes Hollywood South

With increased land speculation also came increased industry—one of which came close to changing the fate of a city forever.

Today, many people can barely find Jacksonville on a map. Though the largest city in Florida by population—and the largest in the continental United States by land—it still remains shadowed behind the fame of Florida's three other major cities: Miami, Tampa and Orlando. This, however, was not always the case. In fact, by the turn of the 20th century, Jacksonville was not only Florida's biggest tourist attraction, but was home to the world's largest film industry.

Yes, before Hollywood was ever Hollywood, Jacksonville was the "it" place for film production. Its warm climate, moderate seasons and easy access by boat and train proved attractive for burgeoning directors seeking to escape the dreary winters of New York.

The first such production to open was Kalem Studios in 1908. This studio made the first adaptation of *Dr. Jekyll and Mr. Hyde*. After Kalem's success, many more studios followed due to the region's "natural setting and its bustling downtown area, which offered vibrant crowds, cooperative civic leaders, cheap real estate, inexpensive labor, and readily available talent."[8]

By 1916, "more than 30 studios had relocated to the city, including a small, unknown company called MGM, which sat in what is now Jacksonville's Metropolitan Park."[9] Famed comedian Oliver Hardy became the poster child for the city's movie industry, which saw huge technological advancements including the production of the world's first-ever Technicolor picture: *The Gulf Between*, produced in 1917.

While many lauded the city's new identity as the "Silent Film Capital of the World," others were angered by it. The deeply conservative nature of many of the city's citizens clashed with the loose morals of the industry, and a campaign was mounted to chase them out once and for all.

The election of anti-film, religious zealot John Martin to the mayorship in 1917 effectively severed all ties between the city and the industry, with many of the studios packing up for the relatively unknown town of Los Angeles. Conservative Jacksonville residents had had enough of the daily disruptions brought on by film crews, disruptions such as pulling fire alarms or parachuting from tall buildings.[10] Add to the fact that the women in these films were taken to "wearing pants" and "frequenting bars"[11] and it just became all too much for the conservative citizens of Jacksonville, leading many of the spurned studios to seek an escape out west to the Hollywood Hills.

Thus, with the decline of the film industry, Jacksonville's reputation as a magnet for commerce and culture would forever take a backseat, as it would seek out other forms of industry.

Black Actors Flock to Jacksonville

While Martin's election led to an overall decline of the film industry in Jacksonville, it didn't happen overnight. In fact, even as other studios were making their exit, new ones were being founded, the most famous of which was Norman Studios.

Founded in 1920 by Richard E. Norman, a white man and native of Middleburg, Florida, Norman Studios was a pioneer in Black cinema. Catering to Black audiences at a time when most studios were content to solely market to Whites, Norman Studios was unique not only for its production of "race films," a term for films with all Black casts, but also for its depiction of Black Americans in a positive light.

These films helped generate a lot of clout for the Studio at that time, becoming a big hit with Black audiences and drawing in a lot of Black actors into the city. While Norman's reason to produce race films was largely financial, he was also influenced by the situation of race relations. He rightly felt that Black actors could compete on the silver screen with White audiences, and he wanted to showcase the untapped talent that the other studios were missing.

Some films from Norman Studios include: a drama about the railroad called *Green-Eyed Monster* (1919); the comedy *The Love Bug* (1919); two westerns, *The Bull-Dogger* (1921) and *The Crimson Skull* (1922); plus, *Regeneration* (1923), a shipwreck adventure, and *Black Gold* (1928), an oil industry drama.

Flying Ace, produced in 1926, was Norman's most successful film to date. It is the only film from Norman Studios to be inducted into the Film Registry of the Library of Congress. Called "the greatest airplane thriller ever filmed,"[12] the movie was filmed completely on the ground with camera strategies to suggest flight. Aviation pioneers like Bessie Coleman inspired the film. Coleman wrote to Norman Studios about the idea of making a film of her life experience.

Like other silent studios, Norman Studios began to flounder after the introduction of sound in film, with his means of filmmaking becoming obsolete by the 1930s. Soon, more and more of his time was spent on film distribution rather than film making itself; although as time went on, he would still produce industrial films and Joe Louis fight films at the studio.

By the 1990s, much of the studio's history had been largely forgotten until a local resident of Arlington began advocating for its preservation and conversion into a museum. Now owned by the City of Jacksonville, Norman Studios was declared a National Historic Landmark and is in the process of being transferred to the National Park Service.

An Empire in the Everglades

Not all of Florida's environmental woes during these years were the result of individual actions from land speculators, railroad barons and hunters; some actually came from the realm of politics. One such leader was Florida Governor Napoleon Bonaparte Broward.

During the 1904 gubernatorial campaign, Broward made draining the Everglades an official priority, adopting it into his platform. Calling the Everglades "that abominable pestilence-ridden swamp," Broward compared the potential of draining such a huge mess to that which had been undertaken by countries such as Egypt and Holland. He stated that "it would indeed be a commentary on the intelligence and energy of the state of Florida to confess that so simple an engineering feat as the drainage of a body of land above the sea was above their power."[13]

Optimistically referring to this plan as "the Empire of the Everglades,"[14] Broward envisioned a new and different looking South Florida, one in which construction for housing developments would not be hindered by lack of available land along its western fringes. He introduced this measure in more detail during his inaugural year, drawing up plans for drainage just one year later.

Forcing his plan through the legislature, he began by taxing the counties to be impacted by the drainage at "5 cents an acre."[15] Afterwards,

7. Boom! Goes the Landscape

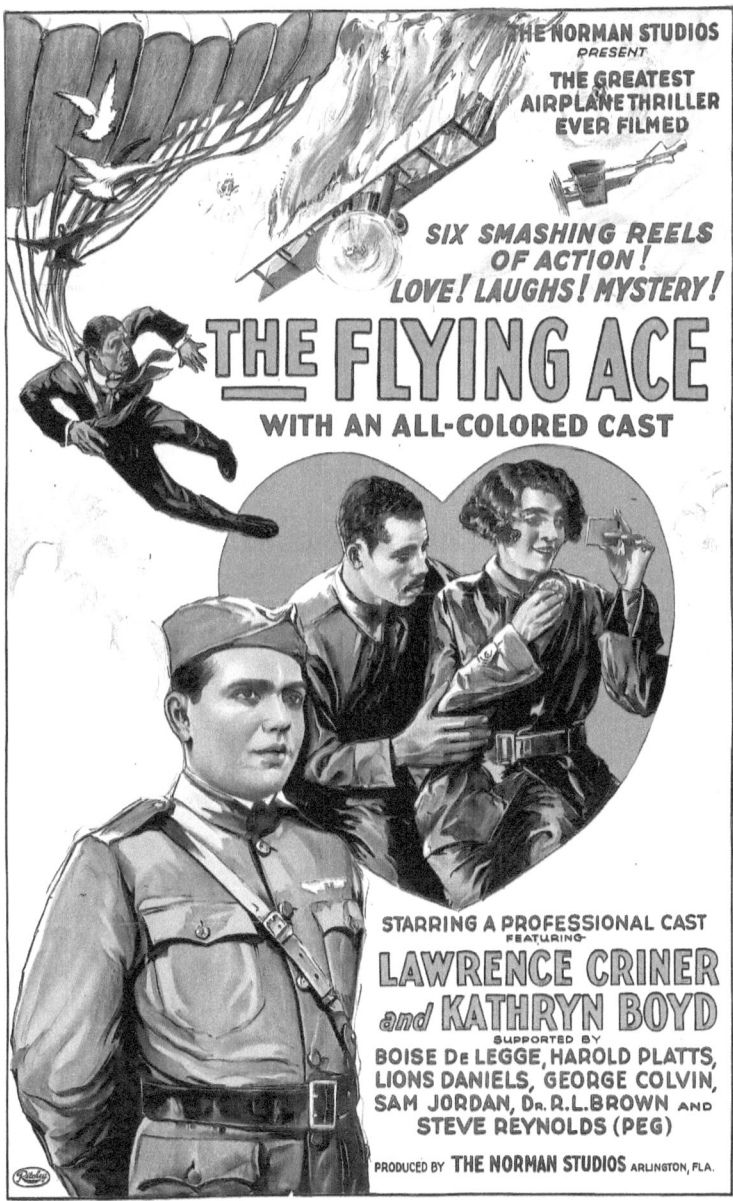

In a rarity for the time, Norman Studios created films for Black audiences featuring all Black casts with protagonists in positive roles, helping to make Jacksonville a mecca for Black actors. During its run, the studio produced eight feature-length films and numerous shorts. Its only surviving film, *The Flying Ace*, has been restored by the Library of Congress (Wikimedia Commons).

he appointed James Wright, an engineer from the USDA's Bureau of Drainage Investigations who was working with Florida, to develop blueprints.

Drafting a report showing how eight canals could be used to effectively drain off the excess water in the Everglades, "at a cost of a dollar per acre,"[16] Wright went to work immediately dredging up two of the canals. Before he could really get going, however, Wright's supervisor began to note errors in his report based upon shaky weather data. Most notably, his supervisor found that "Wright's calculations concerning how much water the canals should be able to hold were off by 55%."[17]

While these revelations made no difference to real estate companies who began drawing up blueprints for housing developments, it did in fact make a difference from a construction perspective. As more and more people came forward dissenting with Wright's findings, including a colleague who stated, "I regard Mr. Wright as absolutely and completely incompetent for any engineering work," the project came to a halt, and Wright retired.[18] Afterward, the entire project ran out of money and the two canals dug in at "only six miles in length" were left uncompleted.[19]

Anti–Semitism in the New Florida

Environmental and industrial changes weren't the only things sweeping through Florida as a result of the population boom; there were serious changes in racial policy as well. These changes usually came piggybacked to the land developers and real estate moguls who made their way down from the North, introducing an entirely different way of thinking to the Sunshine State.

Though anti–Semitism might've seemed like a given with Florida's reputation as a staunchly Catholic colony under Spain, the colony was actually surprisingly lenient with regard to Jews. In fact, it's been speculated that some of Florida's first settlers under Ponce de León and Pedro Menéndez were in fact, "marranos," or Jews in disguise, seeking to escape the Inquisition. While they couldn't worship publicly, there is some evidence that they were allowed to practice in private making St. Augustine and Pensacola the ancestral home of Florida's first Jewish communities.

After the arrival of the Americans, Jews were also similarly accepted, with many land-hungry settlers forced to do open business with the likes of one of Spanish Florida's largest landholders, Moses Elias Levy, an Orthodox Jew from Morocco. So influential was his family that Moses' son, David Levy Yulee, became one of the territory's first representatives and later its first elected Senator to Congress. Consequently he was "also the first Jew to ever hold that position."[20]

Yulee was instrumental in Florida's statehood process and though he was a personal Unionist, he stood with the decision of the Florida legislature to secede, becoming a close confidante of Jefferson Davis. Throughout all of this Yulee never denied his Jewish heritage and for many of the voters it was simply a non-issue. In fact, upon his death, the Florida legislature unanimously named the county of Levy and the city of Yulee in North Florida, in his honor.

By the 1880s, it seemed that every major community in Florida boasted some kind of Jewish presence. In Jacksonville, the Congregation of Ahavath Chesed opened, becoming a landmark of the city. "Its 400-seat capacity was quickly overtaken by fresh newcomers ultimately forcing the congregation to move into a larger building."[21]

In Tampa, Jewish immigrants played an active role in politics, with Herman Glogowski and Frederick Salomonson, Jews from Germany and the Netherlands, serving as the city's mayors. Both were instrumental in the community developing into a major port, with Glogowski serving four terms.[22]

Unfortunately, this historical attitude toward Jews did not carry over into South Florida.

Along Came a Tuttle

Known today as a virtual playground for Northern Jewish retirees, it's hard to believe there was ever a moment when Jews did not play a role in South Florida life. This was not the case at the turn of the century, however, with anti–Semitic clauses being as much a part of the social fabric as segregation was for Blacks.

While anti–Semitism was certainly present in the Keys at the time of Florida's first land boom, "with many Jewish peddlers turned away by the City fathers, and a $100 license fee being imposed upon them for stealing business away from local shops,"[23] it wasn't until the founding of Miami that it actually became law.

Founded by Julia Tuttle, the ambitious widow of the great Cleveland industrialist, Frederick Tuttle, the city was little more than a small collection of fishing shacks composed of transplants from all across the country, before her arrival.

A stern Christian woman through and through, Tuttle came to the area that would later become Miami for one reason and one reason alone: to civilize the jungle. Her idea of civilization consisted of wide boulevards, white church steeples and well-manicured lawns where society could throw garden parties and everyone could dine on cucumber sandwiches and lemonade. It would be a perfect utopia, one where everyone was rich, happy and, oh yeah, White. Not the Catholic, Southern European type, just the Protestant, Anglo-Saxon type. *And oh yes, no Jews.*

Trying in vain to convince Henry Flagler, by that time one of the leading real estate moguls, to invest in the area by bringing his railroad and his hotel down to the area, she met stiff resistance—that is until the Great Freeze of 1894–95 hit. As a result of a surprise, long-lasting freeze that destroyed every citrus crop north of Miami, Tuttle was able to finally convince him to go further south.

Offering him half her land in return, she had two conditions: no booze and no Jews. Because he was desperate, he agreed, only serving alcohol in his hotel during the tourist season, and barring anyone not of Caucasian and Gentile descent from staying. The regulations imposed by him in his hotel, as well as by Julia in her city, ultimately became solidified into the *Caucasian Clause*—a policy by which "Jews were excluded from owning property."[24] Such clauses mirrored those later adopted by the swank development of Bal Harbour, which prohibited those with even ¼ Hebrew blood from leasing or purchasing property within its limits.[25] "Two other clauses of the warranty deed link Jews with Syrians, who also are excluded from the exclusive residential area."[26]

While such clauses proved unpopular among the residents, they were heavily enforced by landowners. This was demonstrated most powerfully when Isadore Cohen, a haberdasher by trade, daringly knocked on Tuttle's door to ask about purchasing land for his shop. Not disguising either his name or his heritage, he was told in no uncertain words to take his business across the river to a relatively undeveloped barrier island.

Seeking Acceptance in Miami Beach

Barred from establishing themselves in Miami proper, many Jews began to congregate in Miami Beach, back then a narrow snake-infested mangrove swamp across the bay.

Attracting the likes of Carl Fisher, an Indianapolis automobile millionaire, the island began to take on the modern-day image of itself, as mangrove jungles were replaced with fancy hotels, while low-lying bay areas were dredged up to make room for small residential islands.

Though claiming that he was not personally anti–Semitic, Fisher, like Tuttle and Flagler, imposed a strict *Caucasian Clause* on the island, barring Jews from settling on his property. As a result, signs popped up all over the island with various *No Jews Allowed* and other restrictive placards. Despite this, Jews found traction on a part of the land owned by the Lummus Brothers.

Soon, a stark division overtook the island with Jews occupying land below Fifth Street and non–Jews owning land to the north. Today, the once-largely Jewish section has grown to become the most popular and colorful part of Miami Beach, known as South Beach.

While Miami and Miami Beach were famous for their restriction of Jewish ownership, they were not the only areas to pass discriminatory measures during this period. Evidence of anti–Semitism was also noted in the city of St. Petersburg.

> The early 1920s saw a rampant rise in anti–Semitism. High ranking figures in the city made public statements about Jews and other immigrant groups. The secretary of the St. Petersburg Chamber of Commerce, for example, declared that "the time has come to make this a hundred percent American and gentile city as free from foreigners as from slums."
>
> Perhaps the most shocking, however, was that public signs were erected to directly discriminate against Jews. When the Gandy Bridge was completed in 1924, a car crossing toward St. Petersburg side would see a sign that read "No Jews Wanted Here." Signs at resorts and restaurants that read "Restricted Clientele" or "Gentiles Only" reflected the exclusionary policies of many local institutions. Throughout much of the early and mid-century, the city was considered one of the most anti–Semitic in all of the United States.[27]

Such policies resulted in many of the Jews in the area having to hide their names and their heritage in true marrano fashion. Ditto in Coral Gables and Palm Beach, those communities expressly built for the wealthiest of residents. There, social barriers remained in place preventing Jews from staying at any of the hotels or participating in any of the social clubs.

William Jennings Bryant, an extreme Protestant Christian and a noted anti–Semite, would actually deliver sermons in front of Miami's Royal Palm Hotel touting the benefit of Christianity by comparison. These sermons, along with George Merrick, the city's founder and developer, forced famous Jews such as Sol Solomon, a noted professional high diver, to hide his heritage when performing at the city's grandiose Biltmore Hotel. "He did this, concealing his identity under the auspicious, non–Hebraic name of Tom Sellers."[28]

Though Jews would eventually come to be accepted in Central and South Florida following World War II, it would be several decades before they would become completely accepted in the public sphere. Even today, certain country clubs still have restrictions imposed upon non–Gentiles, albeit in more subtle ways.

Governor Catts and the Politics of Hatred

Jews were not the only ones to face blatant discrimination at the hands of Florida's elite; Catholics also found themselves in the line of fire.

Given Florida's longstanding association with the Catholic faith while under Spain, it comes as somewhat of a shock how quickly things turned at the beginning of the twentieth century. While a lot of this had to do with the rise in nativism all across the country, which was heavily anti-immigrant and therefore anti–Catholic, a great amount of the blame can be placed at the feet of Governor Sidney J. Catts.

As one of the most racist and bigoted governors this side of George Wallace, Catts, an Alabama native and noted Baptist convert, seemed to have it out for Catholics right from the start. A populist and staunch social conservative, the Alabama-born Catts catapulted to the forefront of Democratic politics by riding a wave of anti–Catholic bigotry in the Florida countryside.

Taking advantage of a resolution introduced by R.B. Sturkie of the State Democratic Executive Committee, which expressed support for a measure that would prevent discrimination based upon religion in the primary voting process, Catts traversed the state, proclaiming a vast conspiracy.

Befriending the likes of Ku Klux Klan members and anti–Catholic crusaders, Catts riled up opposition for the resolution arguing that it amounted to little more than an attempt by established Democrats to "Romanize" Florida for the pope.

Like Hitler would later do with the Jews, Catts argued that Catholics were trying to overthrow the established order in the state and claim it for the papacy. He stated that they were disloyal and, despite their small numbers, "making up around 12% of the total population at the time," were bent on disenfranchising Protestants at the polls.[29]

While Catts tended to avoid the bigger cities like Jacksonville and Miami, he traveled frequently to the rural interior of the state, promising those at his rallies that he would "open convents for inspection, make the Catholic churches pay taxes, and make the priests turn their collars right."[30] Of course, only the ignorant believed he could actually do this.

Nevertheless, in one of the most divisive elections in state history, he ended up winning after a recount. During his inaugural address, he proclaimed:

> Your triumph is no less in this good hour in beautiful Florida, for you have withstood the onslaughts of the county and state political rings, the corporations, the railroads, the fierce opposition of the press and organization of the negro voters of this state against you and the power of the Roman Catholic

hierarchy against you. Yet over all of these the common people of Florida, the everyday cracker people have triumphed.[31]

Although there was a protest among justices, who because of Catts' extreme views did not feel disposed to attend his inaugural ceremonies, they ultimately relented, swearing him in on January 2, 1917.

Interpreting his victory as a victory for the common man, Catts continued his ramblings against Catholicism, adding in a dash of anti–Black language for good measure.

Throughout his blessedly short term as governor, Catts met resistance at every turn from the state legislature, making him one of Florida's most embattled politicians. Making good on his anti–Catholic and anti–Black sentiments, he relocated Florida's ancient military headquarters from the St. Francis Barracks in St. Augustine to Tallahassee, a slap in the face to the largely Catholic city, and ignored the plight of two lynched Black people because he did not count them as equals.[32]

As a result of Catts' victory, like Jews, Catholics largely went into hiding outside larger cities, becoming pariahs in a state which had traditionally once been one of the most staunchly Catholic areas in North America. It would be a long while before they would once again become the dominant religion.

The Tragic Case of Father Conoley

In the years following World War I, hatred for Catholics exploded across the state of Florida. This was of course in no small part to the staunchly anti–Catholic Catts, who served as governor during this period, but was also highly attributed to a sharp rise in Ku Klux Klan membership.

Because of the popularity of movies such as *Birth of Nation*, which glorified Klan activity during Reconstruction, a call went up all across the nation for the formation of a new and strengthened Klan. Like the old one, this new organization would seek to protect White values and womanhood by targeting Blacks. However, this time, they would also incorporate White religion into the mix, adding Catholics, foreigners and Jews as threats to its survival. This was the environment Father John Conoley returned to after serving as an Army chaplain during World War I.

A Jacksonville native, Conoley began his religious career in Gainesville after spending a year in study at the University of Florida. He had a soft spot for the university town and asked to be reassigned there upon his release from the Army.

Wishing to minister to the few dozen Catholics living in the community, Conoley began taking up money for the creation of a drama club and the construction of a dormitory for Catholic students—a move encouraged by University leaders because of their woeful lack of dorm space.

A champion of student causes, he began to travel around the city encouraging business owners to provide more employment opportunities for local students. In his speeches, he argued that students needed to earn money to stay in school, and that the small community had too few jobs for their budding minds, as is. Many of them became directly endorsed by the *Gainesville Daily Sun*, which soon published his activities on the front page, carrying favorable editorial remarks from the staff.

As a result of his newfound popularity among the press, Conoley began to be targeted by community bigots. Within days of his story being published, fliers criticizing Conoley and his "Papism" began to appear on his doorstep.

Several months after the publishing of the *Sun*'s article, three men burst into the church rectory and cornered the surprised Conoley. After savagely beating him black and blue, they took out a knife and castrated him,[33] right there within the confines of his home.

Driving him to the riverside community of Palatka, they shoved his bloodied, broken body out of the car, dumping him on the steps of the local Catholic Church. It would be several hours before the face-down Conoley would be discovered and it would take him roughly a year to recover.

> When the bishop learned of Fr. Conoley's fate, he appointed a priest to fill in for him at St. Patrick. The priest arrived at the St. Patrick rectory to find the windows manned by the Knights of Columbus armed with shotguns. The Knights were responding to the KKK's threat to burn St. Patrick Church and rectory. After one year of hospitalization and two additional years in a monastery, Fr. Conoley was accepted as a priest in the diocese of Portland, Maine. He served as a diocesan priest there until his retirement in 1956. Fr. John Francis Conoley died July 25, 1960, and he is buried at the Veterans Cemetery in Togus, Maine.[34]

No police investigation against the perpetrators was launched and there was no report or public response in the Gainesville area to the attack.[35] While two of the men were later identified, neither was ever charged or brought to justice. Just who were these men in question? Why none other than Gainesville Mayor George Waldo and Police Chief Lewis Washington.

Today, the memory of that awful incident lies hidden in the depths of obscurity, a testament to the cold hard realities faced by much of the state's Catholic community during the height of Florida's Boom Years.

Gone with the Wind

For a state which prided itself on being able to manipulate nature for settlement purposes, it seems somewhat ironic that it was a series of natural events that brought the activities of land developers to an end.

In the summer of 1926, it seemed that there were few barriers standing in the way of Florida becoming the next New York State. Residential and commercial building had exploded, and it soon seemed that every real estate entrepreneur on the East Coast was rushing to the area to outdo their predecessors. In addition, population figures doubled in cities like Miami, with Northern migrants cramming into the new construction. Then on September 17, a hurricane struck, catching everyone off guard and reversing all of the progress made since the 1890s.

First spotted in the central Atlantic on September 11, the massive storm strengthened as it drifted west, developing into a monstrous Category 4 behemoth. Though U.S. officials were aware of the storm, no warnings were issued to the people of Miami from the Weather Bureau in D.C. until September 17, less than 24 hours before the storm's effects were expected to be felt. It was only at noon that the Miami Weather Bureau was finally given permission to post storm warnings for the area, alerting the population of Miami to winds of 48–55 knots, and only around 11 p.m., well into the storm's landfall, that hurricane warnings were issued. The story of their tribulation as the eye of the storm passed over the city was captured by eyewitness accounts from storm survivors, such as Mr. Francis M. Perry:

> At some time after midnight while Mama was sitting on the bed beside her four sleeping children, the wind just picked up the house and carried it some 50 to 100 feet and deposited it on an adjacent vacant lot. As the house settled in its new location, it disintegrated. Mama found herself and all four of us children still on the mattress. The roof was gone and rain was pelting us.... Wall sections of the house were sticking up around us partially protecting us from the wind....
>
> We sat there on the mattress in the wreckage of our house for some time until the wind began to die down. Actually, the wind died down rather suddenly. Later we learned that it was the calm in the "eye" of the hurricane.[36]

When the storm's winds finally relented the following day, survivors picked their way through wreckage and floodwaters as far as the eye could see. In a sick display of calm, the weather was peaceful and sunny.

Following the storm, 372 people lay dead and an additional 6,000 injured.[37] Poor, shabby construction and general unawareness of hurricanes among the population accounted for a majority of the deaths and injuries. While support for the victims poured in from all across the nation, reactions differed drastically.

Overzealous newsmen at first exaggerated the extent of the disaster, the Miami Tribune being a major instance. Other sources moved by concern for the coming tourist season tried to play it down.

Peter O. Knight of Tampa saw the effort to raise money by appeals for help doing more harm to the Florida image than relief could do good. Likewise, the mayor of Miami embarrassed Red Cross officials by minimizing reports of the damage.[38]

All of these conflicting reactions further exacerbated the plight of the people, and likely led to increased suffering and loss of life, as proper aid could not reach them. To this day, it's hard to tell just how many people were killed by the storm itself, and how many might have died as a result of neglect at the hands of tourist-minded officials. In the end, "the great hurricane of 1926 ended the economic boom in South Florida and would be a $90 billion disaster had it occurred in recent times."[39]

The Final Nail in Florida's Building Coffin

While Miami's Great Hurricane of 1926 did not put an end to the *entire* state's building boom, it did deliver a severe blow. The knockout punch, however, came two years later in 1928, with the onset of yet another major hurricane.

At the time that the San Felipe hurricane was spotted in the mid-Atlantic, Florida was still in the midst of a serious recovery from the previous storm.

Reaching the Caribbean as a major Category 3, the behemoth grew to unprecedented intensity, striking Puerto Rico as a Category 5.

Churning directly toward south Florida, the eye of the storm passed just north of Palm Beach, causing a 10-foot storm surge to inundate the island. "More than 1,711 homes were damaged as a result, with the Jupiter Inlet lighthouse reportedly 'squeezed like toothpaste' between the bricks during the storm, swaying the tower 17 inches off the base."[40] Nevertheless, because of advanced warnings, the number of lives lost was kept to a minimum within the area. The same, however, could not be said for the inland communities surrounding Lake Okeechobee.

Storm of the Century

No other area of Florida was as woefully unprepared for this storm as inland Florida. While residents had been warned away just as in other parts of the coast, many who had evacuated returned unexpectedly early.

7. Boom! Goes the Landscape

Believing the storm to have missed them when it did not arrive on time, they returned to their low-lying houses around the lake. The storm was supposed to have arrived a day earlier, but had slowed significantly as it made landfall. When the winds finally did pick up, it was too late.

As the storm crossed the lake, a surge of water rushed over the small earthen dike that had been dug some years before. In a circumstance that would later come to be witnessed in New Orleans, the communities became completely submerged, some drowning in as much as twenty feet of water. These depths caused numerous houses to float off their foundations and forced hundreds of families to their roofs out of desperation to escape the torrents.

With the storm's rear eye wall passing over the main part of the lake, residents were blasted with sustained winds of 140 miles per hour which dashed their houses to pieces, while yet another flood unleashing itself along Okeechobee's northern coast.

The disastrous Lake Okeechobee hurricane made landfall as a Category 4 storm near West Palm Beach, with sustained winds of more than 140 miles per hour. With an eye 25 miles wide, the massive storm surge that ensued caused water to pour out from the lake, submerging homes and farmland in 20 feet of water. The resulting damage, estimated to be $1.6 billion in today's money, effectively ended the building boom in Florida (Wikimedia Commons).

By the time the storm passed, the settlements of Belle Glade, Pelican Bay, Pahokee, Canal Point and South Bay were reduced to rubble. As in Katrina's aftermath, floodwaters remained for several weeks, seriously impeding aid and cleanup. Devastation was near total, with death estimates as high as 2,500, 75 percent being Black farmers and migrant workers, many from the Bahamas.[41] In many instances, "bodies were carried far into the saw grass and their skeletons were discovered years later by workmen clearing the land."[42]

Unlike in Miami, politicians, including the governor, made no effort to try to hide the devastation from the press. The area affected was extremely large and the enormous costs, estimated at $25 million,[43] were financially crippling for a state that had suffered its worst hurricane in history just two years prior.

This time, the cleanup from the storm, combined with Florida's solidified reputation as a state that was clearly the target for destructive and deadly cyclones, put an effective end to any lingering land speculation across the entire state. No longer could Florida claim to be a land of fun and sun. With the passing of the Okeechobee Hurricane, those days and the days of the boom were effectively at an end.

Out with a Bang

The Florida boom times, beginning sometime after Reconstruction and concluding rather abruptly with the Miami and Okeechobee hurricanes, was a time unparalleled in the history of Florida. In fact, no other state epitomized these times more, with Florida being the epicenter of the freewheeling and high-dealing Roaring Twenties. So influential was it that it inspired a 1925 Broadway musical called *Cocoanuts*, followed by a 1929 film of the same name. Still, in spite of all the good times, there were even darker ones, and if all of the building did anything, it was to help expose the dark underbelly that was Florida in transition.

While anti-environmental ventures, religious intolerance and natural disasters were nothing new to a state that had seen almost four hundred years of continuous settlement and strife, the boom times did in fact bring Florida to the forefront of the nation's attention, making it more scrutinized than ever before. This scrutiny, while uncovering all of the dark aspects of the peninsula, nevertheless assured its position in the national press—a position it was unwilling to give up for better or worse.

8

The Era of Blood and Retribution

Florida in the Days of Prohibition and Wise Guys

It might come as a surprise, but Florida had a pretty active mob presence in the 1920s and '30s.

Now ignored in the annals of gangsterdom, stories of Florida's sordid reputation in the 1930s were well documented in the press at the time, with vendettas, drive-bys and blood feuds being an active occurrence.

Now referred to as the "Era of Blood" due to its high mortality rate and increased incidences of disappearances, this troubled time witnessed murder upon murder, as the state entered into a new era of darkness.

Mob City, USA

For those into mob lore, one city outshines all others for sheer volume and scope of gangster activity, leaving all others in the proverbial dust. So move over Chicago, New York and Miami because Tampa has called your bluff.

Now generally known for retirees and Midwestern tourists, the Tampa of the 1930s and 1940s was known for far more than its polished image of today may suggest. In fact, as early as 1912, Tampa had acquired a reputation for grit and vice with one crusader journalist from Jacksonville referring to it as the most wicked city in the U.S.

While it may seem strange that a city relatively small and isolated, in comparison to the huge, industrialized centers of the Northeast, became such a haven for organized crime, it tends to become a little more believable when examining the large immigrant populations who settled there.

Because of the relocation of the cigar industry from Key West, as well as the numerous years of unrest resulting from the Ten Years War in Cuba, Tampa became flooded with immigrants from Cuba, who brought with them their skills at rolling and manufacturing cigars. Soon, they found themselves joined by Spanish and Italian immigrants.

Settling in the tiny enclave of Ybor City, a neighborhood east of downtown originally built for the specific purpose of housing those employed in the cigar industry, these workers, like their counterparts in the Northeast, existed in a state of relative isolation from the much larger community that surrounded them. Unlike in Tampa proper,

> though many of the residents [in Ybor City] were Hispanic, immigrating from Spain or Spanish Cuba, there were also Italian, German, Rumanian Jewish, and Chinese immigrants.... Ybor City's concentration of diverse ethnic groups was uncommon in the American South and added to the unique character of the town. While most of the Hispanic residents worked in the cigar factories, these immigrants also produced the beautiful boxes that held their cigars, operated small shops, and supported the service industries.[1]

This isolation naturally led to the establishment of various social clubs based upon one's particular ethnicity; these served as both social gatherings as well as a community awareness force.

As a result of being confined to the limits of Ybor City, the neighborhood, in essence, began taking on more and more characteristics of an actual independent city, complete with its own grocery shops, security forces and unions.

While the obvious upside to this relative isolation was the formation of a strong, tight-knit community of Latin kinship, the downside was an area fraught with increasing amounts of crime. For, largely outside the control of Tampa officials, the area quickly came to be regarded as a free-for-all, anything goes kind of place. Such an atmosphere encouraged a flush of outside interest and influence in the neighborhood, leading to the development of every kind of illicit activity one could think of. The biggest of these was bolita:

> A prelude to the modern lottery, wooden or ivory balls numbered 1 through 100 were placed in a sack by someone working the game. One winning number was pulled.
> The game spread to Spain, Cuba and Key West before Tampa, where bar owners initially used it as a promotion.
> With an 80–1 payoff, the numbers game known as bolita could be lucrative.
> But due to long odds, it was more lucrative to operate, with millions of dollars wagered annually in Tampa at its peak in the mid–20th century.
> That brought bloodshed as crime syndicates battled for control.[2]
> Gaining popularity and spreading to the rest of the city, the game went

largely unenforced, opening it up to manipulation from crime bosses. Such a lack of enforcement led to an increase in rivalries and ultimately deaths. Late historian Tony Pizzo estimated there were "at least 40 bolita-related killings in Tampa during the first half of the 20th century. Numerous others were injured."[3]

Enter Charlie Wall.

The Devil in Ybor City

It seems a little funny that the founder of one of the most active and organized crime families in America was (a) Southern and (b) a Blue Blood. In fact, Charlie Wall, perhaps the most infamous and underrepresented figure in all of mob-laden history, was downright respected by the locals.

Born into one of the oldest and wealthiest families in the Tampa Bay area, Wall grew up surrounded by high society and gentility. As the son of a physician, he was sent to some of the best area schools, and hobnobbed with some of the wealthiest and most influential figures, many of them his cousins, including politicians, civic leaders and industrialists.

> Perry Wall, his grandfather, was a pioneering resident of the Tampa Bay area who in the mid–1800s settled in Hernando County and served as a probate judge and postmaster. His father, John P. Wall, was a Tampa doctor who served as mayor from 1878 to 1880.[4]

For much of his early life, Wall's position in society seemed rather assured. This all changed when he hit adolescence, however, as his mother died and Wall's father got remarried to a woman he detested, leading Wall to spiral and turn to crime.

> "He was probably already the black sheep of the family," Tampa mob historian Scott Deitche said. "That made it worse."
> In June 1895, at the age of 15, Wall shot and injured the family cook, according to the *Weekly Tribune*. That was his first arrest. "The affair is seriously regretted by the whole community," reads the article.[5]

Following his expulsion from military school and the mysterious death of his stepmother (rumored to have been committed by Wall himself), Wall began to frequent the gambling dens of the Latin Quarter in West Tampa and Ybor City, where, through a mix of monetary and food donations to striking workers, he began to cultivate friendships and trust. "He became known as 'The White Shadow,'" Atkins said. "He was the Anglo who looked out for the poor. He was the benevolent don of the time."[6] It was even said by close relatives that he donated up to $1,000 in coins to the Children's Home[7] each Christmas.

Bolita, a lottery-style game introduced to Tampa from Cuba, was one of the most popular gambling games in the 1920s and '30s. Its popularity would trigger two decades of bloodshed as rival dons competed for control over the lucrative racket (photograph by Zeng8r of an exhibit at Ybor City Museum State Park, November 2007, CC BY-SA 3.0, Wikimedia Commons).

Seizing control of the bolita racket, Wall used his growing wealth, family position and working-class goodwill, to buy off local cops and elected officials, expanding the racket to the rest of the city's districts. As the game rose in popularity, so too did its profits, helping hardscrabble Tampa fund a number of civic projects.

While Wall eventually tapped into bootlegging and pimping in the '20s and '30s, it was the highly lucrative bolita racket that was most coveted by local dons because of its simplicity to cheat:

> One way, passed down and retold for generations, was for the game organizer to place a ball in the freezer, so that it was identifiable through the sack....[8]

Because of these fixes, Wall amassed a huge fortune, attracting the ire of many. No less than a dozen times, Wall dodged an assassin's bullet as eager rivals seeking to gain control tried to off him—a feat he attributed to a protection pact he had made with Satan. He often bragged to the press that he survived because "the devil looks after his own."[9]

As one of the few men with connections, Wall outlived rival dons,

Ignacio Antinori, Velasco and Lumia, who all met early deaths at the hands of drive-bys or hits. Some of these were carried out in full view of the public, such as Ignacio Antinori, who was gunned down at a local restaurant while sipping on his morning coffee, purportedly under the orders of Wall, himself. "Over twenty-five gang members died this way over a period that stretched roughly from 1930 until 1959."[10]

Wall's luck soon ran out, however, as he succumbed to a morphine addiction, steadily losing his grip on reality. Santo Trafficante, Sr., who rose to lead one of the city's most powerful crime syndicates by the 1940s, soon made a deal that if Wall stepped aside, he'd let him live.

> Wall did, but not graciously.
> The late Ellis Clifton, who led the Vice Squad's investigation of Wall's murder, once told the *Tampa Bay Times* Wall would publicly badmouth the Trafficante family.[11]

Squealing about Tampa's criminal networks to the Feds, perhaps out of moral consciousness over the rising violence, and perhaps partly out of bitterness due to his lost prestige, Wall emerged from retirement in 1950 to testify at the Kefauver Hearings on Organized Crime. There, on live, national television, he graphically described Tampa's criminal network, implicating its rackets and activities. Not long after in April of 1955, Wall was found dead at the age of 75.

"He was beaten with a blackjack, his neck cut with a knife, and his head battered with a baseball bat." The crime remains unsolved, though Clifton, who investigated the murder, maintained it was a hit ordered by Trafficante's son.[12]

A Violent End for a Violent Era

The murder of Charlie Wall shocked Tampa to its utter core. Not only was Wall a prominent citizen, coming from one of the oldest and most distinguished families in the city, but he was also a notorious gangster and in spite of being retired, was still widely regarded as the undisputed king of the Tampa underworld.

Last seen having a drink with his close confidante and fellow gangster, Nick Scaglione, his "blood alcohol level, according to the autopsy included in the report, was .145."[13]

Right from the start, police faced a formidable puzzle. How did the killer or killers get into Wall's home? There was no sign of a forced entry into his bungalow. Their conclusion: "Apparently he either was friendly with the killer or the assailant surprised him while he was preparing for bed."[14]

His wife and former wife were each early suspects as part of a love triangle theory, according to the report, as were former bodyguards and drivers Joe "Baby Joe" Diaz and Johnny "Scarface" Rivera, who allegedly worked for the Trafficante syndicate at the time.[15]

Another suspect was Emory Lee Scott, who the report says had been recently released from prison and "once ran dope for Charlie Wall."

Clifton told the *Times* that he believed Joe Bedami, described as a Trafficante hitman, was responsible for Wall's murder, but he is not mentioned as a suspect in the report.[16]

Birdseed was also discovered at the murder scene, according to the report, a possibly symbolic gesture alluding to Charlie's "singing" to the Feds.[17]

Despite the fact that no clear killer or motive would ever be established, Wall's sudden death would benefit his chief rival, Santo Trafficante, Jr., in a very big way, clearing the way for a new chapter in Florida mob history.

Tampa's Godfather and the Birth of the Sunshine Mob

Call him the Godfather of Tampa or the Angry Assassin, but when referencing the likes of Santo Trafficante, Jr., in Tampa, just be sure and don't call him a wise guy.

As head of a "family" of criminals that endured for over thirty years, Trafficante, in many ways, embodied the heart and soul of one of the largest and most extensive mob families in the U.S., rivaling the better known Bonannos, Luccheses and Gambinos.

Born to Sicilian immigrants in Tampa, it seems Trafficante was predestined for the mob life, growing up under the tutelage of his father, Santo Trafficante, Sr., one of Tampa's most powerful bosses, and serving as a personal protégé to Ignacio Antinori. Involved in the racket from an early age, Trafficante inherited his father's vast grip on the city after the elder Trafficante died of stomach cancer in 1954.

Arrested and convicted that same year by a jury for running illegal bolita operations in Ybor City, Trafficante escaped a five-year prison sentence when his conviction was overturned by the Florida Supreme Court. Thus began his lifelong habit of legally dodging jail terms.

As a principal stakeholder in the Cuban gaming industry from an early age, Trafficante gained a ton of wealth by holding key interests in the Hotel Habana Riviera, the Sevilla-Biltmore, the Tropicana Club, the Habana Hilton, the Capri Hotel Casino, the Comodoro, and the Deauville, some of Havana's most frequented casinos. It was in this latter capacity that Trafficante was able to gain a presence in the international mob scene, even garnering an invitation to the ill-fated Apalachin Meeting, with other leading mobsters.

In 1959, Trafficante's fate, along with the fate of all other mobsters, changed dramatically after Castro's successful revolution. Almost overnight, all of Trafficante's holdings were seized, and not long after, he was expelled from Cuba.

Eventually, Trafficante partnered with members of New York's Bonanno family, dividing the remainder of his later years between New York, New Orleans and his two homes in Tampa and Miami.

His death in 1987 marked a power shift away from Florida, resulting in Trafficante's remaining "family" to ally themselves under the direction of their Northern counterparts.

Santo Trafficante and the Assassination of JFK

Is it possible for one man to play a direct role in some of the biggest scandals in American history, including the assassination of a U.S. president, all while keeping it concealed from authorities? Some conspiracy theorists think so, and there's a good bit of evidence that backs them up.

It might seem like something straight out of the plot from Oliver Stone's *JFK*, but there are quite a few documents that support Mafia involvement in the assassination of John F. Kennedy. These documents allege a close connection with Kennedy and the Mafia stretching back to before the Cuban Revolution:

> Havana also became a destination for junkets, where politicians could do things they couldn't in the United States. Sex was a big part of that. [While still serving in the Senate and before he was elected president], John F. Kennedy went down there with another young senator, from Florida, named George Smathers. Santo Trafficante, one of the leaders of the mob in Havana, later told his lawyer about how he had set up a tryst with three young Cuban prostitutes in a hotel room. What Kennedy didn't know was that Santo Trafficante and an associate watched the orgy through a two-way mirror. Trafficante reportedly regretted not capturing it on film as a potential blackmail resource.[18]

While many of these documents implicate an intricate network of interlinked gangsters, they nevertheless reveal a common source that appears over and over again. That source? None other than Santo Trafficante, Jr., himself.

On January 14, 1992, an article was published in the *New York Post* claiming that Trafficante, Jimmy Hoffa and Carlos Marcello were involved

Santo Trafficante was the founder of the Trafficante crime syndicate in Tampa. Taking over the bolita racket from Charlie Wall, he is rumored to have ordered Wall's brutal murder. He established extensive business relations in Cuba prior to Castro's takeover and later confessed on his deathbed to having orchestrated the Kennedy assassination. Here he is pictured at Sans Souci's Bar in Havana around 1955 (Wikimedia Commons).

in the assassination of John F. Kennedy. Their main source for this article was Frank Ragano, an attorney of Trafficante's, who upon organizing a meeting with Trafficante and Marcello, recounted in detail:

> "You won't believe what Hoffa wants me to tell you. Jimmy wants you to kill the president." He [Ragano] reported that both men gave the impression that they intended to carry out this order.[19]

While this very well could have been the angry ramblings of a spurned comrade, further testament from Marcello to the FBI in 1988 adds to the conspiracy. According to their documents, Marcello, never a friend of Bobby Kennedy, who during his time as attorney general aggressively prosecuted organized crime bosses, shouted, "Take the pebble out of my shoe!" As he stated, he wished to destroy the "tail of the dog," referring to Bobby, by having "the dog," referring to John, assassinated. He would then plant a "nut" to take the blame, "the way they do it in Sicily." He later concluded, "I had the little son of a bitch killed, and I'd do it again.... I wish I could've done it myself."[20]

Yet another confidante of these men, Jose Aleman, would later come forward to the FBI implicating Trafficante in the plot once again.

Aleman, a wealthy Cuban exile living in Miami, served as an undercover FBI informant, meeting with Trafficante in September 1962. As Aleman would later repeat to the FBI, Trafficante broached the subject of Kennedy, stating:

> "Have you seen how his brother is hitting Hoffa, a man who is a worker, who is not a millionaire, a friend of the blue collar? He doesn't know that this kind of encounter is very delicate. Mark my words, this man Kennedy is in trouble, and he will get what is coming to him."[21]

When Aleman argued on the viability of Kennedy's reelection chances in 1964, Trafficante bluntly said: "No Jose, he is going to be hit."[22]

While Trafficante later refuted these claims, stating that his conversation with Aleman occurred in Spanish and that no such words were uttered, Ragano claimed that Trafficante, upon his deathbed made a remorseless confession: "Carlos f—ked up. We should not have killed Giovanni (John). We should have killed Bobby."[23]

Castro Bankrolls a Revolution

As was stated, Trafficante's obsession with Kennedy largely stemmed from his resentment over Kennedy's failures during the Bay of Pigs, earning a lifelong vendetta from the Tampa mobster. Trafficante should've blamed, however, the people of Florida and himself, for while Trafficante was busy frolicking in corrupt casino money, Castro was bankrolling a revolution right underneath his nose.

Though it's not exactly the nicest thing to point out, especially to a community that has endured so much, Castro's rise to power can largely be placed at the feet of Miami's early exile community. For it was through the aid of this community that a young orator in the 1950s was able to charm the people into bankrolling his upcoming revolution.

Paying a visit to Miami's Little Havana, just west of downtown, Castro was able to wow a crowd of thousands with his anti–Batista rhetoric, speaking from a platform in the Flagler Theater. In one of his most heated speeches, delivered on November 20, 1955, Castro ironically made a big deal of the then 26,000 exiles living in Florida, making a boast to the Miami Herald that he was in the process of organizing a movement of 100,000 persons for a revolution. "If Batista remains in power by force, then there is no other way but to remove him by force," he was quoted as saying.[24]

By the time he left Florida, Castro had amassed thousands of dollars from the Cuban community and had added three more chapters of his rebel group, the Movimiento 26 de Julio (26th of July Movement), in Miami, Key West and Tampa. This group, though small in size, was influential in his eventual success in toppling the Batista regime. They were particularly influential in Tampa, where the radical *La Gaceta* newspaper continued to run editorials on the revolution and helped recruit more rebels to the cause.

Though Castro's takeover was initially met with exhilaration, the joy among Florida's exiles did not last. Within two years, Castro had announced a full change of course to Socialism, with pre-revolutionary leaders and those suspected of complicity rounded up, beaten and imprisoned in gulag-like camps.

The abolition of private property, the oppression of free speech and the daily executions, as headed by Castro's head henchman, Che Guevara, soon turned the tide of goodwill he had received in Florida against him. Many in the community felt duped, as the indefinite delay of elections led them to rightly believe that they had traded one bad dictator for another.

The birth of a new communist regime, which, in fact, did not officially become so until 1961, altered the course of Florida and U.S. history forever. For those gangsters who had the most to lose, such as Trafficante, it would elicit a lifelong vendetta.

Santo Trafficante and the Attempted Assassination of Fidel Castro

Although Trafficante's alleged involvement in the Kennedy assassination is damning enough, there is also ample evidence he was involved in plots against Castro's life. For this, he had particularly good cause, having lost all of his stake in Cuba's hotel industry following Castro's revolution. His loss was met with further humiliation when he was jailed and exiled by Castro's orders.

The plot against Castro involved the CIA, who conspired with Trafficante and Giancana Roselli to have him knocked off.

Known as "Operation Mongoose," these attempts involved the use of poison pills, cigars filled with poison, exploding conch shells and even "a wet suit impregnated with a special fungus that would cause a disabling rare skin disorder, which was to be presented to the Cuban leader, well-known for his love of diving."[25] All ended in miserable failure.

Though it happened under the radar, history has revealed that Operation Mongoose was, in its own way, every bit as disastrous as the Bay of Pigs. "It was an expensive and embarrassing failure," summed up [Bobby Kennedy biographer Evan] Thomas. "Castro after all is *still* alive in Cuba, and the people who tried to get him are long since gone. And the way they went after him, by hiring the Mafia, was something that has long-term effects on U.S. foreign policy. People still see the CIA as this sinister, nefarious force. It was a fundamentally foolish thing to do and Bobby bears real responsibility for it."[26]

While his plots against Castro were never successful, Trafficante purportedly continued his work with the CIA throughout the remainder of his days. One such plot that he was later linked to was the Iran-Contra Affair under Reagan, a connection he would personally become implicated in because of his continued dealings in Latin America.

The Near-Assassination of Franklin Roosevelt

It might come as a surprise, but Santo Trafficante's flirtation with presidential assassination was hardly a first for the Sunshine Mob, for exactly thirty years prior, Giuseppe Zangara attempted to assassinate a newly elected Franklin Delano Roosevelt during a goodwill trip to Miami in 1933. An Italian immigrant who became naturalized in 1929, "Zangara suffered from mass delusions, espousing a hatred for kings and capitalists, alike."[27]

Making his move while Roosevelt was speaking to a crowd in front of Bayfront Park, Zangara attempted to do the deed with a .32 caliber U.S. Revolver he had purchased at a local pawnshop. His attempts to get a clear shot proved feeble, however, as the chair he stood on wobbled, and the crowd subdued him after he fired a single shot.

Though he missed Roosevelt, he shot wildly four more times from the ground, hitting Anton Cermak, the mayor of Chicago, and fatally wounding him in the process. Before dying Cermak turned to Roosevelt and said: "I'm glad it was me instead of you."[28] Zangara later claimed "I don't hate Mr. Roosevelt personally I hate all officials and anyone who is rich."[29]

In the aftermath of the shooting, Zangara pled guilty and received the electric chair for Cermak's murder. His final words were: "Viva Italia! Goodbye to all poor peoples everywhere! ... Push the button!"[30]

While Zangara was ruled delusional by the judge, many have since speculated whether he was indeed sane, and acting on the advice of Chicago crime boss Frank Nitti. Nitti, after all, had been the target of his own assassination attempt three months earlier and blamed Cermak for the hit. Coupled with the fact that Zangara had been an expert marksman in the

Italian Army, some have since wondered if Cermak, and not Roosevelt, had indeed been the intended target, all along.

Northern Gangsters in South Florida

Tampa wasn't the only area in Florida to attract a significant mob presence; South Florida did so as well. For its case, however, South Florida didn't produce mob activity, but rather imported it from abroad.

Like Tampa, all of South Florida's mob woes can pretty much be laid at the feet of one person—Al Capone. While Chicago may get the credit for Capone's Prohibition escapades, it's really Florida that should garner the credit for keeping him protected.

Born to Italian immigrants in Brooklyn, Capone showed all the signs of an emerging criminal as a child, displaying violent behavior with other children and even punching his female teacher in the face at the age of fourteen. Dropping out of school, Capone shuffled between various street gangs before hooking up with Frankie Yale, who employed him as a fellow racketeer as well as a bouncer in his Brooklyn nightclub. It was there, during a scuffle with a patron, he had his face hideously slashed, earning him the lifelong moniker "Scarface."

In the early 1920s, Capone departed New York for more lucrative opportunities with Johnny Torrio and his Five Points Gang in Chicago. Taking on the infamous Black Hand, Capone quickly went to work murdering different members of the gang until control of the city became safely encompassed under his and Torrio's authority. A noted example of the extent of this control can be found during the Cicero mayoral elections of 1924. Capone, using thugs as enforcers, rigged the election in favor of one mayoral candidate in particular, who later turned on Capone by publicly decrying his criminal activities only weeks after the election. As a result, Capone met with the mayor and shoved him down the town hall steps, nearly killing him.

Inheriting all of Torrio's rackets the following year, after the former departed for Italy, Capone quickly expanded his racket from mere bootlegging to prostitution and gambling. Around this time, his place in the underworld looking increasingly secure, Capone traveled to Miami via a hideout in Jacksonville, where he purchased a palatial estate on luxurious Palm Island, just off the sunny shores of Miami for $40,000.[31]

From the comforts of his seven bedroom, seven bath Miami mansion, Capone started an all-out Italian vs. Irish war back in Chicago, culminating in the infamous St. Valentine's Day Massacre, where seven prominent Irish gangsters were brutally gunned down in a Lincoln Park garage.

Though Capone was never implicated in the massacre, as he was in Miami at the time, he was nonetheless made a scapegoat by the unabashedly corrupt Mayor Bill Thompson, and presumed responsible since the victims were people who opposed him.

For the next few years, Capone dedicated himself to establishing himself as a legitimate citizen of Miami. Despite the outward show of respectability, however, he quietly made plans to solve pressing problems caused by his old boss Frankie Yale, and divided his time between the Lexington Hotel in Chicago and his home in Miami. His luck soon ran out when he was convicted of tax evasion and sentenced to 11 years in prison in 1931. His sentence was shortened to six and a half years, again for good behavior.[32]

After his parole, Capone returned to his Florida home where he lived out the remainder of his days in relative seclusion. There he died of a fatal cardiac arrest in 1947, surrounded by his wife and family.

Although publicly "retired" during the majority of his Florida sojourn, Capone was nonetheless extremely active in the business, even arranging a meeting of his top six guys to discuss business affairs in the Windy City. His presence in South Florida, while never fully appreciated by the population, is nonetheless widely credited with the sparking of increased real estate investment among fellow gang members, who became entranced with the many gated communities dotting the islands of Biscayne Bay.

The Real Hyman Roth

Italians weren't the only ones to get in on the lucrative gangster business during the Prohibition years; Jewish-Americans like Meyer Lansky also took a swing at it, playing a major role from his home base in South Florida. Unlike Capone, however, Lansky never feigned retirement, actively launching his ventures into Cuba from his home.

Born in Belarus, Lansky immigrated to the United States at the age of nine with his parents, and they settled in the Lower East Side of Manhattan. It was in this neighborhood Lansky made a lifelong connection with the likes of Bugsy Siegel and Lucky Luciano.

Over the years, Lansky grew particularly close with Siegel, having the same familial and religious background as him, and took to forming the Bugs and Meyer Mob. This gang, officiated over by Luciano, quickly grew to be one of the most feared street gangs during the heyday of Prohibition, with members supplying bootleggers with stolen trucks and drivers, as well as handling the protection, hijacking, murder and illegal gambling operations of the business.

After the repeal of Prohibition, Lansky narrowed his racket to focus on the establishment of casinos. By 1936, he had opened casinos in Florida, New Orleans and Cuba. He invested a particularly large amount of interest in his Cuban operations, making it a point to connect other northern bosses with the golden opportunities the island nation presented. He also took an active interest in Las Vegas, encouraging Siegel to look into the area.

Ironically, during this time, Lansky, who was usually careful about keeping his hands clean in physical matters, stepped out from his comfort zone to help break up pro-Nazi rallies in Manhattan. At one particular rally in Yorkville, Lansky and fourteen others threw attendees out windows and proceeded to beat them up and chase them down the street. Lansky stated that he "wanted to show them that Jews would not always sit back and accept insults."[33]

After World War II, Lansky renewed his interest in the Cuban gaming industry, establishing a personal connection with Fulgencio Batista. Several of his casinos, the Montmartre Club, the Habana Riviera and the Nacional, soon became synonymous with decadence and corruption, notorious for their connections to the Italian Mafia. As was the case with Trafficante's Cuban holdings, however, Lansky's multimillion-dollar ventures came to an abrupt end when Castro outlawed gambling and nationalized all foreign companies following the Revolution.

Forced to rely solely on his earnings from Las Vegas, which he had inherited upon Sigel's assassination in 1947, Lansky began to keep a low profile, settling in a modest home in Miami Beach. Though he attempted to escape federal tax evasion charges by fleeing to Israel, his criminal record and his well-known underground associations resulted in his deportation back to Florida. There, he died quietly of lung cancer in 1983.

While little hard money was left following his death, the FBI estimated that up to $300 million in assets was hidden in a number of Swiss bank accounts and relative's names. Despite this, no such fortune has ever been found.

Lansky's colorful life would later be fictionalized, both in writing and on the big screen, in Francis Ford Coppola's *The Godfather Part II*, inspiring the character arc of Hyman Roth. Parts of Roth's fictional persona even had layers of truth, including his money laundering activities through casinos and his gathering with other mob bosses in Havana in 1946.

The Key Bank Scandal

While most of Florida's mob activity seems to have peaked in the period between the thirties and early sixties, there is ample evidence that

8. The Era of Blood and Retribution

Meyer Lansky was one of the most powerful Jewish gangsters during Prohibition, known for operating casinos in Florida, New Orleans, Las Vegas and Cuba. He is pictured here (far right) with his wife and Cuban President Fulgencio Batista just prior to the Cuban Revolution. His exploits would forever be immortalized through the fictional Hyman Roth in *The Godfather Part II* (Wikimedia Commons).

it is still omnipresent, particularly in Tampa. This was most evident in a 1992 bank scandal that had national ramifications.

Immediately following Santo Trafficante's death in 1987, there was a squabble over who would take over as don. While mob rivals sought to take advantage of the situation and divide the family against itself, the Trafficantes ultimately pulled themselves together and emerged once more as a unit to be reckoned with.

Smaller than before and headed by Vincent LoScalzo, who took to initiating a new group of members, the family turned toward white-collar crime, allegedly using their accounts in Key Bank as a front for money laundering, fraud and a whole host of other financial crimes. The Feds, suspecting illicit activities, placed 65,000 wiretaps in the bank, finally catching them in the act in a discussion about a $30,000 deposit with Bank President Frank Pupello, which the Trafficante associates desired to use to purchase a certificate of deposit.[34]

> "Would I be better off just giving you ten at a time?" Bernstein asked, according to wiretap transcripts.
> "Well, even less," Pupello answered.
> "See, I thought I could bring you five every day," Bernstein said.[35]

Breaking right open, as a result of wiretapping, 15 people were arrested[36] for the crimes, including Santo Trafficante III, a nephew of the late boss, and a reputed underling of LoScalzo, and Michael J. Freedman, a lawyer for the bank, who was incidentally the husband of Tampa Mayor, Sandy Freedman. The latter was arrested on charges of making false banking entries and delivering false documents.[37] Both charges carried a maximum punishment of five years in prison. In addition, the bank president and vice president were charged with falsifying bank materials, with hundreds of boxes of documents being seized at the main branch.

Luckily for all accused, the investigation was thrown out in court, due to the incorporation of warrantless wiretapping by the prosecution. Though LoScalzo managed to walk away free, his victory would be short-lived, as he would once again be arrested one year later on allegations of fraud in an unrelated case, serving out probation for the next five years.

Florida and the Mafia—Fuggedaboutit!

Florida's association with gangsters in both Tampa and South Florida makes it one of the most colorful states with regard to the Mafia. Nevertheless, history has turned a blind eye to this chapter in the state's past, ignoring the fact that throughout the thirties and forties, Florida had one of the most active rings of gangster activity of any state in the country, rivaling the likes of Chicago and New York for both sheer brutality and power. Still, throughout all of it, Florida's mob chieftains seemed to have risen above the fray, achieving an elusiveness not generally witnessed among the more famous families in the North. It's this elusiveness that has kept Florida's Sunshine Mob out of the spotlight and out of the jail cells, allowing them to continue their activities through a relative veil of secrecy. Even today, while we may speculate about the general whereabouts and involvement of these individuals, there is little we actually know about the true extent of their reach and power.

9

We Shall Overcome

*Florida in the Dark Days
of Xenophobia, Segregation
and Purple Panic*

Xenophobia and racism didn't disappear with Sidney Catts' departure from the governorship in the 1920s. If anything, it became more entrenched and accepted.

Long a place of welcome for newcomers and entrepreneurs, Florida became even more closed off following World War II, joining the ranks of other Southern states as a society closed off from the rest of the world. This pattern of hostility toward differentness would mark the state through the post-war years, and well into the '50s and '60s.

Casualties of War

By now, most of us have a passing knowledge of the conditions imposed on the Japanese in the aftermath of Pearl Harbor, particularly in California, where one's heritage was the only factor to land one in an internment camp. Did you know such camps existed in Florida, too?

Though there were several areas of Florida which housed internees, the largest of these was located at Camp Blanding in Starke. It was here in January 1942, barely a month after the U.S. entry into the war, that the first batch of internees arrived.

> [T]his group consisted not of soldiers, but rather a number of German civilians who were living in Latin America. These not so fortunate few were interned and brought to the United States as enemy aliens. At Camp Blanding they were separated by sex. Interned without trial, they had been transported to Florida against their will, forced to wear fatigues with the letters "E.A." (Enemy Alien), and left to camp out in the hills of northern Florida, with

little assurance of what the future held for them. Mixed within this group were sixteen Jews, who received the same treatment as the most ardent Fascist sympathizers....

Approximately 1,000 prisoners found themselves incarcerated in the Army compound at Camp Blanding, and the Post administered for eleven original, and an eventual fifteen branch camps. These held between 250 and 300 men, thus totaling nearly 3,000 prisoners collectively.[1]

There, they remained until being transferred to more permanent camps in Oklahoma and Texas.[2]

Forced into signing pledges not to take up arms against the Allies, they were ultimately expelled, not back to their native Latin American countries, but rather their ancestral homes in Germany or Italy. Toward the end of the war, almost all of the internees were out of Florida, and the ranks of Camp Blanding became increasingly composed of actual prisoners of war.

German U-Boat Attacks

While Florida's shameful treatment of enemy aliens, as they were called, was a serious blot on state history, its reactions, while despicable,

Just as the Japanese were imprisoned out West, Germans and Italians were both subject to internment in Florida during World War II. Here, a group of POWs are gathered outside a dwelling in Camp Blanding in 1944 (Camp Blanding POW Camp, CC BY-SA 2.0, Wikimedia Commons).

become more understandable given the context of the events occurring in the immediate presence of the peninsula.

Florida, unlike other states during this time, was at the forefront of the war, having the longest contiguous coastline in the Eastern United States. This made it vulnerable to an increasingly high number of German U-boat attacks. As part of a campaign to initiate fright and despair in the American psyche, the Germans launched these attacks right off the coast, in plain sight of tourists and residents within the state; the most dramatic of these took place on the night of April 10, 1942, when German U-123 torpedoed the tanker *Gulfamerica* off the coast of Jacksonville Beach.[3] The resulting explosion killed 19 crewmembers and was seen by many, prompting Governor Spessard Holland to order a blackout of lights[4] across the shore.

In general, high death tolls were not associated with these attacks, though overt precautions taken by the United States increased accidents and worry, leading to the Gulfbelle incident. In this incident, two U.S. tankers off the coast of Jupiter Inlet ordered to travel without lights for fear of German attacks collided, causing an explosion that killed 88 of the 116 men aboard the ships.[5] The resulting flames lit up the night sky for seven weeks, to the gaping horror of all those ashore.

Operation Pastorius

Though Hawaii may be able to claim a surprise aerial attack by the enemy during World War II, it's Florida that can justifiably claim an all-out invasion.

Happening right around the time of the infamous U-Boat attacks, the sparsely populated shores of Florida, still one of the least populated states in the South, provided the perfect opportunity for the Nazis to launch an invasion and sabotage the Allied effort. Known simply as Operation Pastorius, the invasion served dual purposes: to launch attacks against American economic landmarks and to fatally cripple American morale to continue on with the war effort. Sporting a two-prong invasion of the East Coast, one at Amagansett, Long Island and the other at Ponte Vedra Beach, the invaders, eight in total, were given crash courses in sabotage, equipped with $175,000 cash and a number of targets to attack.[6]

Such targets included hydroelectric plants at Niagara Falls; the Aluminum Company of America's plants in Illinois, Tennessee and New York; locks on the Ohio River near Louisville, Kentucky, and Cincinnati, Ohio; the Horseshoe Curve, an important railroad pass near Altoona, Pennsylvania; the Pennsylvania Railroad's repair shops at Altoona; a cryolite plant in Philadelphia; Hell Gate Bridge in New York City; and Pennsylvania Station in Newark, New Jersey.[7]

Divided up into two submarines, the first group, landing in New York on June 13, 1942, stormed the beach in uniform, burying enough explosives, primers and incendiaries to support an extended two-year campaign. After doing so, however, one of their crewmembers, John Dasch, was discovered by a Coast Guardsman and compromised. As a result, they abandoned their plans altogether, boarding a train to New York City.

The second batch of crewmembers, landing just off the coast of Ponte Vedra Beach three days after the New York landing, fared a little better. Coming ashore on a raft in the predawn hours of twilight, the four men went about burying their deposits of explosives before boarding a bus to New York, walking their way down Highway 140 before splitting up in Jacksonville.

Checking into the Mayflower and Seminole Hotels under assumed aliases, the four saboteurs quickly discovered that they had lost contact with their counterparts in New York. Furthermore, the FBI had caught on to their scheme.

Sending agents to apprehend the saboteurs the following day, the FBI narrowly missed the men before they boarded a train to Cincinnati. This was in preparation for their rendezvous meet-up set to occur on July 4.

Blithely unaware of how badly the New York mission had gone, and also unaware their counterparts had turned themselves in to the FBI, the Florida comrades were captured and later brought into custody with the other spies. Concerned a civilian court might be too lenient, Roosevelt had them tried by military tribunal.[8] Though their lawyers attempted to reverse Roosevelt's decision, they were denied and the trial proceeded. Six, including all Florida crewmembers, were given the electric chair after being found guilty,[9] while the two New York spies who had helped foil the plot were given 30-year jail sentences. Harry Truman later showed both men clemency,[10] commuting their jail time and deporting them back to the American occupied zone of Germany.

Other Incidents

While Operation Pastorius proved a tactical failure, it did show Americans, in a very public way, that even they were not exempt from invasion. Of course, most Floridians watching burning ships directly from their beachside homes were already fully aware of this.

From Miami to Jacksonville reports had streamed in throughout the war of Germans coming ashore. One of these incidents was recounted by Stafford Beach, a local resident and member of the Coast Guard Auxiliary who recounted in 1987: "I did duty on sentry posts up and down the beach, Singer Beach, watching for anybody coming in. They did have some landings detected.... We were aware that Germans were landing, but we never heard much about it, and I never saw any."[11] Furthermore, Miami Beach residents recounted how anti–Semitic literature was showered upon their doorsteps with the docking of a German cruise ship just before U.S. entry into the war. In addition, historian Bessie DuBois, who lived next to Jupiter Inlet wrote that "Frank Webber, a Marine from the Jupiter Naval Radio Station, told of the capture of a German submarine crew on the sand bar across the inlet. The Marines put them aboard a train to a Kentucky prisoner-of-war camp."[12]

All of these accounts helped galvanize Floridians into a xenophobic frenzy leading them to fear anyone and everyone associated with the Axis powers, even those deemed as loyal residents. Such was the case with the few Japanese farmers remaining in the tiny Palm Beach County village of Yamato, whose land was confiscated by the government to help with the war effort.

Florida in the Era of Jim Crow

As bad as Florida's reputation was with foreign aliens, things were much worse in the state for Black Americans. This was especially true from the 1920s to the 1960s, culminating in numerous acts of violence for the sole purpose of keeping Blacks and Whites separate in the public sphere.

While no Alabama or Mississippi (or even Boston), Florida was nonetheless a very active player in the maintenance of racial separation. Within the state itself, legal segregation had been the norm since at least the end of Reconstruction, becoming codified in different municipalities and cities at different times. In Miami, for example, Blacks were forbidden from owning land under the Caucasian Clause of 1896, while in Jacksonville, segregation on public transportation began in earnest on July 1, 1905, with the separation of races on streetcars.

Such discrimination affected all facets of Black life in the Sunshine State from voting to housing and even interpersonal relationships, and it culminated in widespread, endorsed hate that would eventually come to affect all targeted minorities.

A Simple Right

While the Fifteenth Amendment extended the right to vote to Black citizens in 1870, its application was anything but guaranteed. Loosely protected in the South for as long as Northern soldiers were there to enforce it, its practicality all but ceased to exist by the turn of the century. With wave after wave of new and restrictive laws introduced in the 1890s, including poll taxes and literacy tests, Blacks suddenly found it difficult to exercise their previous rights. So profound was the impact of these laws that by 1910, "registered voters among African Americans dropped to 15 percent in Virginia, and under two percent in both Alabama and Mississippi."[13]

This didn't stop determined voters from exercising their Constitutional rights, however. By the Election of 1920, with women having recently gained the right to vote, a new zeal was sparked in the Black community to reclaim their lost right. Much of this zeal came from women like Mary McLeod Bethune, founder of the Daytona Educational and Training School for Negro Girls, who urged everyone to "Eat your bread without butter but pay your poll tax!"[14]

The ensuing rush to register by Blacks overwhelmed precincts in half of Florida's most populous counties, setting off a panic among Democrat legislators and the media. Some prominent Democrats in Liberty County cried, "'We have one of the greatest crises facing us at the present time we have had since the Reconstruction Days.' The *Orlando Reporter-Star* warned: 'The struggle for white supremacy in the South now confronts us.'" "Suddenly, the 'solid South' no longer seemed solid."[15]

Things Heat Up

On November 1, the day before the election, with robes and crosses, the Klan paraded through the streets of the two Black communities in Ocoee late into the night. With megaphones they warned that "not a single Negro will be permitted to vote"[16] and if any of them dared to do so there would be dire consequences.

Election Day came and at least some Blacks did attempt to vote in Orange County; however, none were permitted to enter their respective polling places. White enforcers camped out around the centers and poll workers were given instructions to deflect their attempts.

With little other option, most returned to their homes without casting their ballots. Mose Norman would not be so easily deterred. After being turned away that morning in his Ocoee precinct, he rode to Orlando to seek the council of Judge Cheney. The attorney instructed him to write down the names of any African Americans who were not permitted to vote and also the names of the poll workers who had denied their Constitutional right. Cheney said a lawsuit against the county could be brought to contest this violation.

Norman returned to Ocoee with these instructions, along with a handful of Black citizens again seeking to vote; as you can imagine, things did not go well. After again being forcibly turned away, he demanded the poll workers' names and exclaimed: "We will vote, by God!"[17]

A Massacre in Ocoee

While the exact sequence of events following Norman's impassioned demand to exercise his right at all costs has become somewhat muddled, most historians agree that it began when "Col. Sam Salisbury gathered nearly 200 men to hunt down Norman, surrounding the home of his friend July Perry. Perry was dragged from his home, beaten by the mob and lynched on a light pole."[18] His killing sparked an orgy of violence that spread across the community, leading to the deaths of 30–80 Black residents.[19] Fires were set on Black properties all across the community to deter any residents from returning.

While the *Orlando Sentinel* gave the incident some press, the

Mary McLeod Bethune was an early Civil Rights and suffragist pioneer who founded and ran the Educational and Industrial Training School for Negro Girls in Daytona. Serving as the Florida chapter president of the NACW from 1917 to 1925, she worked tirelessly to register Black voters in the state and suffered harassment and threats from the Ku Klux Klan. Here she is pictured with one of her classes (ca. 1911) (State Archives of Florida, Florida Memory).

massacre was largely ignored statewide. Still, its effects were omnipresent, for by the following year, only two Black citizens remained in Ocoee out of a pre-massacre population of 255. "It would be another 66 years, in 1986 that the press would again mention the massacre."[20]

History Repeats Itself

A mere three years after the Ocoee Massacre, history once again repeated itself, this time in the tiny village of Rosewood.

The whole incident began somewhat innocently enough, with a 22-year-old wife and mother of two, named Fannie Taylor, taking an interest in a railway worker named John Bradley in the tiny railroad community of Sumner.

Rendezvousing with him in the afternoons, while her husband was out, she became increasingly elusive, keeping to herself during the days and shutting herself in by night. This ended suddenly and violently on New Year's Day 1923, when a neighbor busted through her door after hearing "Taylor scream."[21]

Finding her bruised and beaten on the floor, the confused neighbor was told that an unknown Black man had kicked open the back door, beating her about the face. Though she claimed that he did not rape her, and in fact no evidence of the fracas was found minus some scuff marks on the floor, the community quickly rallied behind Taylor.

With rumors circulating that Taylor was raped and that a Black man matching her description had recently escaped from a chain gang, Levy County Sheriff Robert Elias Walker rounded up a posse and turned the town's attention to the predominately Black community of Rosewood, a few miles west.

Singling out the family of Taylor's washerwoman, Sarah Carrier, a mob, believing that Carrier's family had hidden the culprit, gathered at her house on January 4, and a standoff ensued. After a full day of fighting, the Whites, having lost two members of their own, kicked the door in to find Carrier and her son Sylvester dead from gunshots and several others wounded.

News of the clash circulated around the state, as well as the nation, with both White and Black publications grossly exaggerating the facts and causes of the conflict. The media coverage caused more Whites to descend upon the town; they began razing community buildings, starting with the church.

As the Black residents emerged from the burning structures, many were shot point-blank by the angry crowds. Though several White residents, including train conductors John and William Bryce, as well as John Wright, a general store owner and his wife, took to hiding several of the

Black victims from the angry mob, it was too little too late for many of the ill-prepared residents.

By January 7, all of the structures of Rosewood had been set ablaze and 27 of its residents were found dead. Almost universally, the violence was condemned by both northern and southern newspapers, but as the victims were unwilling to talk about it, and a special grand jury found no one in particular to prosecute, the incident slipped into obscurity.

After the massacre, Taylor moved to another mill town with her husband and children. There, she succumbed to cancer, being described by neighbors as a "very nervous"[22] woman in her later years. The victims of her lie would eventually receive a settlement by the state through a class action lawsuit, although real justice would never come to any member involved in the mob attacks.

Ax Handle Saturday

By the middle of the twentieth century, large-scale massacres of the kind experienced in Ocoee and Rosewood had for the most part dissipated

The small community of Rosewood, Florida, was razed to the ground by an angry White mob in January 1923. The community was composed primarily of middle-class Blacks and the riot resulted in the deaths of dozens of residents (*Literary Digest Magazine*, 1923, State Archives of Florida, Florida Memory).

across the state. With a post-war economy driving a renewed housing boom in Florida, relations between races settled into an uneasy détente. This ended in a very abrupt way after legal segregation was struck down in 1954. Nowhere in Florida was this felt more than in the city of Jacksonville.

Formally instructed to pursue integration with "all deliberate speed," the city was slow to act, making the most minimal of efforts. This came to a head in a very violent manner in the summer of 1960.

Encouraged by Martin Luther King, Jr., and his desegregation attempts in other parts of the South, several teenagers decided to stage a sit-in at a local downtown eatery, the Desert Rider.

Sitting down at an all-White counter on a hot Saturday on August 27, they put in orders for hamburgers and egg salad sandwiches. Informed that they were violating the law and would not be offered service, the protestors remained in place, refusing all calls to leave. This set off a confrontation when a group of 200, mostly older White men gathered in Hemming Plaza armed with baseball bats and ax handles and began attacking the protestors.[23] The violence quickly spread as the mob began attacking any and all Black Americans, including women and children, regardless of their participation in the sit-ins, prompting some to launch a defense:

> A local black street gang called the "Boomerangs" attempted to protect the demonstrators. Although police had not intervened when the protesters were attacked, they became involved, arresting members of the Boomerangs and other Black residents who attempted to stop the beatings.[24]

Nat Glover, whose 37-year law enforcement career in Jacksonville included eight years as Sheriff, recalled:

> He was quickly surrounded and ran to a white police officer nearby.
> "What he told me was: 'You better get out of here before they kill you.' And I took off running, and I ran. And they did not chase me. They did not run after me. And I ran and ran and I ran home. And I was really frightened. I had never been that frightened in all my life," Glover said.
> "And I remember going home and I went to my room and I was laying across the bed and I was still crying."[25]

Because of the nature of the riots, police were extremely slow to respond, in some cases watching or even cheering on White rioters as they beat down innocent Black bystanders. The resulting injuries totaled were in the dozens, resulting in over 60 arrests:

> Several whites had joined the Black protesters on that day. Richard Charles Parker, a 25-year old student attending Florida State University was among them. White protesters were the object of particular dislike by racists, so Parker was hustled out of the area for his protection when the fight began.
> The police had been watching him and arrested him as an instigator,

charging him with vagrancy, disorderly conduct and inciting a riot. After Parker stated that he was proud to be a member of the NAACP, Judge John Santora sentenced him to 90 days in jail.[26]

The story made headlines across the country, including in *The New York Times*, giving Jacksonville a reputation for intolerance and violence. Nevertheless, effective sit-in demonstrations were halted across the city as a result and not resumed until the following spring. It would not be until the end of 1961 that all lunch counters within the city limits would agree to finally desegregate.

The Story of American Beach

Segregation meant more than just separate bathrooms and separate water fountains for Blacks and Whites, it also meant separate beaches.

One of the most overlooked aspects of Florida's segregated days is the fact that almost all of the state's beaches were segregated by color. Because of this, many Blacks could not partake in summertime recreation. Barred from swimming at the same places, much as they were in South Africa during Apartheid, Blacks began opening up their own beach access resorts. One such place was American Beach on Amelia Island.

Founded in 1935 by Abraham Lincoln Lewis, the state's first Black millionaire and one of the seven founders of the Afro-American Life Insurance Company, Florida's first insurance company, the land that now makes up American Beach was purchased with a vision of providing Black American travelers and residents with direct beach access.[27] Rather than just allowing Blacks a place to swim in the ocean and spend their vacations, Lewis believed that Blacks should own a piece of property and gain a chance at achieving the American Dream.

Divvying up plots of land, he allowed development for both real estate and commercial interests, turning the place into the preeminent resort destination on the East Coast for Black families.

As a result, throughout the 1940s and 1950s American Beach welcomed families, children and church functions each summer. It also included hotels, restaurants, bathhouses and nightclubs, as well as scores of other Black-owned businesses.

In addition, the resort played host to numerous period celebrities including folklorist Zora Neale Hurston, singer Billie Daniels, Cab Calloway, Ray Charles, Billy Eckstein, Hank Aaron, Joe Louis, and actor Ossie Davis. Even James Brown made an appearance, though he was actually turned away from performing outside Evans' Rendezvous, a local nightclub.

Eventually, the beach suffered a decline in popularity coinciding with the landfall of Hurricane Dora and the passage of the Civil Rights Act in 1964, which desegregated all beaches in the state of Florida. Falling into neglect, most of the hotels closed down and the businesses soon followed. The community remained, however, and fought for preservation.

Helping them in this cause was Lewis' great-granddaughter MaVynee Betsch, who returned to the area in 1977. Earning the nickname "Beach Lady," MaVynee worked tirelessly to preserve and promote the beach until her death in 2005.

While American Beach has remained a recognized historic site by the National Register of Historic Places, it still remains endangered of becoming enveloped by new development. Amelia Island Plantation has been particularly troublesome as its nearby residential area and golf club threaten to swallow up the remaining portion of the little community. Such development was the subject of the film *American Beach*, as well as *Sunshine State*, starring Angela Bassett.

The Violence Spreads to Florida's "Birmingham"

Jacksonville's Ax Handle Saturday was certainly not the first case of bloodshed to occur during the Civil Rights period, but it definitely wasn't the last either. In many ways, it represented a catalyst for more.

In the world of 1960s Florida, north Florida was Alabama and St. Augustine was its Birmingham. A city with institutional segregation at its very core, everything from swimming pools to neighborhoods and even beaches were segregated, resulting in it becoming the main target for the NAACP's Florida campaign.

Beginning first in the summers of 1960 and 1961 with a series of sit-ins, members of the group attempting to defy the city's strict lunch counter rules were met with fists, bats and chains, much in the same way as in Jacksonville. Unlike Jacksonville, however, no arrests were made. This tense situation became even more exacerbated in 1963 when Dr. Robert B. Hayling took over leadership of the Youth Council of the NAACP.

The movement's demonstrations at various eating establishments around the city that summer began to face stiff resistance from residents, including the local chapter of the KKK, which began to employ increasing forms of intimidation against the protestors. Many of these demonstrations were broken up with cattle prods and German Shepherds much as they had been in the Birmingham and Selma protests. It was events occurring in 1964, however, that really put St. Augustine in the spotlight.

A Shining City of Hatred

In early 1964, a series of events rocked the city to its core, exposing its fleshy underbelly of hatred to the entire nation. Beginning with the firebombing of Charles Brunson, a deaf-mute who was involved in the local PTA, violence spread to others involved in the movement including the Robinson family who had their house burned down for supporting integration in public schools.

For his part in the protests, Dr. Hayling's home was shot into, killing his dog.[28] On another occasion, Dr. Hayling, along with Mr. Clyde Jenkins, Mr. James Hauser and Mr. James Jackson were kidnapped by the Klu Klux Klan, who beat them, leaving them semi-conscious. "Dr. Hayling received the most serious injuries suffering hospitalization for fourteen days, losing eleven teeth, and several broken ribs. Scars he is known to have said, 'I'll take to my grave.' He and the others were charged with assault but charges were dropped because the Klan never showed up to court. The Klan was never prosecuted in this case."[29]

Traveling to the SCLC Conference in Orlando in order to gain the assistance of Martin Luther King, Jr., the NAACP took to calling for more demonstrations in the city. The biggest of these began on May 30, in response to another house burning and the local newspaper publishing the home addresses and names of those Black students attempting to integrate into all White public schools. Many of these demonstrations were met with angry violence at the hands of White mobs, with police sometimes joining in.

With the onset of summer, more violence broke out as Blacks began to stage wade-ins at segregated St. Augustine Beach and swim-ins at Monson Swimming Pool. At each event, they were arrested and met with Whites carrying pipes, bats and other sharp objects. In the case of the Monson Pool incident, the manager was actually seen pouring acid into the pool, to burn Black demonstrators. The photo of him pouring it into the water was captured by a photographer and splashed across headlines worldwide. It was this incident that roused Congress to finally act and pass the long overdue Civil Rights Act. In recounting his story, J.T. Johnson, one of the protestors in the pool that day, shared:

> [A]ll of the news media were there, because somehow I guess they'd gotten word that something was going to happen at that pool that day. And I think that's when President [Lyndon B.] Johnson got the message.[30]

Even with the passage of the Civil Rights Act, however, true equality continues to remain elusive.

Martin Luther King Gets Arrested

While St. Augustine earned the distinction of becoming one of the most segregated cities in Florida, it also earned a more infamous moniker: that of being the only city to jail Martin Luther King.

Joining in solidarity with the demonstrators, King came to the Ancient City in early summer of 1964, staging a sit-in with Dr. Ralph Abernathy at Monson Motor Lodge on the bay front. Sitting down at the Whites-only counter, he asked to be served by the waitstaff. Below is a transcript of his conversation with the manager, James Brock:

> KING: I and my friends have come to lunch....
> BROCK: You are on private property. We reserve the right to refuse service. I ask you on behalf of myself, my wife, and my children to leave.
> KING: We are sorry you have that attitude. You are doing a disservice to the nation.
> BROCK: You can't push this thing. We are a small business. We are caught in the middle of something. We find ourselves between two armed camps. If we integrate now it would hurt our business.
> KING: We will stand here and hope that in the process that our conscious efforts will make this a better land.
> BROCK: We will integrate under two conditions: by federal court order, or if a responsible group of citizens ask us to open to all customers.
> KING: We are glad to know that you would do it under those conditions.[31]

Following this surprisingly cordial demonstration, King was taken into custody and sentenced to 10 days in a St. Augustine jail. So intense were the mobs that gathered outside his cell, however, that King would later have to be transferred out of the city to Jacksonville in order to serve out the rest of his sentence. It was said even the jail guards feared for his safety.

Throughout the entirety of the movement, St. Augustine and Chicago, remained the only unsuccessful attempts at desegregation during King's lifetime.

The Red Scare

While Black people during this period faced significant opposition for demanding equality under the law, they also faced fierce resistance for something far more insidious: that of being Communist sympathizers. This was especially true of Civil Rights leaders, university professors and anyone else in charge of organizing protests.

Piggybacking on the McCarthy Hearings, which were sweeping the nation at the time due to the Red Scare, the Florida government launched its own witch hunt to root out Red sympathizers in the state.

Established as the Florida Legislative Investigation Committee in 1956 and headed by Democratic Senator Charley E. Johns, the Johns Committee, as it became known, began a personal hunt into politically subversive activities by academics, civil rights groups and suspected communist organizations. Its officially worded purpose was defined as a committee formed to:

> [R]id the state of Communists, homosexuals and the NAACP. For many conservatives in the Deep South, the three groups were linked by their desire to turn American culture upside-down, thus making the nation (theoretically) more vulnerable to Soviet infiltration and invasion. In a state with a tradition of political persecution, religious invective and racial segregation, organized opposition to the Johns Committee was understandably sparse and sporadic.

The committee scrutinized public schools first, but quickly moved on to higher education in the early 1960s. As a brand-new urban university, USF threatened the old order. That order was reigned over by Florida's "Pork Choppers," rural legislators determined to curb the influence of the "Lamb Choppers," legislators representing more progressive city folk.[32]

Separating legislators into two groups, "Pork Choppers" and "Lamb Choppers," the former consisting of conservative rural politicians from the northern half of the state and the latter group consisting of progressives from the urban and southern portions, the fundamental goal of the committee was to effectively curb all the influence of liberalism. This included blocking initiatives and agendas that supported Civil Rights boycotts. In fact, there was actually a law on the books stating that Blacks could not organize carpools.

Using these guidelines as a basis, the committee's first victim was the faculty and staff at the historically Black college of Florida Agricultural and Mechanical University in Tallahassee. These professors had the audacity to support the Tallahassee Bus Boycott of 1956–1957 to protest segregation policies in the state and were thus suspect for maintaining communist goals of equality.

Attempting to gain access to NAACP membership lists, of which a large portion of said faculty were a part, the committee was resisted and ultimately blocked from doing so by the U.S. Supreme Court. Rebuffed on this measure, they also sought to gain access to membership access to the SLCC, of which Martin Luther King, Jr., was a part. This attempt also met with similar outcomes.

The Lavender Scare

As bad as the committee's attempts to disenfranchise active members in the Black community who supported Civil Rights causes were, their persecution of homosexuals within the state was just as intense.

Going after individuals whom the Johns Committee viewed as promoting a perverted agenda, the committee broadened its reach in 1961 to include homosexuals and "the extent of [their] infiltration into agencies supported by state funds," particularly at the university level. Though laws for persecuting homosexuals at the university or state level were already in the books at the time of the Johns Committee, "they were not implemented rigorously until the 1960s."[33]

Sending out informants to infiltrate the University of Florida based upon testimony from Johns' son Jerome, who told him that "effeminate instructors had perverted the curriculum," a massive campaign was launched to root out gays from the university. Soon, embittered students from the university were identifying professors as gay for such flimsy reasons as eating lunch together or sporting Bermuda shorts. These unfortunate few would later be subjected to "forcible removal from their classrooms by the highway patrol, late night phone calls, and harassing interviews."[34]

Students too, did not escape the wrath of the committee, being subjected to threats and psychological harassment. While they could not be dismissed from the university in the same manner the committee sought to remove professors accused of homosexuality, they were nonetheless forced to submit to psychiatric treatments at the infirmary in order to remain as students. One victim, University of Florida honors graduate Art Copleston, described his interrogation as follows:

> I arrived at the University of Florida on my 25th birthday in September 1957. Having completed four years in the Air Force, I was anxious to move ahead quickly and get on to a working career.... I was called into be interrogated three or four times during the next two years. Each time, it was the same setting, and the same set of questions. Each time I was unceremoniously marched out of class, in front of the instructor and all my classmates, by a uniformed policeman. Once this occurred during a final exam in accounting.... At each interrogation, I refused to tell them anything. Each time I was amazed that, while I was truly terrified by their tactics and threats, I was able to stonewall their questions.... I came to realize that they, as a group, were really a very dumb bunch of redneck, illiterate people.[35]

The investigation ruined almost every life it touched.

Over 15 University of Florida professors were dismissed as a result, and countless students received the Copleston treatment. One such victim,

Professor Sigismond Diettrich, a married man, even attempted suicide after being interrogated and forced to resign by university president, J. Wayne Reitz. Many of their colleagues just stood by in horrified silence, unwilling to speak out against these crimes for fear of putting their own selves under committee suspicion. Nevertheless, Johns remained committed to eradicating this "disease" as he thought of it, no matter how many people he hurt along the way. As he stated in a 1972 interview, "I don't get no love out of hurting people. But that situation in Gainesville, my Lord have mercy. I never saw nothing like it in my life. If we saved one boy from being made homosexual, it was justified."[36]

The Investigation Heads South

The University of Florida was not the only institution subjected to such scrutiny. The University of South Florida came under the gun, as well.

Integrated and set in a city rather than a rural community, the university posed an enormous threat to state precedent. For with no traditions, education at USF could be dangerously subversive, opening it up for liberal faculty to introduce evolution, atheism, a broader post–Cold War view and racial equality into the classroom.

Invited by university president John Allen, the committee came in 1962 in search of communists and homosexuals. Their presence this time met with a large degree of cynicism from students and faculty alike, who were in the beginning stages of the '60s counterculture movement. A prime example of this was the sarcastic editorial written in the *Campus Edition*, commemorating their arrival:

> What we admire most about these people is their vocabulary.... Communist, homosexual, pornography; Communist, homosexual, pornography. There is a rhythm, beat and emotional impact in the chant. It will serve as the perfect background music for any play they wish to direct on campus during the next few weeks. We do hope it won't be *The Crucible*. That was a clear case of righteous townspeople vs. the witches, and by the end of the play we didn't like the townspeople very well.[37]

Once in Tampa, the committee began to single out students and professors, much as they did at the University of Florida. This time, they went after professors who dared to assign obscene or controversial literature, such as banned books.

Compiling over 2,500 pages of witness testimonies,[38] often based on groundless accusations, their reports were blasted publicly by deans, staff and students alike. Still, certain professors ended up paying the price, such as Sheldon N. Grebstein, who was suspended after the committee found out that he was assigning Beatnik literature and a book on the Scopes "Monkey Trial" to his class. His departing quote upon leaving for employment in NYC was "the greatest boost that higher education could get in this state would be for the Johns Committee to be put out of business."[39]

A further 10–20 professors lost their positions or were prevented from being hired altogether, with one professor lamenting that the unjust hunts had led them to become physically ill.[40]

In the end, university president Allen turned against the committee action saying enough was enough by delivering a 25-minute speech against the Fascist overtones of the committee. His speech received a standing ovation from the student body and marked an effective end to Johns' presence on the university campus. Still, in spite of this, almost 100 professors were discredited,[41] as well as countless students, from the actions of the previous spring.

The Purple Pamphlet and Pornography

While the Johns Committee was laughable enough due to the sheer ridiculousness surrounding their witch hunts, things got downright hysterical with the publication of their pamphlet book, *Homosexuality and Citizenship in Florida*.

First published in 1964 and dubbed the "purple pamphlet" due to its lavender hue, the booklet represented the last major undertaking by the Johns Committee to root out and destroy homosexual activity in the state of Florida once and for all. The committee quotes at length

> …a letter from a young lesbian who wrote that she leads a "quiet, and apparently normal, life. I have a well paying, responsible job, I own my own home, I am active in church and community affairs and I command the respect of those who know me."
>
> Beyond acknowledging the acceptability and respectability of *some* LGBTQ people, however, the Johns Committee was quick to frequently condemn *most* queer people, especially gay men, whom the committee believed represented the "other side of the homosexual coin…."
>
> The committee, searching for an appropriate definition of homosexuality, settled on this: "We would … suggest that that the Biblical description of homosexuality as an 'abomination' has stood well the test of time."[42]

Featuring detailed photos and descriptions of men engaged in various homoerotic acts, the booklet also contained bogus statistics and dire warnings such as:

9. We Shall Overcome

The widely published Kinsey studies suggests that 50% of the unmarried males under 35 in America have engaged in homosexual practices, and that of the general population, one out of six men had experienced at least as much homosexual, as normal, or heterosexual experience for at least three full years between their 16th and 55th birthday. The Kinsey reports estimated that one out of 25 men is exclusively homosexual after the onset of adolescence.

The best and current estimate of active homosexuals in Florida is 60,000 individuals. Several of our consultants have suggested that this figure would be more appropriate if limited to male homosexuals and ought to be doubled if to accurately reflect the female homosexuals in our population.[43]

In addition, the pamphlet contained a dictionary, defining the following words:

Queer—a homosexual, usually of low class and habits
Dog's Lunch—either a normal person or a gay person whose looks
    and actions are unattractive to the point of non-association
Dinge queen—a negro homosexual
Sea food—a homosexual in the Navy
Crushed Fruit—a homosexual who tries to deny he is a homosexual[44]

" ... This illustrated monograph on perversion is a new low ... We feel that the immediate resignation of every state official who had a hand in it, and full investigation of possible violation of obscenity laws, is called for." (Miami Herald, March 19)

" ... It will become the object of curiosity in every school in the state and could engender perversion," Dade County State Attorney Richard Gerstein, after directing the committee to keep the manual out of the G r e a t e r Miami area or face possible prosecution!

" ... The physical make-up of the book ... the far-out covers and the location of the pictures without real interpretation of what these pictures represent, in my opinion was in poor taste ... " State Senator C. W. Young

The purple pamphlet became a synonymous symbol of the gay witch hunt launched by the Johns Committee in 1960s Florida. In an ironic twist, its depiction of various homoerotic acts resulted in its distribution as pornographic material in the LGBTQ+ community, leading to the committee's ultimate disbandment (Guild Press, "Advertisement for Purple Pamphlet," State Archives of Florida, Series S1486).

Though originally meant to be educational in nature, the 2,000 or so copies printed by the committee eventually had the opposite effect, becoming ridiculed and lampooned across much of the country. In New York City, this lampooning took on a whole other level of irony as the copies became adopted into the local Gay community and later incorporated as a part of LGBTQ subculture, with some reportedly using it for "pornographic purposes."[45]

As revelations of such activity became known, the media began to decry Florida's version of "state-sponsored pornography."[46] As a result of the increasing pressure, lawmakers forbade the printing and distribution of any more copies, eliminating any and all funding to committee activities on July 1, 1965.

> In 1975 the Civil Service Commission announced new rules stipulating that gay people could no longer be barred or fired from federal employment because of their sexuality. The Lavender Scare was finally officially over (at least for civilian workers).
>
> In his testimony before the Hoey committee in 1950, psychiatrist George Raines emphasized the danger of further alienating anyone who was already a social outcast. "That sort of individual," he warned, "is ripe for revolution."
>
> He was correct. Although the "revolution" was of a different sort than Raines (or McCarthy) imagined, Kameny and his fellow activists, under the pressure of rising discrimination, brought about their own kind of revolution: a changed world for gay federal workers.[47]

Though initially sealed, pressure from local Florida historians eventually secured their release of documents tied to the scare in 1993 and today these records can be seen in the Florida State Archives in Tallahassee—a chilling testament to the abuse of state power.

A New Frontier

Following the signing of the Civil Rights Act of 1964 and the Voting Rights Act of 1965, Florida became increasingly more integrated. While such integration finally allowed for the chance at true equality under the law, it hardly meant the practice of true equality in everyday life. For, even despite these new laws, Blacks, Gays and other immigrant groups would find themselves the targets of discrimination for years to come. Much of this discrimination in the later years would reverse the course of all the progress made in the Civil Rights Era, heightening racial and ethnic tensions to new and disturbing levels.

10

Drugs, Disco and Decadence
Florida in the '70s and '80s

Following the turbulent years of the '50s and '60s, Florida entered into a long period of moral and economic decay. Drugs, particularly cocaine, played a major role in this downward turn, resulting in a spike in murders and violence.

During this period of "Wild West" carnage, Florida was more of a frontier than ever with drug enforcement and police forces helpless to stop the spreading violence. As the body counts increased, Florida soon took on an aura of danger. Popular programs like *Miami Vice* would later capture this carnage in all its pastel glory, propelling Florida once more into the cultural zeitgeist for all the wrong reasons.

Murder in Broad Daylight

In the late 1970s, the Dadeland Massacre brought Miami to its knees, setting off a nearly decade-long war. Occurring at 2:30 p.m. on July 11, 1979, at the Dadeland Mall in Kendall, the infamous shootout began with "dozens of rounds ... throughout the mall parking lot, riddling cars with bullets. When the smoke cleared from what police and witnesses described as a wild-west style shootout, the drug dealer and his bodyguard were dead and two liquor store employees were wounded."[1]

Beginning at Crown Liquors, an anchor store just outside the mall's entrance, the gruesome event saw two men rush inside the storefront entrance pursued by two others in an armored van. The heavily armed pursuers caught up with them carrying out their murders in full view of customers and store attendants, seriously wounding several innocent bystanders in the process. After offing their two targets, they then sprayed the parking lot with bullets, "emptying 86 rounds into the crowded space."[2] The gunmen fled the scene in a phony delivery van marked "Happy Time Complete Party Supply," which was abandoned at the far end of the mall parking lot. Police later described the van as a "war wagon"[3] after an arsenal of firearms and bulletproof vests were discovered inside.

Though there were many witnesses, police found little in terms of character description from the people, other than the fact that they appeared to be Latino and showed up quite suddenly in an armored van labeled with a "'Happy Time Party Supply' logo splashed across the side."[4] They also found little initial motive. Closer identification of the two victims, a Cuban exile and a Colombian national, however, ultimately led them to conclude that foul play was at work, as the two were part of an underground gang of drug dealers.

Putting two and two together, police were able to develop both a motive and a suspect for the crime, linking them back to one of Miami's most infamous drug rings. In spite of this, they would never catch the culprits, leaving the door open for more bloodshed and violence in the city.

As *Miami Herald* staffer Howard Cohen recalled:

> Dadeland and the Cocaine Cowboys changed everything if you lived here. Loud noises in a parking lot became cause for alarm. Paranoia set in. Maybe it was just backfire from a car.
>
> To my knowledge, the Omni incident [referring to the Omni International Mall] never even made the news.
>
> "[The media] didn't have the resources to cover it," says film producer Alfred Spellman, whose documentary Cocaine Cowboys...covers the bloody period when the drug trade exploded here and Miami drug lords made the Mafia seem like peacemakers. The local media couldn't possibly recount every incident.
>
> "[Last week] every 24-hour news station cut in with breaking coverage on the Turnpike and the family that was killed. It's extraordinary how that story is that important the world over. In the '80s, that would not be the most important story of the day," he says.[5]

Dadeland indeed changed everything. The good times were over. The Cocaine Cowboy Wars had just begun.

Cocaine Cowboy Wars

Arising out of the popularity of cocaine, which had exploded onto the disco scene several years prior, the Cocaine Cowboy Wars, as they came to be called, were a direct result of heightening tensions in the drug world.

Taking place in Miami, which at that point had amassed a reputation for excess and decadence, the dealers found a city ripe for the taking. Once a mecca for retirees and spring breakers, Miami had transitioned into a city of nightclubs and strip bars. The seedy nature of these places, along with the area's proximity to the Caribbean and large collection of private banks, made it the perfect spot for congregation.

Soon an all-out struggle exploded between rival gangs of dealers, as established Cuban exiles fought for control of the lucrative industry with upstart Colombians seeking to muscle their way into the business. This feud eventually made its deadly presence felt in public, spilling out into the streets, giving Miami a reputation as one of the most violent cities in the country.

As homicides peaked and tourism suffered, desperate civic leaders sought a means of protecting their image. The Dadeland Mall massacre proved the final straw for many, bringing to light the savagery of the participating gangs. For, unlike previous criminal activity, the Cocaine Cowboys did not keep themselves hidden, fighting in open public venues. If an innocent bystander happened to get in their way, they'd simply do away with them as well. Such cold-bloodedness brought Miami's war to national prominence, prompting the DEA to take action against the dealers. The nation was at war, it was later announced, but this time it was a war on drugs.

La Madrina Brings the Rage

While not as famous as the fictional Tony Montana from *Scarface*, Griselda Blanco earned the dubious distinction of becoming the "Godmother of Cocaine."

Affectionately called "la madrina" by her peers, Blanco headed an organization that, at the height of the seventies and eighties coke craze, oversaw the shipment of thousands of pounds per month through the port of Miami, alone. Initially brought up in poverty-stricken Medellín, Colombia, Blanco became involved in illicit activities early on in her childhood. Abused at home and left to her own devices, she had already earned a criminal record at the ripe old age of 11 when she "kidnapped a boy from a wealthy neighborhood near her hometown, and shot him in the head when the ransom she demanded was not paid."[6]

Running away from her physically abusive mother at the age of 14, she engaged in prostitution and petty theft to get by. Marrying twice, she ultimately shifted her residence from South America to Queens, New York, with her second husband.[7]

Ruthless to a tee, Blanco grew to admire the stylized crime families she witnessed in movies such as *The Godfather* and named her son Michael after the main character.During the midst of the Cocaine Cowboy Wars, which took place in Miami at the end of the 1970s, Blanco was said to have amassed over half a billion dollars, seeing as much as eighty-million-dollars worth of cocaine pour into the port each month.[8] During this time, she is thought to have masterminded the murders of over 200 people.[9] Her reputation for ruthlessness knew no limits and, among many, she was simply portrayed as a bona fide psychopath.

Authorities were finally able to catch up with Blanco in Irvine, California, in 1985, sending her back to Florida where she was later tried and implicated on second-degree murder charges in the deaths of three Miami residents, among whom was a two-year-old boy. Convicted of these murders, she went to prison. It is said that while incarcerated, she was still involved in the business and even took on a lover, Charles Cosby, from the outside. A petty drug dealer, Cosby first learned of Blanco from the arrest report on the news, and despite her habit of killing off lovers and husbands, he took the risk to date her. Throughout this time, she bribed guards and officials to allow her regular conjugal visits with Cosby.[10]

Blanco and the Almost Kidnapping of JFK Jr.

As crazy and intimidating as Blanco was as a free woman, she wielded even more power behind bars. This played out in a very strange way with a near attempt at kidnapping JFK Jr., the son of former president John F. Kennedy. As Nelson Andreu, former Miami homicide cop and chief of police at the West Miami police department, explained:

> Blanco planned for Cosby to have someone "kidnap somebody very prominent," Andreu explains. "And hold that person ransom in exchange for her release and return to Colombia ... but it never materialized."[11]

At some point, it seems JFK Jr. became her primary target.

> Reporter León Wagner, who spent years covering the Kennedy family, said of JFK Jr.,... "The FBI at one point uncovered a plot to kidnap him and demand millions in ransom, and it was deadly serious."[12]

Flying in six Colombian men to carry out the deed,

> the plan fell through because Blanco's advisors thought kidnapping JFK Jr. would result in "a massive military response from Colombian armed forces" that could destroy their entire operation.[13]

10. Drugs, Disco and Decadence

This paranoia at setting off such a response led to her lover ratting her out to the FBI:

> "Kidnapping JFK Jr. would effectively mean starting a war with every law enforcement agency in America," he says. "And what exactly would he get out of the deal?"[14]

While the plot might have seemed half-baked to many, it was not entirely out of the realm of her power, as investigative journalist James Robertson recalls: "She was at that level"[15] referring to hits on other famous people like Pablo Escobar and El Chapo. Furthermore, it was noted that JFK Jr.'s security was far from serious and was described by McClaren as being "rotten."[16]

Released from prison in 2004—a mere five years after the tragic plane crash which killed JFK Jr.—Blanco was deported back to Colombia and became a born again Christian. Going off the grid, she was shot to death in a drive-by execution in September 2012.

Cannabis and Black Tuna

While cocaine got all the press during the '70s and '80s, Florida was also experiencing serious problems with marijuana imports. One of the earliest distributors, the Black Tuna Gang, was among the first to get the trend started.

Responsible for bringing in roughly 500 tons of cannabis into the United States over a 16-month period the gang conducted a large amount of their operation out of Miami Beach's luxurious Fontainebleau Hotel.

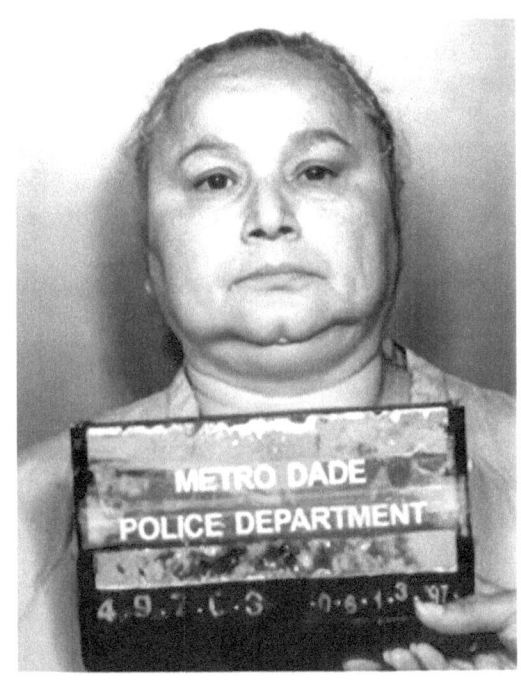

Griselda Blanco, nicknamed "La Madrina" or the Godmother of Cocaine, is thought to have masterminded the murders of 200 people, 100 of them in Dade County alone. Her reach was so powerful that she even developed a plot from behind bars to kidnap JFK Jr. (Metro Dade Police Department, 1997, Wikimedia Commons).

In the 1970s, [Robert Plathorn] was a leader of the Black Tuna Gang, a pot-smuggling crew [he] assembled with two pals that became law enforcement's first big catch in the War on Drugs. In its heyday, the Black Tuna Gang transported 500 tons of high-grade Santa Marta Gold cannabis from Colombia into the United States, which spawned a 36-count criminal indictment against Platshorn and his cohorts.

"When we started bringing in that really good Colombian Gold, that became the mother strain for every good medical strain in the U.S. today," Platshorn boasts. "The Colombian Gold we used to bring in was about 18 percent THC. That's the stuff that makes you feel good, makes you smile, gives you a good night's sleep, and helps get rid of the pain. It is also the part of the plant that is most effective against cancer and a whole lot of other things."[17]

Arranging bulk deliveries to a houseboat, the gang members affiliated with the contraband were then transported to waterfront houses in well-to-do neighborhoods so that it could be stashed away.

To keep tabs on police anti-drug activity, the gang established a central and elaborate monitoring system which allowed them to listen in on law enforcement channels. They were also creative, communicating in code and symbols. One such symbol was the inclusion of necklaces with gold medallions and a crude black tuna carved in the middle. This symbol allowed them to tell members from non-members. In addition, messages were often communicated to their boss via code. A box of diapers, for example, was symbolic of the drugs being ready to be picked up.

Directed from a base in Colombia and operated by the drug lord Raul Davila-Jimeno, the smugglers met with tremendous success over the months, eluding even the savviest of authorities. Eventually, however, fortune caught up with them and their leaders, all partners at a Miami used car dealership, were indicted.

Known as Operation Banco, which began in 1977, funds hidden by the smugglers in a Miami Beach bank ultimately gave them away. When they were busted in 1978 for attempting to smuggle 500 tons of marijuana, the DEA proclaimed it to be among the most sophisticated drug operations ever encountered. Both Platshorn and Meinster received stiff sentences.

On April Fool's Day 2008, Platshorn was released to a halfway house in West Palm Beach after 28 years in the pen. Though he had absolutely nothing to show for his stint as one of America's most wanted smugglers—no money, no job, little remaining family—he did have a manuscript he had written while serving time, later titled *The Black Tuna Diaries*. Published in 2009, the book went on to critical acclaim, shining fresh light on the debate over marijuana legalization and the War on Drugs.

Notorious P.O.T.

On the heels of the Black Tuna Gang came yet another marijuana mastermind, this time in the form of a nerdy stoner named Donald Steinberg.

Like any other small-town kid with a dream, Steinberg fantasized about making big money out of doing something he loved. So it was that his lifelong love affair with Mary Jane slowly grew into a multimillion-dollar business along the sunny shores of Florida.

Starting out in his hometown of Carpentersville, Illinois, Steinberg stumbled into the drug trade somewhat haphazardly, simply looking for a way to finance his recreational pastime. After discovering how profitable the industry was, he continued in this measure, expanding his marijuana trade into the South Florida market.

Largely recruiting close friends and relatives rather than outside agents, he sought safe houses in the greater Miami area in which to store his product. The success of his close-knit relationship with friends and family soon paid off, allowing Steinberg to become one of the largest marijuana distributors in the country.

At the height of his power, which peaked in 1978, Steinberg was responsible for approximately one sixth of all marijuana shipments into the United States,[18] and he often spent frivolously on cars, liquor and food.

As with most drug dealers, however, his money and power slowly caught up with him as his partners, believing themselves increasingly invincible, grew reckless in their precautions.

> The downhill slide started when Steinberg directed one operation from a Fort Lauderdale hotel room. Calls to his extension tied up the entire switchboard; a suspicious owner called the police. The gang scrambled out the windows but left behind marijuana, 7 lbs. of cocaine (value: $180,000) and $1.2 million....[19]

After escaping to San Pedro, California, the DEA was able to catch up with him by tracking calls to a veterinarian who was overseeing care of his dog.[20]

Arrested and convicted under an organized crime statute, along with other senior members of his operation, Steinberg eventually lost everything, including his money, his company, his wife and his friends. Following his trial, he was handed down a life sentence.[21]

In spite of his involvement in illicit activity, Steinberg is regarded as one of the gentlest drug lords to have ever graced the industry, relying on good business ethics and fair market values, rather than force, to achieve his ends. The antithesis of "La Madrina," Steinberg never at any point resorted to brutality, shooting or killing to achieve his objectives.

If at First You Don't Secede.... Throw a Party!

Drugs weren't only breeding crime in the '70s and '80s, they were also breeding resentment, particularly from those communities which became the target of heavy-handed federal actions. One such community grew so fed up that they even seceded from the country!

Secession is a word that isn't taken too lightly in the United States. After all, the last time it was used, it resulted in the deaths of over 600,000 people. Still, certain instances have proven so odious to the mindset of Americans that it has appeared as the only viable option left. This was certainly the case for the little secession movement staged by the Florida Keys in 1982.

Born out of an attempt by the Federal Government to control narcotics and illegal immigrants following the Dadeland Massacre and the onset of the Cocaine Cowboy, the movement at first started peacefully enough, with a failed injunction by the City Council of Key West to remove it from their borders. When this action failed and their economy began to suffer, due to massive traffic jams and a less than robust tourist season, local authorities decided to take matters one step further.

Gathering in Mallory Square with other prominent members of the City Council, Key West Mayor Dennis Wardlow read off a list of grievances; to the shock of everyone, he declared the birth of a new nation—the Conch Republic.

After breaking a loaf of stale Cuban bread over a naval officer's head,[22] he promptly surrendered and applied for a billion dollars in foreign aid from the United Nations. All of this took place in a matter of a minute!

While tongue-in-cheek in nature, the PR move proved very effective in gaining enough press to effectively remove the roadblock and return the island to normalcy. As a result, the threat of secession became a regular occurrence for the island chain, being used multiple times throughout the following decades.

One of the more famous of such events occurred on September 20, 1995, after it was reported that the 478th Civil Affairs Battalion of the United States Army Reserve was to conduct a training exercise that would simulate an invasion and occupation of a foreign island.[23] Wind of such exercises incensed the local population, who were not made aware of these activities by the Defense commanders beforehand. So once again, sovereignty was reasserted and war declared.

Firing water cannons from boats and hitting people with stale Cuban bread, the Conchs succeeded in ultimately forcing an apology from federal leaders the following day, subjecting them to a brief, but symbolic, surrender ceremony on September 22.[24]

10. Drugs, Disco and Decadence

The flag of the "Conch Republic" (Wikimedia Commons).

Fed up with heavy-handed tactics by the Reagan administration during the War on Drugs, residents of Key West declared their secession from the United States and formed "The Conch Republic" in 1982. Each year, this secession is commemorated by a ten-day festival (Florida Keys History Center, Ida Woodward Barron Collection, CC BY 2.0, Wikimedia Commons).

While Key West's flirtation with secession spurred a series of moral victories over federal authorities, it also manifested a deep-seated pride in Key West residents. Today, this pride is showcased each year with the Conch Republic Independence Celebration, a ten-day spectacle you have to see to believe.

Kicking off in late April on the Friday before the anniversary of secession, this "anything goes" festival features a party, a flag raising ceremony, a military reception and a conch shell blowing contest, complete with prizes, music and food. And that's just the first day!

In the ensuing 10 days, activities almost too numerous to name go on nonstop from sunrise to sunset. These include a miniature golf tournament, a royals ball, a naval parade, a battle reenactment of the Conch Republic's past triumphs, the "world's longest parade," a music festival and a red ribbon bed race, where participants motorize their mattresses and race down Duval Street. The hedonistic festival finally concludes the following Sunday, leaving its participants in a hangover-induced coma that can only be described as legendary.

> Key West's Conch Republic Independence Celebration is a fun annual event that honors our eccentric community with 10 days of fun races and parties. Every April, people come from all over to celebrate the independence of Key West and the entire Florida Keys.[25]

Since its inception in 1983, the party has drawn tens of thousands of visitors to the Keys annually, making it one of the largest and most outlandish festivals in the state. Such bacchanalian features have continued to add a gross amount of revenue to the island chain, all resulting from a small protest movement born over thirty years ago.

Cocaine, Heroin and Rock 'n' Roll

The explosion of drugs onto the scene in the 1970s not only gave birth to a new breed of criminal, but also to a new breed of music, one fueled in part by the decadence of the era, but nonetheless intricately tangled up in its trappings.

While few people today may realize it, Florida is the birthplace of Southern Rock, a blend of rock and roll, country music and blues focused generally on electric guitars and vocals. First coined in 1972 by Mo Slotin while writing for Atlanta's underground paper, *The Great Speckled Bird*, the genre quickly came to define the rock scene in the latter half of the decade. In fact, the 1970s saw the emergence of the Allman Brothers, .38 Special, Molly Hatchet and others, all of whom got their break playing in

Jacksonville venues. Of all the aforementioned acts, however, none shone quite as bright as Lynyrd Skynyrd.

Born and raised in Jacksonville, members Ronnie Van Zant, Bob Burns, and Gary Rossington started playing as early as 1964. Calling themselves Leonard Skinner (later spelled Lynyrd Skynyrd), in mocking tribute to their strict PE teacher at Robert E. Lee High School (now Riverside High School), who used to give them grief about their long hair, they quickly built up a fanbase becoming one of the most in-demand acts in Jacksonville by 1970. Striking it big in 1973 with the release of "Simple Man," they followed in quick succession with "Gimme Three Steps," "Sweet Home Alabama," "Free Bird," "Saturday Night Special," and "What's Your Name," all of which hit the U.S. Top 40.

It was an uncharted song, "That Smell," released in 1977, however, which would prove to be their most personal, as it dealt directly with the dalliance of drugs emerging in the rock scene at the time. Inspired by a car crash off Jacksonville's Mandarin Road, in which guitarist Gary Rossington, fueled by drugs and alcohol, veered into an oak tree, "That Smell" contained lyrics such as:

> Whiskey bottles, and brand new cars
> Oak tree you're in my way
> There's too much coke and too much smoke[26]

Reflecting back on the writing, Van Zant said: "I had a creepy feeling things were going against us. So, I thought I'd blow lines, slam some H and write a morbid song."[27]

Unfortunately for Van Zant, however, the song would prove a little too prophetic as he would die in a plane crash just three days after its release, along with guitarist Steve Gaines, vocalist Cassie Gaines and several members of the crew, effectively killing off the band's tour and leading to their disbandment for the better part of a decade.

Digitalizing the Drug Trade

For most of its existence, the drug trade in Florida was conducted via a careful network of trusted associates who would communicate in brief, coded messages via telephone or letter. This changed toward the end of the '80s with the development of the Internet and cell phones, allowing for dealers to cast an even wider net for business, while still being discreet and anonymous.

In many ways, Alejandro Bernal Madrigal could be called the Steve Jobs of drug dealing. Smooth, polished, yet surprisingly under the radar,

Bernal seemed to represent the antithesis of the earlier drug dealers from the seventies and early eighties.

As a young man, Bernal was mentored by Pablo Escobar before entering into a partnership with the youngest son of the cocaine peddler, Ochoas. Moving to Los Angeles in 1981, Bernal kept a relatively low profile, selling toilet fixtures by day and smuggling in drugs from Mexico by night. This double life eventually caught up with him when, in 1989, Mexican authorities busted him with over 500 kilos of cocaine.

Spending the next three years in a Mexican prison, Bernal managed to save his upstanding reputation by refusing to rat out his friends, returning to Colombia in 1995 as a hailed hero. His time away proved to be a godsend, as Escobar and the majority of the cocaine cartels had begun to suffer serious reversals in their fortunes, largely through a series of arrests and infighting, leaving a vacuum open for new leaders.

Seizing upon the opening, Bernal went about assembling a crack team of systems analysts to create secure channels for internal communications. To give his new business an air of legitimacy, Bernal enlisted the support of Alberto de Jesus Gallego, a former vice president of marketing for the Colombian airline Aces, to take over the role of his chief financial officer. Together, they pirated cell phone ID codes assigned to legitimate customers in order to make their conversations more difficult to trace, and used the then-burgeoning Internet to set up chat rooms with firewalls designed to foil any hackers working for the cops.

The success of this narcotrafficante setup made Bernal one of the most successful drug lords in the post–Escobar era; he was responsible for roughly 25 percent of all cocaine exports into the United States by the late '90s.

Unlike Escobar, however, Bernal kept a relatively low profile, choosing a well-to-do, yet more scaled back, upper middle-class lifestyle away from politics and violence. This lack of flashiness allowed him to blend in better with surrounding society, increasing his success.

> Alejandro Bernal Madrigal was the very image of respectability—at least by the strict but skin-deep standards of Colombia's upper-middle class. The light-complexioned, blue-eyed businessman, 40, lavished millions of dollars on his pampered stable of top-of-the-line show horses.... His three children attended one of the best private schools in Medellin. His wife, Blanca Estela, kept fit playing tennis at the city's exclusive Ceylan Racquet Club. By the late 1990s, Bernal had reached the top of his profession. According to Colombian law-enforcement officials, he was using satellite phones and the Internet to run an export network that handled at least 10 tons of cocaine every month—roughly 25 percent of Colombia's total production....
>
> [V]iolence was scarcely Bernal's style. Urbane and smooth, he preferred to go about his daily affairs unencumbered by obtrusive bodyguards. Without

them he could blend in perfectly with the other impeccably tailored customers at the finest restaurants in Bogota and Cartagena.[28]

As with all good things, Bernal's success came crashing to a sudden end in 1998 when DEA agents entered the north Miami apartment of an alleged Bernal money launderer named Carlos Jaramillo. Though Jaramillo was not captured, his computer files, revealing the vast technological setup, including email and Internet chat room instructions for deliveries, were hacked and quickly traced back to Bernal in Colombia. Less than three months later, Colombian police succeeded in bugging Bernal's Bogotá office suite, rented in Jaramillo's name, giving a federal grand jury enough evidence to indict him for drug smuggling and money laundering. Not long after, Bernal and two of his associates were captured in a surprise police raid in Colombia.

Arrested and extradited to Florida, Bernal was convicted and served time in a Florida prison. It's unknown whether his former network continued in the trade during his incarceration. "He was a big boy," said Special Agent Joe Kilmer, spokesman for the Drug Enforcement Administration in Miami. "He was known to ship cocaine in quantities of no less than one ton at a time."[29]

Although Bernal's reign as king of Colombia's coke industry did not last as long as Escobar's, his tactics of using non-violent methods, as well as new technological innovations such as the Internet to achieve shipments and deliveries, have made him a legend among Colombia's next generation drug traffickers.

Like so many other drug lords before him, Bernal would be assassinated in his native Colombia in 2012 after only a one month stay.

The Unintended Consequences of Florida's Drug Scene

No other state has been impacted by the drug trade quite like Florida. In the ten years between 1978 and 1988—roughly the time when cocaine was at its most popular—Florida witnessed a 47 percent increase in violent crime and a 67 percent increase in murder.[30] Such a sharp increase in crime gave Florida the reputation of a seedy and dangerous place to live, an image it has never successfully shaken off.

In addition, the flooding of billions of dollars in illicit imports into the state led to a building boom across much of the state, particularly in South Florida, where places like Brickell in Miami became home to luxury high rises for the kingpins. As a result of this, Florida will forever be a changed place.

11

Blood and Riots

*Serial Killers and Destruction
in the Twilight
of the Twentieth Century*

Drug violence wasn't the only phenomenon to sweep the nation toward the end of the twentieth century; violent crime saw a rapid increase, as well.

Spurred on by a range of issues such as White flight, a poor economy and a weakened political system, crime spiked to levels never before seen in this country, culminating in a rise in rape, gang beatings and murders. This latter aspect was a particularly troubling scenario for much of Florida, which saw a notorious amount of bloodshed from bloodthirsty serial killers.

Ted Bundy: The Sorority Slayer

Take a school-sponsored tour of Florida State's campus, and you're not likely to hear about the campus' most infamous serial killer, Ted Bundy. Nevertheless, his presence in Florida State lore was so magnanimous as to forever change the face of campus security across the country.

Born Theodore Robert Cowell to Eleanor Louise Cowell and an undisclosed father, Bundy grew up in difficult and often disturbing circumstances. From an early age, he was tricked into believing that his unwed birth mother was actually his older sister.

Reared from youth by his grandfather Samuel, who in all likelihood was his birth father, and his meek-mannered and depressive grandmother, Bundy grew up in a highly dysfunctional environment. While Bundy spoke warmly of his grandparents, telling Anne Rule that he "identified with," "respected," and "clung to" his grandfather, he and other family members told attorneys in 1987 that Samuel Cowell was "a tyrannical bully and a bigot who hated blacks, Italians, Catholics, and Jews, beat his wife and the family dog, and swung neighborhood cats by their tails. He once threw Louise's younger sister Julia down a flight of stairs for oversleeping. He sometimes spoke aloud to unseen presences, and kept a large collection of pornography, which Ted and a cousin would peruse for hours. At least once he flew into a violent rage when the question of Ted's paternity was raised."[1]

It was during this time that Bundy first began to exhibit early symptoms of psychopathology. The earliest of such incidents occurred when he was three during a holiday visit from his aunt who, upon reclining in bed for a nap, woke up with the perimeter of her body outlined in kitchen knives.[2]

Taking the name of his stepfather, Johnny Bundy, in 1951 after his mother remarried, Bundy continued to remain a reclusive child, ignoring his stepfather's pleas for father/son-type outings. He carried this aloofness with him into high school, where his young addiction to pornography, first present as a child, took on a darker form. It was during this time that he became increasingly obsessed with books about sex crimes and rape.

Attending college at the University of Washington, Bundy entered into Republican politics, becoming the manager of presidential contender Nelson Rockefeller's Seattle office in 1968. While there, Bundy began seriously dating a girl named Stephanie. Though he was enamored with her, she backed off a bit, eventually ending the relationship. His breakup with her began several years of drifting until he ultimately ended up at the University of Utah Law School. It was there that a new string of homicides began the following month "with two that went undiscovered until Bundy confessed to them shortly before his execution."[3] Later that September, he raped and strangled a still-unidentified hitchhiker in Idaho, then returned the next day to dismember the body and photograph his handiwork. "On October 2 he seized 16-year-old Nancy Wilcox in Holladay, a suburb of Salt Lake City,"[4] and dragged her into a wooded area, intending to "de-escalate" his pathological urges, he said, by raping and releasing her. However, "he strangled her—by accident, he claimed—in the process of trying to silence her."[5]

On October 18., Melissa Smith, the 17-year-old daughter of the police chief of Midvale, another Salt Lake City suburb, disappeared after leaving a pizza joint. Her naked body was later found in a nearby mountainous area nine days later. Postmortem examination indicated that "she may have remained alive for up to seven days following her disappearance."[6]

On October 31, 25 miles south in Lehi, Laura Aime, also 17, disappeared after leaving a café just after midnight. Her naked body was found by hikers nine miles to the northeast in American Fork Canyon on

Thanksgiving Day. "Both women had been beaten, raped, sodomized, and strangled with nylon stockings."[7] Years later Bundy described his post-mortem rituals with Smith's and Aime's remains, "including hair shampooing and application of makeup."[8]

Arrested in Utah, Bundy escaped from a law library window at the Pitkin County Courthouse and into Colorado before being taken into custody once more six days later. It was there, in Glenwood Springs, the night following his trial announcement that Bundy escaped through a small access hole he had sawed, crawling through the roof and into the jailer's apartment before escaping. From there, he drifted across the country, ultimately setting his sights on Florida.

Settling in Tallahassee, Bundy rented a room in a boarding house under the alias "Chris Hagan" and attempted to find a job and go straight.[9] When he found none, he reverted to shoplifting and petty theft to support himself. Soon, boredom took over and Bundy began to look for the next kill.

Early Sunday morning, January 15, 1978, "Bundy snuck in through a rear door with a faulty lock at the Chi Omega sorority house at Florida State University."[10] Inside, he found two sleeping women, Lisa Levy and Margaret Bowman.

> Beginning at about 2:45am he bludgeoned Margaret Bowman, 21, with a piece of oak firewood as she slept, then garroted her with a nylon stocking.[11] He then entered the bedroom of 20-year-old Lisa Levy and beat her unconscious, strangled her, tore one of her nipples, bit deeply into her left buttock, and sexually assaulted her with a hair mist bottle.[12]

"Finding Kathy Kleiner and Karen Chandler in an alarmed state next door, Bundy used the branch to beat them too, breaking Kleiner's jaw, and causing multiple shoulder lacerations before crushing Chandler's finger, breaking her jaw and causing loss of teeth."[13]

> After leaving the sorority house, Bundy broke into a basement apartment eight blocks away and attacked FSU student Cheryl Thomas, dislocating her shoulder and fracturing her jaw and skull in five places. She was left with permanent deafness, and equilibrium damage that ended her dance career.[14]

Police later found a semen stain and a pantyhose "mask" on Thomas' bed,[15] which they used to identify Bundy.

Escaping to Jacksonville, he attempted to repeat his murders by going after a 14-year-old girl in the parking lot of a K-Mart. Failing to kidnap her, he drove to Lake City, where he succeeded in abducting 12-year-old Kimberly Leach from the grounds of Lake City Junior High School. After brutally raping and murdering her, he threw her body under a pig shed, where she was later found rotting.

Caught by police on his way to Pensacola, he was positively linked with the Chi Omega murders and sent to trial in Dade County, but only after some prodding. As described by Pensacola Police Chief Norman Chapman:

> "He was very personable, very charismatic, very unalarming, and see, that's the dangerous thing," Chapman said.
>
> When Bundy's booking photo was taken that 15th day of February, police did not realize who they had in custody, nor did they know what he was capable of doing. Chapman said he would find out later Bundy planned to continue his killing spree.[16]

Ted Bundy is widely regarded as one of the most prolific serial killers of the twentieth century. In the mid–1970s, he is reputed to have murdered over 30 people across seven states. Two of his victims include Lisa Levy and Margaret Bowman, two sorority sisters murdered by Bundy at Florida State in 1978 (State Archives of Florida, Florida Memory).

Acting as his own attorney, Bundy was convicted on all charges and sentenced to death. A separate trial one year later in Orange County over the murder of Kimberly Leach resulted in a similar conviction. Before being sentenced to death, Bundy alleged that he felt that violence in the media was the primary cause for his murdering sprees.

All in all, 30 homicides were linked back to Bundy, with some "estimates stating them to be as high as 100 or more."[17] Bundy met his final end in the electric chair on January 24, 1989.

Aileen Wuornos: Portrait of a "Monster"

Ted Bundy wasn't the only serial killer to gain attention during this time, as Aileen Wuornos also earned a considerable amount of notoriety. Her excuses, however, were far different than Bundy's, and although gruesome, were somewhat justified given her backstory.

Poor, abused and unloved—this was how many people came to describe the sad life of Aileen Wuornos, the woman behind a slew of serial killings that would later garner an eternal place in Hollywood cinema.

Born to an uncaring mother and a jailbird, pedophiliac father, Wuornos was left in the care of her sick grandmother and sexually abusive grandfather at the age of four. By the time she reached adolescence, Wuornos had already been sexually engaged with multiple partners, including her older brother.

Following a brutal rape, "Wuornos gave birth to a baby at thirteen, which she promptly gave up for adoption."[18] Two years later, she began a career as a prostitute, living in the woods near her home after her grandfather had thrown her out.

Hitchhiking to Florida in 1976, it seemed Wuornos' fortunes were about to change when she met the wealthy and influential Lewis Gratz Fell, a 69-year-old yacht club president. That same year they married, but Wuornos' violent history eventually became too much for Fell to take, as she continued to be arrested for bar fights and even abused the elderly Fell with his own cane. After filing a restraining order against her, Fell and Wuornos divorced; they had been married just nine short weeks.

In and out of jail over the next few years for such crimes as assaulting a man with a cue ball and beer bottle, Wuornos moved to Daytona Beach where she met Tyria Moore, a hotel maid, at a local gay bar. They quickly fell in love and moved in together, at which point Wuornos, to sustain their livelihoods, reverted to prostitution.

> According to Wuornos biographer Sue Russell, the couple's fateful encounter in Daytona in 1986 dictated the rest of their lives.

"From then on, they became inseparable," she said. "That was the anchor that Aileen had been looking for"....
But Moore did take issue with Wuornos' tendency to turn to prostitution.[19]

Wuornos was arrested at Daytona's The Last Resort biker bar in 1991 for the murder of Peter Siems. At the behest of ex-lover Moore, who sold her out after making a separate plea bargain with police, Wuornos eventually took the rap for all the murders. At the trial, Wuornos argued self-defense for her actions, describing the brutal way in which Richard Mallory, her first victim, an electronics store owner from Clearwater and a convicted rapist, went about brutally beating and raping her. While she claimed that her other victims had not gone as far as Mallory, she nevertheless stated that they would have had she allowed them to live.

In order to make amends for her crimes, Wuornos eventually plead "no contest" to several of her murders, dropping the self-defense claims for three of her victims, but sticking to her story about the brutal encounter with Mallory. She eventually received six consecutive death sentences before dying by lethal injection on October 9, 2002.

The year after her death, the much acclaimed film "Monster" was released starring Charlize Theron; it revealed many more details of her sad life, particularly highlighting her abandonment and betrayal at the hands of Moore.

A Murder Unlike Any Other

When Athalia Ponsell Lindsley stepped outside to get the mail, she had little knowledge that it would be the last time she would ever step anywhere.

Born into one of the wealthiest families in Toledo, Ohio, Ponsell grew up with every privilege imaginable. This privilege extended to her being raised upon the exclusive Isle of Pines located off the coast of Cuba.

Eventually moving to New York, Ponsell sought fame and fortune as a model and dancer on Broadway before becoming a dance instructor. It was during this time she attracted the attention of Joseph Kennedy, Jr., the eldest son of the Kennedy clan and Joe Kennedy, Sr.'s, handpicked protégé to become the future president of the United States. Falling in love, they began dating and ultimately became engaged. World War II intervened during these years, however, and Kennedy died during service.

Drifting for a while, Ponsell eventually settled in the sleepy community of St. Augustine, where she purchased a home on the Matanzas River. Almost from the start she attracted celebrity status within the community, becoming both a controversial and celebrated figure within the town. This role ultimately became political with her marriage to James "Jinx" Lindsley, a former mayor.

Though married to Lindsley, Ponsell maintained a separate residence, refusing to give up her well-crafted home. It was then her feud with her neighbor, Alan Griffin Stanford, Jr., began to heat up.

Suspicious Circumstances

Circumstances surrounding Ponsell's death proved highly suspicious both because of her outspoken disdain for County Manager Alan G. Stanford, Jr., whom she harassed with zeal at city meetings, and her general unpopularity with the public:

> In life, Athalia could be intimidating, aggressive, and single minded; qualities that were abhorred in women especially in southern society in the 1970s. Many citizens of the city though she was "a troublemaker" and were not sorry that she was permanently gone. Francis O'Loughlin, one of the first officers on the scene, said, "I will always remember the remarks made by some that the woman had earned her own death." Sally Boyles, the widow of former state attorney Steven Boyles, said: "Not that St. Augustine citizens went around killing people they didn't like. But Athalia was not on a level playing field. Nobody liked her, so there was not a big hue and cry when she was killed."[20]
>
> On January 23, 1974, between 6:00 and 6:15 p.m., the 56-year-old Athalia went outside to walk her pet bluejay, Clementine. On her porch, she encountered a man wielding a machete who proceeded to hack her to death. By the time police arrived, Athalia had been nearly decapitated. Police Chief Virgil Stuart said, "she was dead when we got there. She had been badly butchered. Her head was almost cut off." Clementime, the bluejay, was never seen again.
>
> A neighbor, 19-year-old Locke McCormick, said he could [hear] Athalia's screams from his house. When he went to check on Athalia, he discovered her butchered body.[21]

Toward the end of the attack, which lasted only a few moments, Locke McCormick, her next-door neighbor, ran outside to look at the ensuing commotion, before yelling to his mother: "Mr. Stanford is hitting Mrs. Ponsell."[22] As a result, the attack stopped and the perpetrator fled. The McCormicks later found her lying in a pool of blood.

Given the hatred shared between Ponsell and Stanford, as well as Locke McCormick's own recollections regarding the incident, it seemed Stanford's days as a free man were numbered. This was not the case, however. From the beginning police were careless with the crime scene, failing to cordon it off and failing to preserve evidence. Witnesses on the scene said officers tracked blood into the Lindsley house.[23] Furthermore, Phillip

Athalia Ponsell Lindsley was an American model, Broadway dancer, political activist and television personality on the show *Winner Take All*. Lindsley was murdered by an unknown assailant on the front steps of her home in St. Augustine, Florida. Her murder remains unsolved (Stein, H. "Athlaia Ponselle (sic) and Thomas G. Slater, 1941," Wikimedia Commons).

Whitley, a *St. Augustine Record* photographer who shot crime scene photos, recalls that police did not secure the property.

> "People were walking through the yard and climbing over hedges," he said. "The whole thing was a screwed up mess from beginning to end. They were destroying the crime scene." He too saw blood in the grass, "leading all around the south side of the house." At one point, he said, one of the police officers ordered the ambulance attendants to hose down the blood "where it was concentrated to the left of the front door and at the bottom of the steps."[24]

Suspected from the start, due to their volatile relationship in public, Stanford was indicted on charges of murder. Eventually during a low tide, a county worker found a pair of trousers, a dress shirt, dress shoes—all seeming to indicate a male suspect—along with a baby diaper and a watch. All signs pointed to Stanford. He was even reportedly to have said to her in a meeting:

"You're a vicious evil woman," he said, "and one day I'm going to fix you."

Athalia did not take Stanford's threat lightly. She told James about it and also their mutual friend, a contractor named Gavin Laurie Jr. When Geraldine came to visit, she told her, "That man over there that Alan Stanford is going to kill me."[25]

Despite all of the evidence, Stanford was acquitted on all charges during his trial a year later. Even with witnesses corroborating his role, by that point, almost all of the evidence had been improperly tampered with by the police and Stanford was found not guilty.

Though acquitted, many still believe Stanford, without a doubt, was the killer. In fact, to this day, there have been no other credible suspects found and the case remains unsolved. The mystery that surrounds the murder became fodder for media outlets all across the country, ultimately fueling the publishing of a 1998 book called *Bloody Sunset*, a slightly fictionalized account of the murder that forever changed a city.

Race Riots and Rising Tensions

Serial killers weren't the only thing marring Florida in the twilight of the twentieth century; the state also experienced a fair amount of racial tension and prejudice, as well. Much of it was a holdover from the fifties and sixties that came to a boiling point with the enforcement of new laws, leading to violent and bloody confrontations. Among the largest of such flare-ups occurred following the death of Arthur McDuffie.

Arthur McDuffie and the Liberty City Riots

Long before there ever was a Rodney King, a Trayvon Martin or a George Floyd, there was Arthur McDuffie, the oft-forgotten victim whose death sparked one of the worst riots in the nation's history.

In the early morning hours of December 17, 1979, McDuffie was riding his 1973 black and orange Kawasaki motorcycle down a street, when he ran a red light and began to be pursued by the police.

Leading them on an eight-minute, high-speed chase through some residential areas, with speeds in excess of 80 miles per hour, McDuffie lost control of the motorcycle after failing to make a left turn. He then allegedly fled on foot. Surrounded on all sides by four of the officers involved in the chase, the police succeeded in subduing him to the ground, where, according to testimony, he fought back and kicked one of them. A scuffle ensued and the officers later cracked his skull with a baton.

11. Blood and Riots

Transported to a nearby hospital, McDuffie died four days later as a result of his injuries. The coroner's report stated that he had suffered from multiple skull fractures after being struck by a blunt object.

Details of the McDuffie's death began filling papers and newscasts all across the Miami area, and soon accusations of racism against the four White officers began to appear. These accusations intensified when it was later found that McDuffie was a workingman, a father and a military veteran. His driving on a suspended license and his failure to pay past traffic tickets were the main initiators of the chase that led to his death.

Indicted on charges of manslaughter, the four officers were also charged with tampering and fabricating evidence. Two other officers at the scene were later charged as accessories to the crime and were fired along with the others less than a month after the incident.

Due to the volatile nature of the incident, which at the time was described by the presiding judge as a "time bomb," the trial was moved to Tampa and overseen by Janet Reno, who would one day become the Attorney General under President Clinton.

During the trial, several officers, given immunity for their testimony, reported that McDuffie had actually surrendered prior to making that faulty left turn. The police officers, then pulled him off his bike, yanked his helmet off and beat him about the head with their clubs and fists until he lay motionless and bleeding. It was later corroborated that the police then proceeded to run over McDuffie's bike to make it look like an accident.

Despite all the testimony to the contrary, the presiding judge stated that the State had failed to prove its case. Nine days later, on May 17, 1980, the all–White jury acquitted all officers involved in the cover-up of all charges after a mere three hours of deliberation.

The verdict resulted in a massive protest in the Miami streets which turned into an all-out riot by nightfall, resulting in several deaths and injuries. With rioting spreading to the areas immediately north of downtown Miami, including Liberty City, Overtown, Black Grove and Brownsville, access to these areas became extremely hazardous. Drivers brave enough to frequent the areas experienced rocks being thrown at their cars and violent beatings.

Fires, lootings and burglaries added to the chaos, forcing authorities to seal off the areas to fireman and policemen due to sniper fire. Many were forced to sit helplessly by behind barricades in Coconut Grove as they watched the carnage ensue.

By the third day, the violence started to abate as an additional deployment of 2,500 troops and temporary bans on alcohol and firearms sales led to an abrupt calming among the city's most hard-hit neighborhoods. These measures put an effective end to the violence, but only after "18 people were dead and $100 million in damages"[26] were done to the city.

Eventually, the federal government declared all of Miami a disaster area, allocating funds for the rebuilding effort. Miami suffered from a massive PR backlash as a result, with many in the media—the Dadeland Mall Massacre still fresh in their minds—decrying the city as a haven for violence.

Two months after the rioting another trial was held to determine if the officers had violated federal civil rights statutes. Once again, all officers were acquitted and surprisingly reinstated to their old positions after a pending strike by the Miami Fraternal Order of Police.

The Plight of the Marielitos

In addition to Black frustrations with authorities, recent Cuban émigrés were venting their anger at the Law, as well.

Beginning as a trickle after the Cuban Revolution, the steady stream of immigrants slowly but surely increased throughout the sixties and seventies, until becoming a torrent in 1980. In that year, Castro allowed all dissenters, "lumpens" (undesirables) and "escoria" (scum), as Castro termed them, to leave the island.

Though given the official go-ahead by the government, dissenters found themselves the immediate targets of violence at repudiation meetings, "where the participants screamed obscenities and defiled the facades of the homes, throwing eggs and garbage, for hours."[27] Those who tried to stop them faced similar consequences, creating an unstable environment and an even stronger desire to leave in some Cuban citizens.

Allowed to leave through the port of Mariel Harbor, these refugees were given the opportunity to flee if a sponsor would take them in. To their aid came the Cuban refugees already settled in Miami and, later, the United States government, which authorized a mass flotilla to carry them to Miami to be processed.

While the vast majority of these refugees were genuinely interested in obtaining freedom, Castro, behind the back of the United States, stocked within their crowd many criminals and former patients from asylums for the criminally insane. As he later stated:

> The United States is the most to blame because it encouraged illegal exits from the country and this is why the whole situation turned against them. Cuba benefited greatly from the departure of these persons [lumpen]. The boats came from the United States. The Cuban community in the United States

Mariel Boatlift refugees at an emergency shelter set up in Boca Chica, Florida, 1980 (U.S. Coast Guard Historian's Office).

sent boats to pick up their relatives and friends. We authorized all those who wanted to leave to go. I think it was the greatest cleanup in history.[28]

These miscreants blended in seamlessly with the others aboard the ships, bringing their reputations for violence and criminal activity with them. In fact, it is estimated that of the thousands who migrated, 25 percent had some form of criminal background.

The Mariel wave of 124,700 Cubans arrived between April and October of 1980. Four groups of immigrants made up the Mariel wave: (1) ex-political prisoners and other dissidents that were pressured to leave by government officials and members of the state-run Committees for the Defense of the Revolution; (2) "several thousand social undesirables comprised of petty criminals, mentally disturbed persons, homosexuals (sic) and juvenile delinquents"; (3) "antisocials" in Cuba (a category which included religious evangelists such as Jehovah's Witnesses, alcoholics, prostitutes, vagrants charged under the "Dangerousness Law" of 1979); and (4) individuals with family members already living in the U.S. who had an expressed desire to join them (by far the largest segment) (Boswell, Rivera, et al. 1980).[29]

As a result of Castro's deception, Americans began to monitor all new arrivals from Mariel, placing them in temporary housing until their backgrounds could be better determined. This housing was typically overcrowded and required lengthy months-long stays, with little to no information being passed along to the crowds.

Desperate to get their new lives started, dissent began fomenting within the ranks of these camps, resulting in a huge riot in one of the detention centers at Fort Chaffee, Arkansas.

> After the demonstrators got outside the gate, they tried to race up Arkansas Rte. 22 to nearby Baring, but were turned back by state troopers, who beat them with billy clubs....
>
> The Cubans responded by hurling rocks and chunks of concrete—some six inches square—at the troopers.
>
> After being pinned down behind cars and trucks for about 10 minutes, troopers fired about 20 rounds with shotguns and pistols, forcing the refugees back into the sprawling Army base....[30]

The migrants finally relented after 10 minutes, but not before setting fire to two mess halls and some barracks. The rioting added to the allusion that the Marielitos were a different breed of Cubans than the ones who had arrived before, casting them in an even more negative light.

The Dark Side of Cuban Immigration

The Fort Chaffee Riots, as well as the much-publicized accounts of Castro stocking Marielito ranks with undesirables, led to a perception that all refugees were tainted. This stigma proved all the more difficult for refugees to break through, as they were already marked by other differences. For, unlike Cubans who had previously settled in Miami during the First Wave of immigration following Castro's takeover, these new immigrants looked different and thought different. The most marked of these differences was skin color, as earlier waves of Cuban refugees tended to be wealthier and lighter skinned than the Marielito arrivals.

In addition, Marielitos also came under the gun for their perceived ignorance. For, while a majority of those immigrating were physicians, doctors and attorneys, they were nevertheless viewed with suspicion. They had actually experienced an entire generation of their lives under communism and were more likely to have a harder time adapting their trades to the American labor market. Furthermore, they were viewed by the media, as well as by the people of Miami, as having increased the unemployment rate from 5.0 to 7.1 percent.[31] This made them a heavy political target for politicians, who espoused these rising numbers as proof that U.S. policy regarding the Marielitos was poorly handled. Further adding to this target was the fact that a significant portion of

Marielitos were Black and were not of the same economic fortune as earlier migrants.

Although processed in all different parts of the country, around 50 percent of the Marielitos ended up settling back in Miami.[32] This helped increase the Cuban population of the city exponentially, shaping Miami into the modern city that it is today. Still, among many, the stigmatization of the Marielito is alive and well within the community and continues to remain a deep divide between First Wave and Second Wave Cuban exiles in Florida.

Florida in the Twilight of the Twentieth Century

The 1970s and 1990s marked a defining turn for Florida in the national spotlight. Long viewed as a resort destination for the wealthy and health conscience, the state denigrated over the 1960s into an ailing retirement community, becoming a cesspool for drug lords, criminals and serial killers by the end of that decade.

Fueled in part by the rising popularity of drugs in American culture, as well as its close geographic association with drug-producing Latin American countries, the state entered into a period of anxiety and uncertainty. Such emotions would later be captured in hit TV shows and movies, such as *Scarface*, showcasing the very violence that Florida had fallen victim to, ingraining even more so the image of the state as a drug-riddled swampland.

In addition to Florida being perceived as a safety concern for tourists, the state also began to feel the squeeze from minority groups, which, in response to intolerant actions taken by state police and state government, began to view the area with hesitation. This was a reversal of sorts for a state, which while violent during the Civil Rights Era, paled in comparison to the problems associated in other Southern states, such as Alabama and Mississippi. Such a reversal showed that Florida's path to progress through tolerance and equality still remained highly untraveled, and that the state's overt conservative attitudes were still very much prevalent among the fixtures of government.

12

Politics, Terror and Economic Ruin

Florida Leaves Its Mark on the World

Florida's transition into the 2000s will forever be ingrained in the national consciousness. This transition would leave an indelible mark that would have ramifications not only for the state, but for the nation and the world as well, affecting everything from politics and travel to housing and immigration. Such an impact on international conscience would begin almost immediately in the year 2000, and nothing would ever be the same again.

Florida Sets the Stage

In the twilight of the 1990s, America was at its peak. Unrivaled on the world stage in military prowess following the collapse of the Soviet Union, America had all but recovered from its successful intervention in Iraq and its less than stellar attempt in Somalia two years later and settled into a period of relative peace and prosperity. The housing market had boomed, the Internet was taking off, and entrepreneurship in tech was bursting. To many, it seemed America's best and brightest days were ahead:

> Only recently, after all, did the democracies of the West appear at ease with themselves, the day's great ideological conflicts apparently solved. Governments were liberal, open, and modern, and their countries not yet so full of the angst that seems to define them today. The phrase *War on Terror* had not yet been coined, China had not yet risen, and Europe was on a smooth path to ever-closer union, protected and supported by the only power on Earth that mattered, the United States. This was the 1990s.[1]

When in the late fall of 1999, a small child and his companions were picked up in the Straits of Florida, few could see the radical changes they would bring with them.

And a Child Shall Lead Them

On November 21, 1999, five-year-old Elián González, his mother Elizabeth Brotons Rodríguez, and 12 others left Cuba on a small aluminum boat with a faulty engine. Sailing out of Cárdenas and into the path of a storm, their small unequipped boat began to take on water, leading the crew to place the more vulnerable into inner tubes, Gonzalez among them, so that they could drift away to safety while the others attempted in vain to save the boat. The crew, including González's mother and 10 others, would eventually die while Elián and the other two survivors would float at sea until being "rescued by two fishermen three miles off the coast of Fort Lauderdale."[2] Elián was brought to the mainland and then transferred to the U.S. Coast Guard before being processed by the Immigration and Naturalization Service (INS) and released to his paternal great-uncle, Lázaro, in Miami. This is where things began to take an interesting turn.

A Custody Battle Unlike Any Other

Less than a day after Elián's surrender to his relatives in Miami, an international custody battle began, as Elián's biological father in Cuba, Juan Miguel González (who had been estranged from Elián's mother), along with the Cuban government, claimed that the boy's mother had removed him illegally and that he must be returned. The boy's relatives in Miami, however, resisted the demands and suggested that the Castro regime was playing politics. This move would set off an international custody battle which would play out over the next four months in court battles, the U.S. Senate and the media.

With Janet Reno seeking to secure a peaceful transfer back to Elián's father and the family doing everything they could to stay the transfer, the wrangling continued back and forth dominating headlines until the United States Court of Appeals for the Eleventh Circuit weighed in blocking any potential transfer in April that year.

The Raid That Shook the World

Fresh from their legal victory in the Eleventh Circuit Court of Appeals, the family spent much of the next day negotiating on the phone with Reno and Deputy Attorney General Eric Holder into the wee hours of Easter morning. It was during this time that the Feds swarmed the Gonzalez's Little Havana house and caught the family by surprise. As recounted by witnesses present during the raid, the move came as an unbelievable shock:

> **Donato Dalrymple**, *the fisherman who found Gonzalez and a family friend*: I don't think that [the family] was expecting a raid at all. Because if you really look at it, they were out there negotiating, and basically it was a setup.... They had all the legal people on the phone when I arrived at the house and while they're talking and negotiating, that's when they moved in....
>
> **Tony Zumbado**, *then–NBC cameraman*: It was 4:30 am/5 am and we heard this thunder in the back of the house, like a train. It was agents coming in through the back door, knocking down fences to get through the back door. We saw one of Elián's attorneys run out the door, screaming, "They are here! They are here! The Yankees are here!"[3]

Elián, who was hiding in a closet with his uncle, was taken at gunpoint and immediately flown to Bethesda where his father was waiting. The reaction was instantaneous.

As images of the frightened child splashed across every newspaper and news outlet in the world, massive protests broke out across Florida in solidarity with the Gonzalez's and with utter appall at the heavy-handed tactics used by the Federal Government. Nevertheless, Elián was returned to Cuba. While this would normally be the end of the story, Elián's plight and the way he was handled by members of the Clinton administration would not soon be forgotten by the Cuban community. It was an election year, after all, and Floridians of Cuban descent were about to make their displeasure known in a very big way.

An Election Unlike Any Other

The 2000 U.S. presidential election was an event unparalleled in modern national history. Not since the days of Rutherford B. Hayes vs. Samuel Tilden back in 1877 had the nation seen an election so closely contested, with similarities almost too eerie to be coincidence.

As in that long-ago election, Florida was placed at the forefront of the national stage, with its electoral votes playing the virtual kingmaker for the next president. All election night the state seemed to seesaw back and forth between Gore and Bush, with no clear winner being declared.

In the aftermath of that tumultuous night, hordes of lawyers, politicians and rabble-rousers descended upon the state from all sides. The media, in typical 24-hour news fashion, kept the drama at the forefront every hour on the hour, relaying the minutest personal details possible about each candidate, each candidate's team and, above all, those involved with the electoral recount process.

Covering roughly 171,000 votes out of approximately 6 million cast statewide,[4] the recount focused on a wide range of disputed ballots, largely consisting of under and overvotes. An exceptionally large number of these were located in large retirement areas such as Volusia and Palm Beach counties, where confusion over the state's butterfly ballot—just introduced that election cycle—was blamed for contributing to a Bush victory.

As the days went on, anger built up as Bush and Gore's lawyers publicly squabbled over the methodology used in the recount. Florida Secretary of State Katherine Harris, a Republican—and a close personal friend of George W. Bush's brother, Jeb, and a Bush state campaign co-chairman—announced that she would reject any new totals from the four outstanding counties that were not submitted by November 14, just a week after the election. Her announcement was summarily taken to the Florida Supreme Court by Gore's lawyers, which then extended the deadline by another two weeks. Despite this, neither Palm Beach nor Miami could meet the new deadline, allowing the state canvassing board to declare Bush the winner once again.

Taking the newly certified results to the Florida Supreme Court, Gore's lawyers once again scored a victory with the court ordering a full recount of the votes. Bush, appealing the reversal to the U.S. Supreme Court, ultimately won out, however, when in a historic 5–4 decision, the Supreme Court ordered the manual recount effectively stopped and Bush, through an earlier certification of a 537 vote margin,[5] was declared the victor. While strongly disagreeing with the outcome, Gore nonetheless conceded, opening the way for Bush to be sworn in just one month later.

Irregularities and Race in the Election

For a while after the election, various newspapers sponsored recounts to determine the "what if" scenario that never got to play out as a result of the Supreme Court's decision. Studies conducted by these media outlets generally met with divided results, declaring both Bush and Gore the winner depending upon the recount methodology used.

In a nutshell, they concluded that had limited county-by-county recounts requested by the Gore team been completed, then Bush would have still won. However, they found that a recount of all disputed state ballots would have ended up putting Bush's margin of victory at risk.

> The first survey, conducted on behalf of the *Washington Post*, shows that Mr. Gore had a nearly three-to-one majority among 56,000 Florida voters whose November 7 ballot papers were discounted because they contained more than one punched hole.

The second and separate survey, conducted on behalf of the Palm Beach Post, shows that Mr. Gore had a majority of 682 votes among the discounted "dimpled" ballots in Palm Beach County.[6]

What they found from both cases was that Al Gore would have won Florida's 21 electoral college votes by a narrow majority had the new votes been allowed to be entered, which would have made him the 43rd president.[7]

Although both The *Miami Herald* and *USA Today* found Bush to be the winner in each of these scenarios, their tabulations consisted of a wide margin of undervotes including votes with fairly dimpled indentions, which had not previously been counted or included in the recount process.

While trends such as these would no doubt prove disturbing for Gore, who literally came within a hair-thin margin of scoring victory, his defeat became all the more bitter with the less-talked-about and little-known controversy surrounding the state "scrub list."

Overseen by Katherine Harris and Sandra Mortham, from May 1999 through election day 2000, "the state pumped over $4 million into the process,"[8] all in the effort to rid the system of potential voters. While this was fairly standard, Florida's outsourcing of the process to ChoicePoint, a private company in Texas, George W. Bush's home state, raised eyebrows and alluded to possible roll tampering.

As a result of their actions, "a total of 173,000 voters were immediately docked from the rolls."[9] A disproportionate number of these were Black voters. In Florida, where slightly over one third of Black men cannot vote because of a law banning felons from the voter roles, cries of racism began to echo across the state. While there was much about the lists that bothered the county's election supervisor, Pam Iorio, she felt she didn't have a choice but to use them per the Florida Constitution.

> "We did run some number stats and the number of blacks [on the list] was higher than expected for our population," says Chuck Smith, a statistician for the county. Iorio acknowledged that African-Americans made up 54 percent of the people on the original felons list, though they constitute only 11.6 percent of Hillsborough's voting population.[10]

While Florida's outsourcing of its voter rolls to Texas was suspicious enough, it was discovered that almost 10,000 of the voters on the list were, in fact, innocent of any crime.[11] Their only association, it seemed, was that they shared similar names, receiving letters that they were not allowed to vote. When complaints began to arise, some county supervisors began to look into the accuracy of the list, with a few rogue counties such as Duval and Palm Beach deciding to dump it altogether.

12. Politics, Terror and Economic Ruin 191

Madison County's elections supervisor, Linda Howell, had a peculiarly personal reason for distrusting the central voter file: She had received a letter saying that since she had committed a felony, she would not be allowed to vote.

Howell, who said she has never committed a felony, said the letter she received in March shook her faith in the process. "It really is a mess," she said.[12]

As it turned out, only a fraction of these voters were informed of their docking by letter, allowing them time to correct the mistake. The other, much larger group was not informed until arriving at the polls on election day.

Because of this, it is estimated that thousands of Black voters were denied their constitutional Civil Rights, leading many to conclude foul play. It is now speculated that had these voters actually been allowed to participate, and continued the voting pattern exhibited by 93 percent of all Black voters in the state, their votes could've and would've decisively swung the election for Gore, making him the presidential victor.

The 2000 Presidential Election was one of the most closely contested elections in U.S. history. Florida's 25 electoral votes proved to be the make-or-break for both candidates, causing protests to break out across the state as votes were counted and recounted (photograph by Village Square, October 28, 2010, CC BY 2.0, Wikimedia Commons).

Florida's Role in 9/11

The 2000 presidential election played a significant role in more ways than one. While redefining the electoral system as we know it, its 24/7 media scrutiny helped set America on the path toward the political polarization we continue to live with today. Further still, it set America on course for the War on Terror—the most significant international policy of the twenty-first century—with consequences that have left no corner of the world untouched. This latter aspect can all be traced back to one seminal event that would forever change the course of history—September 11.

While many recognize the significance of this date—certainly Boomers, Gen Xers, Millennials, and perhaps a few older members of Gen Z— few are aware of the direct role that Florida played in its happening. For it was right within the Sunshine State where the plot for September 11 was formed and ultimately implemented.

Terror in the Sunshine State

Often associated with New York City and Washington, D.C., which ended up as the prime targets of the hijackers, Florida's role in their training and coordination is a hardly mentioned footnote in modern history ... until now. For, on August 31, almost two weeks before that fateful day which would forever alter the course of world history, members of a well-to-do Saudi family abruptly vacated their posh luxury estate in Sarasota, to make their way out of the country.

Having inhabited the home, which was located in the prestigious gated community of Prestancia, for much of the prior year, the family, which consisted of Abdulaziz al-Hijji, his wife Anoud and their small children, lived a fairly innocuous existence, until a sudden visit from "friends" began to alert the suspicions of the neighbors. Among these was Senior Administrator for Prestancia, Larry Berberich, whose suspicions prompted a probe following the family's sudden departure in a white van. These suspicions were later enhanced with an email neighbor Larry Gallagher sent to the FBI on the day of the attacks. Like Berberich, he was convinced something was not quite right.

When Berberich and a senior counterterrorism agent finally broke into the house, what they found added to their wonder; inside they found:

> [A] brand new car in the driveway, a refrigerator full of food, fruit on the counter—and an open safe in a master bedroom....
>
> The couple, living with their small children at the three-bedroom house at 4224 Escondito Circle, had left in a hurry in a white van, probably on Aug. 30.

12. Politics, Terror and Economic Ruin   193

September 11, 2001, was a day that will forever alter the course of world history. Much of the planning for the event took place in the Florida neighborhood of Prestancia (photograph by Robert J. Fisch, September 11, 2001, CC BY 2.0, Wikimedia Commons).

They abandoned three recently registered vehicles, including a brand-new Chrysler PT Cruiser, in the garage and driveway....[13]

In addition to all of the materials left behind, the counterterrorism official also found phone records directly linking the 9/11 hijackers with the family. They found these phone records dating back for more than a year, with time lengths directly lined up with "the known suspects."[14] They also found gate records from the guards physically linking them with three of the future hijackers who were renting rooms in Venice, just ten miles away, while they trained to become pilots at Huffman Aviation. This included Atta, the leader of the future hijackers, his companion Marwan al-Shehhi and their accomplice Ziad Jarrah, who took flying lessons a block away at Florida Flight Training. Together, they spent much of their time traveling around the southern portion of the state with stints in Hollywood, Fort Lauderdale and Delray Beach, among others. A fourth,

Adnan Shukrijumah, resided in Miramar. It was these gate records that ultimately turned suspicion into confirmation and led to links being discovered between the family and other terror suspects, including Mohammed Atta and Waleed al-Shehri.

An Unusual Cover-up

After the attacks and their search of the premises, the FBI carefully monitored the movements of the al-Hijji family following their sudden departure. They linked them first with a property owned by Anoud's father Ghazzawi in Arlington, Virginia, before flying to London's Heathrow Airport with Ghazzawi.

Ghazzawi, it appears, had many links to America even before 9/11, owning several properties in the U.S., including the one in Sarasota. In addition, he had taken an American wife.

A middle-aged financer and interior designer, Ghazzawi had managed to make his way onto FBI watch lists well before the attacks.

Though the family managed to make a successful break for it, with records showing them having arrived safely back in Saudi Arabia, the FBI made an attempt to lure them back home, under the guise of unpaid dues to the homeowner's association. Scott McKay, a Sarasota lawyer for Prestancia said the plot ultimately failed, however, because the documents could legally be signed elsewhere by a notary. Records show that they did so via the vice consul of the U.S. embassy in Lebanon, as well as a public notary in Riverside, California.

While the evidence linking Ghazzawi, his wife Deborah, his son-in-law and his daughter to the terrorist attacks is overwhelming, former U.S. Senator Bob Graham, a Florida Democrat, who co-chaired the congressional joint inquiry into the attacks, said he was not told about the findings until many years later.

The fact that the FBI did not tell the inquiry about the Florida discoveries, Graham says, is similar to the agency's failure to provide information linking members of the 9/11 terrorist team to other Saudis in California until congressional investigators discovered it themselves. The inquiry did nevertheless accumulate a "very large" file on the hijackers in the United States, and later turned it over to the 9/11 Commission.

"They did very little with it," Graham said, "I never got a good answer as to why they did not pursue that."[15]

Blame it on the Sunshine: Florida Leads the Nation to Economic Ruin

There's a famous quote by George Santayana that goes *those who cannot remember the past are condemned to repeat it*. So it was with the start of the Great Recession in 2007, where Florida's real estate bust marked an economic downturn in a role eerily similar to the one it played almost eighty years prior.

It's unlikely that anyone will soon forget the economic collapse and subsequent recession brought on by the banking and mortgage industries. Evidence of this collapse lasted well into the 2010s, with the economy not reaching full recovery for nearly a decade.

Brought on by a housing bubble unparalleled since the Roaring Twenties, the Great Recession was a product of greed and overzealous urban planning throughout the country. Nowhere was this more pronounced than along the sunny shores of Florida.

Between 2000 and 2006, the Sunshine State saw housing prices more than double, spurring rapid suburban development and urban renewal projects such as condos and downtown neighborhood revitalizations. At its heart were state and city legislatures built on becoming the next greatest thing.

Keeping ahead of demand, local city leaders allowed real estate speculators to dominate their markets and saturate their cities with a plethora of housing choices. Encouraging them along were restrictive management growth laws. While adopted for noble conservation purposes, these laws helped fuel an unprecedented bubble by restricting land for development:

> The basic problem is that, by delineating and limiting the land that can [be] used for development, planners create guides to investment, which shows developers where they must buy and tells the now more scarce sellers that the buyers have little choice but to negotiate with them. This can violate the "principle of competitive land supply," cited by Brookings Institution economist Anthony Downs.
>
> Downs said: "If a locality limits to certain sites the land that can be developed within a given period, it confers a preferred market position on those sites.... If the limitation is stringent enough, it may also confirm a monopolistic powers on the owners of those sites, permitting them to raising land prices substantially."
>
> [The Brookings Institution cites] higher house prices in California as having resulted from growth management restrictions that were too strong. "... even well-intentioned growth management programs ... can accommodate too little growth and result in higher housing prices."[16]

In states that did not practice such management like Texas and Georgia, the housing bubble did not reach the zenith like it did in Florida, allowing them to evade a catastrophe as experienced by Florida toward the end of the real estate peak.

Bursting the Bubble

In May 2005, Bob Hoffman in his article "Omens of the Coming Real Estate Bubble?" foretold of an imminent burst in market demand that would have a huge impact upon the state's economic future. At the time, few took him seriously, riding a crest of inflated prices and a dearth of available land. Less than a year after the article's publication, the market began to see signs of trouble.

Starting at the end of 2006 and continuing through 2011, real estate across Florida went into a dramatic free fall. Demand dried up, halting construction projects and condo speculators, and the peninsula began to see its population stagnate and even decline in some areas for the first time in modern history. As a result, the state's labor market began to close up, pushing Florida into a deep recession, resulting in skyrocketing foreclosures, with Lee County, home to many new condo developments, being hit the hardest.

> By the spring of 2009, the Circuit Court backlog in Lee County was 29,000 foreclosures, each by the holder of a mortgage note. In many cases, owners were faceless trusts that bought mortgages from the original lender, packaged them into securities and sold them.
>
> In Lee County, the result was the notorious "rocket docket" that brought in retired judges to preside over speedy judgments in foreclosure cases.
>
> Retired judges heard some 300 cases per week and two judges worked full time on foreclosures, handling up to 4,000 in a single month.
>
> Six thousand cases were heard during December 2008. The fact that many homeowners didn't bother to show up made things easier.
>
> The rocket docket helped put thousands of houses on the market at once, and critics said the massive dumping of housing stock on the market depressed prices. The median price bottomed out at less than $90,000 in 2009.[17]

As went Florida, so too followed the rest of the nation, ushering in what became the longest and most economically devastating recession since the Great Depression.

The Tumultuous 2000s

Florida's role in the 2000s was the proverbial canary in the coal mine for the rest of the country. Relegated to the backwater of politics and cultural relevancy for much of the twentieth century, its burgeoning electoral importance along with its rapid growth made ignoring the state all but impossible by the dawn of the twenty-first century, and while not all of it may have been good, there is hardly any doubt that the first decade of the 2000s could firmly be anything but the *Floridian Decade.*

13

Retirees of a Different Kind
Dictators and Death Leaders

Not everything bad happens *in* Florida. Sometimes it just comes to escape there.

Long the butt of retiree jokes and heralded as a place where old people go to die, Florida's vast interior is populated with swaths of retirement villages, canasta halls and golf courses. While many of these retirees are simply there to enjoy the fruits of their labor, others have a more insidious agenda, often escaping a past fraught with cold-blooded murder. As the *Miami New Times* put it in a 2010 article entitled "Latin American Dictators Love South Florida":

> Forget Epcot. Screw the Wizarding World of Harry Potter. Put down that glossy guidebook to Orlando hotel bargains before we sic our guerrillas on your pastel-pants-wearing ass.
>
> This is South Florida, *muchacho*, the retirement home of army strongmen, torturers, and every other unsavory character from the Southern Hemisphere. We make Casablanca look like a Daffy Duck cartoon.[1]

The Bolivian Butcher Claims a Home

It's seldom an event becomes so tainted that it earns the dubious distinction of "Black" in its title. A few instances come to mind. There was the Black Plague, which killed roughly one third of the European population in the Middle Ages, the Wall Street Crash of 1929 on Black Tuesday, which precipitated the Great Depression, as well as Black Friday, where a slew of protestors were massacred by the Shah of Iran in 1978. And then of course, there's Bolivia's very own Black October, where the Bolivian government declared war on its people.

In the fall of 2003, indigenous residents in Bolivia took to the streets, protesting the government's plans to sell off the nation's natural gas reserves. Naturally, they were miffed because they weren't expected to profit at all from this arrangement, even though their native lands contained the most amount of reserves.

Blocking the roads outside the capital, protesters cordoned off a large area, trapping visiting tourists from leaving. In an effort to get them released, and save the country's image abroad, Carlos Sánchez Berzain, Bolivia's acting defense minister, flew via helicopter to Sorata, a backpacker-friendly hamlet on the outskirts of La Paz. The negotiations quickly soured, however, and an order was given to fire on the locals. The first to die was a young girl. Later, more women and children would join her, as the army gave quarter to no one.

As in other countries with similar "shoot first, ask questions later" policies, the event led to a wave of rioting over the next month, causing over 60 deaths as well as a subsequent revolt which led to the ousting of both Sánchez Berzain and his boss, President Sánchez de Lozada.

Seeking out a new life in Pinecrest, Sánchez Berzain at first attempted to retain his place in the limelight by delivering speeches at the University of Miami. Student protests forced him into a quieter role, however, and he now passes his days in relative obscurity, occasionally writing articles for *El Nuevo Herald*, the Spanish equivalent of the *Miami Herald*.

Ultimately, Sánchez Berzain would be brought to civil trial for his crimes and was even convicted by a jury and forced to pay restitution. This marked the first time a former head of state was brought to trial and convicted in such a manner. Nonetheless, his conviction was overturned a month later by the presiding judge:

> "The jury sat in trial for three weeks, deliberated for five days, and we are confident that they reached the right conclusion that the former President and Defense Minister were responsible for these killings. The judge depended on an erroneously high standard of evidence to overturn this verdict—that the defendants needed to have a premeditated plan to kill civilians—which the law does not require," said **Judith Chomsky**, an attorney for the plaintiffs, cooperating through the Center for Constitutional Rights. "This case is not over, and we intend to swiftly appeal this decision."[2]

As of now, the families of the victims who brought him to trial are trying diligently to get the original verdict restored.

Playing with Fire and Getting Burned

Apparently, Telmo Ricardo Hurtado thought he could escape to Florida and forget the past. What he didn't realize, however, is that the past is not so easy to outrun.

A member of an elite paramilitary force in the 1980s, Hurtado spent much of his early twenties hunting for members of the Maoist Shining Path organization, which took to hiding in the Peruvian Andes. In August 1985, Hurtado took part in an operation that killed many unarmed civilians. According to the Center for Justice and Accountability, the massacre occurred as follows:

> The attendees were told that any villager appearing in Quebrada de Huancayoc should be considered a communist terrorist. Then, on 14 August 1985, Lince 6 and Lince 7 entered Quebrada de Huancayoc. With Rivera Rondón's troops blocking a nearby escape route, Hurtado and his soldiers went house to house forcibly removing villagers from their homes. The villagers were beaten with the butts of weapons and kicked with the heels of soldiers' boots. They were lined-up single file and herded into houses of death, where Hurtado and his soldiers repeatedly shot ... family members, and then burned them alive amidst desperate screams for mercy. These acts were personally seen and heard by two 12-year old girls, Teófila Ochoa Lizarbe and Cirila Pulido Baldeón. In all, approximately 100 unarmed civilians were killed by the Army during the operation.[3]

Leaving the charred village, Hurtado sent a written report back to the Peruvian army command that his mission was complete. The company commander thought it best not to mention specific details regarding the victims' demise, in order to avoid future lawsuits. It wasn't until September of that year that two native eyewitnesses decided to come forward about the incident, and it took another two years before Hurtado was found guilty of his crime.

While he was sentenced to six years in jail, it's doubtful Hurdato spent any time behind bars; he was eventually pardoned by Alberto Fujimori, Bolivia's future president. In spite of this, Hurtado thought it best to join his other family members in Florida.

Fleeing to a small apartment block in Miami, he went on to live quite comfortably for the next 20 years, a deep embarrassment to both Florida and U.S. Immigration.

After enough clamor had been made and it became clear that a real international incident was about to occur, Hurtado was arrested on grounds of falsifying information on his visa application.

Pleading guilty to making false statements to the U.S. government and visa fraud, he was sentenced to six months in prison. Commented U.S. District Court Judge Joan Lenard: "The doors to the United States are not open to [foreign torture suspects]."[4]

A year later in 2007, Hurtado was brought before civil court where U.S. District Judge Adalberto Jordan ordered him to pay two of his former victims, one of them a now-grown Teofila. In his remarks he admitted criminal responsibility in the death of 31, however, he denied responsibility for the rest of those people being raped, beaten and burned alive.

Though extradited to Peru to face justice for his brutal past, former neighbors in the U-shaped apartment block that was his former home south of Surfside recall a different kind of character who was reserved and polite. As Marta Dominguez, a cleaner for the apartment complex where Hurtado lived, said, "I guess you never know."[5]

The Bandit of Wellington

America is a lot like Lenny from *Of Mice and Men*. It's not that we intentionally try to mess things up, it's just that our pet countries prove much too pretty to keep our hands off, often ending with broken necks and broken spirits. So it was in the '80s with the training of C.I.A.-sponsored assassins like Juan Hernández Lara.

In its quest to rid Central America of leftist insurgents, the C.I.A. hired a crack team of assassins during the Reagan administration, splitting them up into separate regimens. Among the deadliest was Battalion 3-16, of which Lara was a part.

Recruited as a young man, Lara quickly worked his way up to officer. His admittedly gruesome duties included shoving pins underneath victims' fingernails, firing bullets into people's hands, using plastic bags for smothering his victims and applying extensive electro-shock torture via their genitalia and nipples.

As Miguel Carias, one of the victims of these tortures later recounted: "They started with 110 volts ... then they went up to 220. Each time they shocked me, I could feel my body jump and my mouth filled with a metal taste."[6] Other tortures employed by Lara and his paramilitary cronies were later exposed by former victims in interviews. According to one tortured, the pain was so intense that it was not uncommon to beg for death. Former member Jose Valle described how some prisoners were made to stand naked with a basket tied to their testicles filled with rocks or corn during interrogation. Valle said that Argentinean instructors taught how to use "la capucha"—"The hood,"[7] a rubber mask that was pulled over a person's face to suffocate him. The torturers also recounted numerous examples of rape and assault on female detainees.

While the U.S., particularly the C.I.A., did not officially encourage the use of physical torture, Lara and his battalion were nonetheless provided the equipment, and the knowledge of its use was widespread among the Reagan administration. Women, men, and even young students were all targeted, and the use of electricity during such interrogation methods was paramount.

After the group's disbandment, Lara eventually made his way to Florida, purchasing a home in Wellington, an upper-class suburb on the edge of the Everglades. He was eventually deported back to Honduras in 2001 for making illegal sojourns to the United States, ironically arguing to the judge that his deportation would lead to his torture back home. As was reported in the *Los Angeles Times* at the time:

> After he returned to Honduras, he denied direct involvement in Battalion 316 and said he had been a foot soldier in a U.S.-backed operation in Honduras' Olancho province. A clash there resulted in the execution of nine prisoners and the disappearance of an American priest—and Negroponte [U.S. Deputy Secretary of State from 2007–2009] feared accounts of Honduran human rights violations would alarm Congress if reported. Lara was later posted as a guard at the 316 compound outside Tegucigalpa.
>
> After a fearful month in Honduras, Lara sneaked back into the United States. Another anonymous tip to IEM led to his arrest March 28. He is now being held in a Miami detention center pending trial for illegal reentry after deportation.[8]

To this day, it remains unknown exactly how many people were murdered by Lara and his dreaded battalion.

The Kaibiles Killer of Delray Beach

Most former exiles came to Florida seeking comfort and shelter from retribution. Gilberto Jordan, on the other hand, came to blend in, shunning comfort for modesty, in the hopes that he would not repeat the same mistakes of the past and draw attention to himself.

Reared as a soldier in Guatemala's national army, Jordan was recruited into the elite paramilitary force known as the Kaibiles shortly after his twenty-sixth birthday. These red-beret soldiers were notorious for their reckless treatment of the native peoples during the Guatemalan Civil War, leaving behind a wave of corpses in the process. One such incident highlighted their cruelty, forever changing the fate of an innocent village.

On December 20, 1982, Jordan's unit surrounded the unsuspecting town of Dos Erres and exacted a terrible revenge on the inhabitants. Accusing them of being communist sympathizers, Jordan grabbed a baby and chucked it "into a well"[9] to gain the villagers' acquiescence. Upon gaining their attention, Jordan and his twenty comrades proceeded to interrogate all of the men and "rape the women."[10] After this, he proceeded to massacre them one by one. In all, over 162 townspeople[11] were murdered, many with their heads smashed open with a hammer, and thrown down into a well. The event proved a watershed moment in Guatemala's already notorious civil war.

Fearing a war crime conviction following the conclusion of the conflict, Jordan fled to Florida, choosing a rather run-down section of Delray Beach in which to reside. He lived there in relative obscurity for a while before ultimately moving to other areas south of Delray.

In May of 2010, a full 10 years after the Guatemalan government gave official recognition to the Dos Erres massacre, Jordan was arrested by U.S. authorities for not disclosing the incident during his application process. After some interrogation, he later admitted to his part in murdering a baby, along with committing a number of other ghastly deeds.

> The Department of Justice's Human Rights and Special Prosecutions Section prosecuted this case and in July 2010 Jordan pled guilty, admitting that he had been a Kaibil in the Guatemalan military who participated in the massacre at Dos Erres. Jordan also admitted that the first person he killed at Dos Erres was a baby, whom he murdered by throwing in the village well. Jordan was sentenced in September 2010 to 10 years in federal prison and his citizenship was revoked.[12]

A Tropical Mussolini

Not all of Florida's gruesome retirees played such a direct role in the killing of their countrymen. Some just sat back and gave the orders. This is certainly true for Gerardo Machado, one of Cuba's first dictators.

Taking office in 1925, Machado entered the presidency as a democratically elected leader. His first term actually saw quite a bit of progress: he enlarged the University of Havana, built the Bacardi Building and embarked on a public works program.

> Machado's campaign for national regeneration initially received wide support. He taxed American capital investments, initiated the construction of a 700-mile (1,127 km) central highway and promoted investments in tourism, industry and mining. His image at the time was what many to this day recognize as the most important achievement for a Cuban politician; he combined a genuine support for U.S. interests while defending the idea of Cuban sovereignty.[13]

His second term, however, became far more despotic.

He created La Porra, a secret police force, and began opening gulagesque prisons in the countryside for political opponents. Such heavy-handed tactics were often used against university students, with communist dissident Julio Mella, being one of most high profile of the bunch.

Gerardo Machado was a Cuban dictator who consolidated all government control under his authority. His purchase of a villa and his retirement in Florida helped usher in a trend for future dictators to settle there (*Time Magazine*, 1931, via Wikimedia Commons).

After he was found murdered in Mexico while in exile, Mella's widow aired her suspicions that Machado was behind it. This combined with "the economic crisis that followed the extreme drops in sugar prices during the Wall Street crash of 1929, allowed for opposition against Machado to grow rapidly."[14]

Other political figures were also murdered during this time, apparently in retaliation and on Machado's orders, including three brothers: Representative Gonzalo Freyre de Andrade; Guillermo Freyre de Andrade, an attorney; and Leopoldo Freyre de Andrade, a sugar engineer opposed to Machado's plans for the sugar economy. Representative Miguel Angel Aguiar, who had participated in "the unsuccessful revolt against the Machado government in August 1931, was shot four times, but survived."[15]

Forced out in a coup d'état in 1933, Machado fled to Miami Beach, via the Bahamas, where he lived out the remainder of his days before dying of cancer. He is buried in Miami's Woodlawn Park Cemetery North. His former two-and-half-story Spanish-style mansion still stands in the Allapattah neighborhood of Miami at 1503 NW 26th St.[16]

Batista: The Mafia's President

If Machado brought modern dictatorship to Cuba, Fulgencio Batista perfected it. The hand behind the curtain after Machado's ouster, Batista called the shots in everything but name before bribing his way to power in 1940. "While greatly enriching himself, he also governed the country most effectively, expanding the educational system, sponsoring a huge program of public works, and fostering the growth of the economy."[17]

After his term ended in 1944, Batista traveled abroad and lived for a while in Florida, where he invested part of his earnings in real estate. During those eight years out of power, he made Daytona Beach his new home base.[18]

Becoming a favorite son of the community, Batista later un-retired, returning to Cuba in a U.S.-backed coup in 1952 to unseat a democratically elected president and position himself in power.

Expanding gambling operations, Batista ingratiated himself with both U.S. businessmen and Mafiosi, alike. As a result, Havana became the Latin Las Vegas, "boasting over 11,500 prostitutes in the capital, alone by the mid–1950s."[19]

With mafia interests growing in the booming casino industry, it was soon unclear whether it was Batista or mobsters, Lucky Luciano or Meyer Lansky, calling the shots:

Havana served as a hedonistic playground for the world's elite, producing huge gambling, prostitution, and drug profits for American Mafiosos, corrupt law-enforcement officials, and their politically elected cronies. Drugs, be it marijuana or cocaine, were so plentiful at the time that one American magazine, in a 1950 article, proclaimed: "Narcotics are hardly more difficult to obtain in Cuba than a shot of rum. And only slightly more expensive." In the grandiose hotels and casinos that lined Cuba's beaches, it was common to find U.S. narcotics officials and congressmen hobnobbing with the likes of underworld mastermind Meyer Lansky and crime boss Santo Trafficante Jr., both of whom oversaw the redevelopment of Cuba's lodging and casino industry with over $100 million in assistance from Batista.[20]

By late 1955, student riots and anti–Batista demonstrations had become frequent, and unemployment became a problem as graduates could no longer find work. In response, Batista ordered the closure of the University of Havana in 1956 and began to view young people with increasing suspicion. Purging students and officers, alike, his paranoia mounted as Castro began to launch a revolutionary movement in the countryside.

With a Castro victory assured by the end of 1958, Batista fled Havana on New Year's Day 1959, taking as much as "$700 million in cash and fine art with him."[21]

Denied asylum in the United States, Batista was unable to ever return to his beloved Daytona Beach, and later died in exile in Portugal in 1973. His Florida legacy, however, continues to live on through some of the confiscated artwork he brought over, as it laid the beginning for The Cuban Foundation Museum. As stated on their website:

> The Cuban Museum's primary goal is to give Cuban Americans a rare glimpse into their rich cultural heritage through artworks ranging from the Spanish Colonial period to modern times. MOAS endeavors to share these cultural treasures through The Cuban Foundation Museum with the general public in an attempt to foster a better understanding of Cuban history and tradition.[22]

Tachito Does Palm Island

When it comes to robbing one's country blind, Anastasio "Tachito" Somoza Debayle takes the cake!

Born into a family of dictators who had ruled over Nicaragua since 1936, it seemed Somoza was destined for a life of brutality from the outset. When, in 1967, his somewhat milder brother, Luis, died of a heart attack, Somoza was passed the reins of power, to deadly consequences. His leadership differed from his older brother's and marked a return to a harsher style of dictatorship. Somoza relied on military power and exercised no restraint in using public office for personal enrichment. He encouraged corruption and protected his officers from prosecution, developing a reputation as a human rights violator, and replaced his brother's skilled administrators with unqualified political allies. It was during these years Somoza became affiliated with Plasmaferesis, a company which collected blood plasma from among Nicaragua's poorest persons and up marketed its sale to the United States and Europe. According to *El Diario Nuevo* and *La Prensa*, "Every morning the homeless, drunks, and poor people went to sell half a liter of blood for 35 (Nicaraguan) cordobas."[23] Such a big stake in this plasma company made Somoza look past his people for the benefit of his own pocket, most notably after the Managua Earthquake of 1972, when Nicaragua suffered a severe plasma shortage due to his continued shipments to overseas markets.

By the time the mid–1970s rolled around, Somoza's corruption—and Managua's still ruined state—led to fiercer opposition from the pro-Marxist Sandinista rebels, ultimately forcing loyalists and close family to flee to other countries. On July 17, 1979, Somoza resigned from the presidency and fled to Miami. He took with him "the caskets of his father and brother and, it is claimed, much of Nicaragua's national treasure."[24] The country was left with over a billion dollars in debt upon his departure. After Somoza had fled, the Sandinistas "found less than $2 million in the national treasury."[25]

Denied asylum in the U.S. by President Carter, Somoza later took refuge in Paraguay, then under the rule of Alfredo Stroessner. Less than a year later in 1980, he was assassinated in Asunción by pro-Sandinista rebels.

While he may have been denied entry into the United States in 1979, there is quite a bit of evidence to his connections in the U.S., particularly in the tony suburb of Palm Island in Miami, where he purportedly owned a mansion and spent some time during his dictatorship. Today his legacy lives on in the state through such former real estate.

Prosper-*ing in South Florida Real Estate*

When it comes to Haitian dictators, two figures often come to mind: François Duvalier and his son Jean-Claude Duvalier, otherwise known as "Papa Doc" and "Baby Doc." These two figures wreaked havoc on both the economy and the Haitian people for 29 years, giving birth to the dreaded Tonton Macoute, which was authorized by the Duvaliers to commit violence and oppression against potential dissidents. Some of the most important members were Voodoo leaders, giving the Tonton Macoute a kind of spiritual authority over the populace.

When, in 1986, Baby Doc was forced out of power during a popular uprising, it seemed all would finally be put right in Haiti, with a transitional government coming into power. However, this was not to last, as Duvalier's loyalist and former advisor, Prosper Avril, would overthrow the government, instituting his own brand of terrorism in the form of a new secret police force.

Ruling with brute force, Avril threw the opposition into jail and publicly beat and shamed them. His "thugs beat Evans Paul, the democratically elected mayor of Port-au-Prince, and then paraded the bleeding and bruised politician on national television. Amnesty International says Avril's brief presidency was 'marred by gross human rights violations.'"[26]

While such oppression was bad enough, Avril also bankrupted his country, stealing hundreds of thousands of dollars to personally finance his loyalists and invest in property in Miami.

> In October 1988, "the Intelligent Prosper Avril," as Papa Doc called him, sank $200,000 into a handsome tan ranch home with a red-tiled roof on North Saint Andrews Drive, a winding suburban Miami Lakes road that rings a neatly trimmed golf course.[27]

A mere two months later he purchased a second ranch home nearly identical to the first.

Avril and his wife spent at least a year in the suburb until a civil lawsuit—brought by attorney Ira Kurzban and the Center for Constitutional Rights on behalf of abused opposition leaders—found him culpable of torture and murder. Paul Farmer, co-founder of Partners in Health, a non-profit public health organization that does work across Haiti, wrote:

> A US District Court ... found him personally responsible for enough "torture and cruel, inhuman or degrading treatment" to award six of his victims a total of $41 million in compensation.... Avril's repression was not subtle: three torture victims were paraded on national television with their faces grotesquely swollen, their limbs bruised and their clothing covered with blood. He suspended 37 articles of the constitution, and declared a state of siege.[28]

Fleeing back to Haiti, Avril was ultimately arrested at his home in 2001, but freed when the presidency of Jean-Bertrand Aristide was overthrown by a coup in 2004.

An Unwilling Resident

Most of the dictators and contract killers mentioned came to Florida willingly, either looking for property or for a place to hide their stolen income. In the case of Panamanian dictator Manuel Noriega, however, his arrival in Florida was anything but welcomed.

Looking back through time, it's hard to believe how quickly the tides turned on Noriega regarding his relationship with the U.S. government. First coming to prominence in 1969, immediately following a military coup of a populist president, Noriega was seen as an important ally of the Torrijos administration that had seized power.

Taking on the dirty work of the new government, Noriega was made Head of Intelligence where he launched a campaign against perceived enemies of the state that "resulted in the ouster and exile of over 1300 Panamanians."[29] As the simultaneous head of the secret police and immigration, Noriega was also responsible for the deaths of subversives, including a Roman Catholic priest, whom he had thrown from a helicopter at sea. Most of his work during this period was actively supported, if not outright encouraged, by the U.S. Government, including the CIA, which actually put him on the payroll in 1971 for anti–Communist intelligence.

While minor strains began to erupt between the U.S. and Noriega— especially after it was revealed that Noriega was supplying the Nicaraguan Sandinista rebels with weapons—it recovered somewhat in the early 1980s, when Noriega assumed de facto control of the country.

During this time, Noriega acted as a conduit for U.S. support, including funds and weapons, to the Contra rebels in Nicaragua. He allowed the CIA to establish listening posts in Panama, and also helped the U.S.-backed Salvadoran government against the leftist Salvadoran insurgent Farabundo Martí National Liberation Front. He also allowed U.S. spy ships to use bases in Panama in their operations against the Nicaraguan government, and allowed for intelligence gathered by these ships to be processed in those same bases, permitting such activities despite the Panama Canal treaties forbidding such uses. This relationship made him an invaluable ally to the Reagan administration, who even sent Vice President Bush to meet with him in 1983.

By the mid–1980s, however, Noriega's usefulness as an American asset began to increasingly be called into question. Cozying up to the Medellín cartel, Noriega amassed a personal fortune, laundering money and drugs into the United States through the Port of Miami. Such illicit affairs, coupled with a rising repression of political dissidents, the selling of intelligence to U.S. enemies, and the harassment and murder of U.S. soldiers in the country, eventually led to an all-out invasion on December 20, 1989, by 13,000 U.S. Marines (in addition to 12,000 already present),[30] resulting in Noriega's capture from the Vatican Embassy 13 days later.[31]

Extradited back to Miami, Noriega was hauled before a U.S. court to account for his activities in the drug trade. As was written in a 1990 article:

Manuel Antonio Noriega, last month the invincible leader of Panama, now a humbled defendant in Miami, stood before an American judge Thursday and was formally charged with being a narcotics racketeer.

Afterward, the nation's most prominent prisoner of the war on drugs was taken to his new residence: a jail cell at an undisclosed Miami location. The man who so recently fashioned himself as Panama's "Maximum Leader" now is known as federal prisoner No. 41586.

The ousted head of state, still wearing his military uniform and his military poise and discipline, appeared before U.S. District Judge William Hoeveler late Thursday afternoon but refused to enter a plea or acknowledge the court's right to try him.

Noriega is accused, among other things, of earning $4.6 million by conspiring with Colombia's vicious Medellin Cartel to ship cocaine through Panama to the streets of the United States.

"Gen. Noriega is here today under protest," said attorney Frank Rubino.[32]

Receiving a 40-year sentence, Noriega ultimately served 17 of those years in a relatively luxurious, two-room prison suite. He was then extradited to France for similar crimes in 2010, over the objections of the U.S. District Court of South Florida, where he remained for another two years before being extradited back to Panama. He later died thereat the age of 83 following a botched surgery resulting in a brain hemorrhage.

A Place For All Kinds

Florida's unique position as the southernmost state with the longest contiguous coastline in the continental United States makes it an ideal spot for all kinds, particularly dictators. Easily accessible from much of the Caribbean and Latin America, it shares a kindred culture and history, as well as a tropical climate. Combine

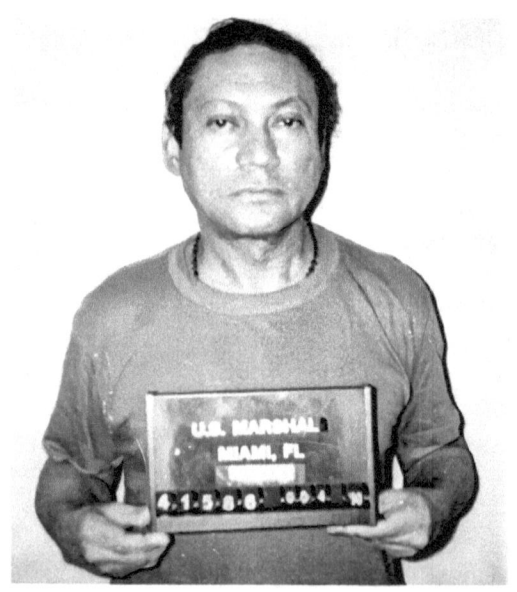

Manuel Noriega was a double agent who acted as the reigning power in Panama. After a U.S. invasion in 1989, he was extradited back to Miami and hauled before a U.S. court to account for his activities in the drug trade (U.S. Marshals Service).

13. Retirees of a Different Kind 211

that with a more affordable real estate market than California or New York, a plethora of gated communities, a large population of Spanish and French speakers, a high respect for privacy, and no income tax, and you have a recipe for a state where you can live out the rest of your days in relative comfort and style. It's no wonder that of any other place in North America, Florida continues to remain the draw for retirees of all kinds: even Latin American dictators looking to escape a sketchy past.

14

Towns Like No Other
Florida's "New" Urbanism

As a relatively new state, Florida had the benefit of experimentation. Undeveloped for much of the nineteenth century, the Sunshine State's millions of open acreage proved tempting for many developers like Flagler and Plant, who went on to fuel the building of new cities along the rail lines. It also led to the founding of new communities with like-minded settlers, such as Cassadaga, a city built in 1895, which later became a haven for psychics and mediums. While most of these cities followed organic settlement patterns, which waxed or waned along economic and technological boom and busts, a new breed of community was born in the late twentieth century, taking firm hold in the state by the early 2000s.

While this new type of community utilized tried and true building practices from the past, its pattern of development proved to be anything but organic, leading to consequences far beyond the imaginations of their founders. These consequences would play out time and again on the national scene, leading many to wonder whether these new kinds of communities were truly groundbreaking, or merely band-aids to cover up the ailments of what was happening in the rest of the world.

A New Community Takes Root

Ever see the movie *The Truman Show*? Even if you're not entirely familiar with all aspects of the plot, chances are you know the basics. It goes something like this: Truman, played by Jim Carey, slowly discovers that life as he knows it is all part of a script—a reality show—which millions across the world watch for entertainment. As such, everyone, from his colleagues to his friends to even his wife, are manipulated at the behest of a director and production team to create drama and sell products. Heck,

14. Towns Like No Other

even his city is artificial, with entire perfectly manicured blocks filled with shops, housing and offices that are all part of a set to further the illusion of reality. The irony of the movie, however, is none of this world is staged. All these picture-perfect houses and manicured streets are in fact part of a carefully planned city on the Gulf Coast of Florida called Seaside. Seaside co-founders Robert and Daryl Davis wanted the community to include homes that were based on a Northwest Florida building tradition—small, wood-framed cottages that were well adapted to the oceanside climate.

> When Robert and Daryl Davis asked Miami architects Andres Duany and Elizabeth Plater-Zyberk to help him [Robert] plan a community which would revive the tradition which had produced these buildings, it was soon clear that considerable research needed to be done. No one knew how to revive a building tradition. So a number of journeys were made through the South, and especially through Florida, with cameras and sketch pads and tape measures....
> Most of the buildings were studied in the context of small towns, and gradually the idea evolved that the small town was the appropriate model to use in thinking about laying out streets and squares and locating the various elements of the community.[1]

Utilizing 80 acres[2] of land near Seagrove Beach, Davis designed a town that would be laid out in a neatly defined radiating street pattern, where every day needs such as shopping, entertainment and work could be accomplished on foot. Testing the market with a couple of homes the following year, Davis found that there was a huge demand for these kinds of houses and continued on with his plan, codifying everything from style to street setback and even the kinds of shrubbery used.

Finally completed in 1985, "modern Seaside features over 423 residences, 42 specialty retail shops and 12 restaurants and eateries,"[3] all within walking and biking distance of area neighborhoods. While much of this may seem like a success on the surface, Davis' vision for an authentic community never materialized, however, as the full-time population never materialized to more than 200 residents, with the rest of the homes being used primarily for renters.

To add to this distorted dream, Seaside soon became discovered by spring breakers, leading to a whole host of problems in the early 2020s as teens took to vandalizing shops, drinking on the beach and getting into fights, most of which ended up on social media:

> "It sounds like the purge at night. There are kids running and screaming and yelling.... It's out of control," Resident Rene Campe said....
> "You know there could be 100 or 200 each group or whatever," [Walton County Sheriff's] Captain Robert Gray said.[4]

Things have gotten so out of hand that people are now encouraged to avoid setting foot in Seaside anytime in the months of March and April. In the spring of 2022, in a bid to quell some of these incidents, town council members passed a curfew for those under 21—a first for the Gulf enclave. However, it remains to be seen whether this curfew will have any lasting effect.

A Reason for Celebration

While Davis' vision didn't turn out exactly as anticipated, his ideas nonetheless gained traction, giving birth to a new movement of community planning called "New Urbanism," and while other Gulf communities similar in style to Seaside would pop up including Alys Beach and Rosemary Beach, it would be a Central Florida community called Celebration that would seize the spotlight.

Disney Designs a Town

When most of us think of EPCOT at Walt Disney World, we think of things like Spaceship Earth (the iconic golf ball-shaped structure), the world showcase where you can experience the cultures and food of 11 different nations, and space simulators. But did you know that was not its original intent? Contrary to popular belief, EPCOT was not conceived as an amusement park, but rather as a master planned city built entirely on utopian and futurist principles. In fact, the name EPCOT is an acronym for Experimental Prototype Community of Tomorrow. In Walt Disney's words:

> "EPCOT will take its cue from the new ideas and new technologies that are now emerging from the creative centers of American industry. It will be a community of tomorrow that will never be completed but will always be introducing and testing and demonstrating new materials and new systems. And EPCOT will always be a showcase to the world of the ingenuity and imagination of American free enterprise."[5]

As outlined in his designs, Walt Disney's original vision for EPCOT was for a model community that would have been home to twenty thousand residents and "a test bed for city planning as well as organization." It was to have been built "in the shape of a circle, with businesses and commercial areas at its center, community buildings and schools and recreational complexes around it, and residential neighborhoods along the

14. Towns Like No Other

EPCOT was conceived by Walt Disney in the 1960s to be a planned city. His original vision was for a model community that would have been home to twenty thousand residents. A test bed for city planning as well as organization, it was to have been built in the shape of a circle with businesses and commercial areas at its center, community buildings, schools, and recreational complexes around those, and residential neighborhoods lining the perimeter (photograph by leamericanos, May 26, 2007, CC BY-SA 3.0, Wikimedia Commons).

perimeter." This radial plan concept was strongly influenced by British planner Ebenezer Howard and his *Garden Cities of To-morrow*. "Transportation would have been provided by monorails and PeopleMovers (like the one in Magic Kingdom's Tomorrowland). Automobile traffic would be kept underground, leaving pedestrians safe above ground."[6]

Denied the permit and funding to construct such a place until he completed the Magic Kingdom, Disney died before his vision could be realized. While some aspects such as the monorail and the futuristic geodesic sphere, Spaceship Earth, were constructed by successive Disney planners, the idea of a community completely funded and controlled by Disney was ultimately scrapped instead for an amusement park.

A mere decade later, however, another opportunity would once again present itself.

On the Edge of Celebration

Eyeing the success of communities like Seaside and Rosemary Beach on the Gulf Coast, the Disney Development Company came to form the Celebration Company in the early 1990s, investing almost $3 billion to fund a community on the edge of its park in a piece of land given to Disney by the Florida Legislature.

Designed and governed under the principles of New Urbanism, all homes would be low density and built according to popular early twentieth-century designs with strict covenants enforced. Everything from street signs, retail signage, manhole covers, fountains, golf course graphics and park trail markers would be codified, with little wiggle room for deviation. The sales brochure summed up the community in the following way:

> There once was a place where neighbours greeted neighbours in the quiet of summer twilight. Where children chased fireflies. And porch swings provided easy refuge from the cares of the day. The movie house showed cartoons on Saturday. The grocery store delivered. And there was one teacher who always knew you had that special something. Remember that place?[7]

Separated into a series of walkable villages, which surrounded a brick-paved community center of faux Victorian embellishments, Disney leaders attempted to amend the mistakes of previous New Urbanist developments by specifically encouraging economic and ethnic diversity among its residents. The company placed advertisements in newspapers and magazines that catered to Black and Hispanic demographics, printed brochures featuring racial minorities, and "hired African-American workers in the community's sales office."[8] In addition, "the owners of the first 350 houses and 123 apartments were chosen by a lottery in an effort to prevent racial discrimination against homebuyers."[9] While these efforts ultimately failed, their attempts at inclusion were applauded at the time, with Celebration even being named "New Community of the Year" by the Urban Land Institute in 2001.

While Celebration quickly grew by leaps and bounds with many of the homes being snatched up by people seeking a refuge from high crime areas, the overt social engineering aspect of the Disney Corporation led to some notoriety, particularly among pop artists, the most damning of which came from Chumbawamba's WYSIWYG album in an aptly titled song "Celebration Florida." The song achieved some mild success and was praised in alternative magazines for its strong stance against overt commercialization and homogenization.

Murder and Mayhem in Florida's "Mayberry"

For a time, it appeared that Celebration was truly visualizing the intent that Walt Disney had laid out. Though the architecture was more nostalgic than he would have liked, the very fact that "the community swelled to a 2010 population of 7,400, and had a crime rate 64% lower than the national average,"[10] proved that the Disney was on to something. In fact, when Disney held a lottery for the first 474 homes, they had 5,000 people apply.[11] It appeared, at least for a while, that it was indeed possible to turn back the clocks and that the good times would last forever.

> Then winter came and a chill wind blew. People lost their jobs, families foreclosed on their homes. One morning you woke up and turned to greet your neighbours but found they had gone. The movie house closed.[12]
>
> The cracks in Celebration's utopian façade had been evident for years: there were major segregation issues; the school, which didn't assign homework, grades, or even books, was losing students by the dozens; the recession had bankrupted local businesses and pushed homes to foreclosure.[13]

As more people woke up to the realities of the Great Recession, things began to take a nasty turn. The first of such occurred on Thanksgiving weekend 2010, when Boston native Matteo Patrick Giovanditto was found murdered in his Celebration condo. The murder sent shockwaves through the community and the world. It was Celebration's first recorded homicide. Though the circumstances of the murder were strange in and of themselves, with a homeless transient, David-Israel Zenon Murillo, eventually confessing to the crime, it was the brutality of the murder along with what led to the murder that proved intriguing. For according to Murillo, it was Giovanditto who brought the murder upon himself after luring Murillo to his residence, ostensibly for a chore,[14] but with the secret intention of drugging him with a beer in order to sexually assault him. Bludgeoning Giovanditto with a hatchet before strangling him with a shoelace,[15] it was later discovered by authorities investigating the crime scene that Giovanditto, a retired teacher, had a questionable history with pedophilia,[16] resulting in a long list of accusers stepping forward.

While Giovanditto's murder was the first of its kind in the seemingly idyllic community, it was hardly the last, as former physical therapist Anthony Todt, 46, was later found guilty of murdering his wife, three children and his family dog:

> The chilling murders came to light on Jan. 13, 2020, when FBI agents and Osceola County deputies knocked on the door of Todt's house ... to serve a federal warrant for health care fraud charges stemming from his physical therapy business.

While they were there, they found Todt inside the house along with the decomposing bodies of his wife, Megan Todt, 42; their 13-year-old son, Alek; their 11-year-old son, Tyler; their youngest child, Zoe; and their dog, Breezy.[17]

In video confessions, Todt, who was suffering major debts, had spoken with his wife about killing his family in order to avoid the coming apocalypse. Todt told detectives he sat on his daughter's bed for hours before he ultimately suffocated her with a pillow.[18] When everyone was dead, he took all of their bodies and "placed them all into the master bedroom."[19]

By the time police arrived Todt had been living with the bodies for weeks. As one of Celebration's real estate agents later reflected: "The people that live here, we're not immune. We have foreclosures, we have divorces. This is still America, even if we do live in a town built by Disney."[20]

Civil Suits

While murder was slowly rotting away at the town's clean image, real life rot was also beginning to take a toll on the city's foundation—quite literally.

When, in 2004, Disney completely divested from Celebration, it sold to a company called Lexin Capital run by New York developer Metin Negrin. Establishing something called the Town Center Foundation—a master association meant to oversee the entire downtown—Negrin acquired 21 buildings in the heart of the community, including a mix of commercial and residential properties. Lexin then converted all the apartments into condos and sold them for premium property. While everything seemed to go well at first, minor repair issues started to arise that eventually turned into a torrent of complaints, resulting in Town Center residents suing Lexin for $15 to $20 million,[21] claiming a steep neglect in maintenance:

> In a transcript of a town meeting submitted to the court, one resident, an asthmatic, described thick black mold stretching from the ceiling to floor of his closet. His staircase had grown so rickety it had to be closed off. Another complained that, after reporting a leak for six straight years, his condo had become "uninhabitable."[22]

For his part, Negrin argued that Disney failed to fully disclose the integrity of many of the structures at the time of purchase arguing that many of their building designs were not up to code, encouraging the growth of mold and rot. "No amount of maintenance could have avoided these kinds of issues because it wasn't built properly. We feel we are victims here too," he said.[23]

Negrin soon became angered with the way residents attacked him.

"They're harassing my team every day. They're cursing them," Mr. Negrin said of the residents. "It's easy to ask for everything new when you're not paying for it." He said the condo association has shirked its responsibility over the years to pay its dues for upkeep of the buildings, demanding he do all of the work.[24]

While Disney still retains some aesthetic input on the town, particularly when it comes to overseeing paint colors, roof tiles and the style of front porches, they have very little sway anymore on the maintenance of their former properties. Now, as blue tarps become an increasing sight in the community, one must wonder whether Disney's dream has turned into a nightmare.

A Catholic Town Takes Root

Remember the town in the movie *Footloose* where dancing was forbidden because of an interpretation of Biblical passages? What if that town actually existed in reality? Well, it turns out there is such a place. Welcome to Ave Maria, Florida, the Sunshine State's very own Vatican City.

Founded by Disney in the 1990s, Celebration was conceived as a slice of Americana in the heart of Florida. As time went on, however, its picture-perfect foundations began to crumble figuratively and literally with high profile murders and derelict infrastructure dominating headlines (photograph by www.traveljunction.com, January 6, 2010, CC BY 2.00, Wikimedia Commons).

Religious enclaves in America are nothing new. Examples of such can be found throughout history from the colonies of the Pilgrims in Massachusetts to the Amish and even the Mormons, all with their idiosyncrasies. But all of these pale in comparison to the strangeness that is Ave Maria.

Built in 2005, a little over a decade after Disney's Imagineers were realizing a slice of Americana in the heart of central Florida, Ave Maria first came about as a dream of Tom Monaghan, the founder of Domino's Pizza. A devout Catholic who had found religion while growing up in an orphanage, Monaghan served as chancellor of Ave Maria College, a liberal arts school in Michigan espousing Catholic values. When the town denied permits to grow the campus, he began scouting new locations in the south of Florida near Naples, catching the eye of the Barron Collier Company, a diversified corporation controlled by the founding family of Collier County:

> The company approached Mr. Monaghan with an offer: If Ave Maria University would locate to land Barron Collier wished to develop outside Naples, the company would give the university 1,000 acres and build a town around the university.[25]

To hammer home the Catholic nature of the community, Monaghan forbid pornography, birth control and all X-Rated shows from within town limits. He also had community builders construct a large oratory featuring a 30-foot relief of the Annunciation in the heart of the city—the only privately owned Catholic church in the country. Such a place of prominence no doubt evokes images of old New England town greens, with their white-washed churches.

Today, the city maintains a private, parochial K-12 school in addition to the university, which has swelled to over 1100 students.

> Most of the people in Ave Maria are retired, work at Ave Maria University or commute to jobs in Naples, 45 minutes away. The community is surrounded by small towns with starkly contrasting demographics. Its nearest neighbor is Immokalee, a poor community of about 20,000 people, most of them Hispanic. It stands in stark contrast to Ave Maria, yet underscores how faith and religion are a thread that unites people of divergent backgrounds.[26]

While the community is now listed among the 25 top-selling master planned communities in the country, it is not without its controversies, mainly stemming from the amount of influence that Monaghan and Barron Collier have over the town's residents.

> [T]he Town of Ave Maria, Florida, is not your normal town primarily because Tom Monaghan and his developers lobbied, and got, the Florida State

Legislature to pass a law that Monaghan wrote, which allows him and his developer to govern the entire town forever....

The law Monaghan wrote, that Florida State Legislators passed and Gov. Jeb Bush signed, turns the town from a normal town, with a mayor etc., to a "Special Interest" town whereby the landowners have zero say in the laws Tom Monaghan enacts.[27]

To further this strangeness, people who challenge the status quo in the community have often faced ostracism from the townspeople. Take the case of Marielena Stuart, a devoted Catholic who purchased her Spanish-style villa in 2007. When she arrived, several things seemed off about the community, including the semi-permanent shuttering of the town's oratory:

> On her first Sunday in Ave Maria, she tried taking her preschooler son and teenage daughter to mass at the church in the center of town. It was locked—the result of a battle between Monaghan and the bishop of the Diocese of Venice, Frank Dewane. Monaghan had built himself a church; now he wanted to name his own pastor. The bishop refused to let him. The building had been largely unused for a year. "The only times they would open it was for tours or concerts," Stuart says. "And that was so people could donate money."[28]

Ave Maria was founded by Domino's CEO, Tom Monaghan, a devout Catholic, who sought to create a community centered on Catholicism. This experiment has had mixed success, however, as the increasingly popular community has been plagued by allegations of homophobia, fascism and xenophobia (photograph Fr. James Bradley, May 16, 2015, CC BY 2.00, Wikimedia Commons).

Another shock came when Stuart received a $1,287 bill to be paid to the Ave Maria Stewardship Community District.[29]

She later learned essentially the Ave Maria Stewardship Community District allowed Monaghan and Barron Collier to control the town in perpetuity as the city's largest landowners. When she raised concerns about this lack of local control at a town meeting, she was publicly barred from stepping foot on the university and suffered public ridicule in the paper. "What's going on here isn't Catholicism," she said. "This town is built around the idiosyncrasies of one man: Tom Monaghan. It's madness."[30] As she went on to state, she soon became barred from any town events.

While Stuart learned the lesson the hard way regarding the way dissent was approached in Ave Maria, she was hardly the first. When one university employee, Katherine Ernsting, alerted authorities of potentially fraudulent activities in the financial aid department, she was hounded into submission. "The whole thing was kind of a nightmare for me," says Ernsting, who nearly went bankrupt because Monaghan's lawyers delayed the trial for five years.[31]

Though the community was founded and has been run as a religious sanctuary for conservative Catholics, there is evidence that things are beginning to change. The town now boasts a number of non-Catholics, including several Gay couples, attracted by the town's affordability.

> "In the beginning, everyone came here for the Catholic community, because we wanted it to be central to daily life," said Ave Maria resident, Dan Dix. "Now people are moving here just for inexpensive housing. Many are Latinos from Miami, and it's kind of nice, because most are culturally Catholic."[32]

The foundation of the community is still centered on Catholic teaching, however, and as a result, Ave Maria still boasts no pharmacy due to its covenant against birth control.

A New City Comes to Grips with the Past

While many of the aforementioned communities were built utilizing urban designs from the past, few if any had real history to draw from. This was not the case for the community of Haile Plantation, however, which dealt with the very real legacy of a past most would soon rather forget.

Begun in the early 1970s, the New Urbanism community of Haile Plantation in Gainesville, Florida, was conceived by the Fleeman Family, Robert B. Kramer and Matthew Kaskel. Like other community developers before them, the founders of Haile Plantation in Southwest Gainesville shied away from designing the typical suburban neighborhood, opting instead for a special place featuring miles of walking and biking trails, swaths of greenspace, and a village center of residences, retail shops and restaurants. Located a mere 10 miles from UF Health Shands Hospital and the flagship campus for the University of Florida, this master planned community quickly grew to over 2,000 homes, featuring two separate subdivisions. Today, it retains a UF Health Clinic and a Publix, along with multiple businesses and shops.

While life in Haile Plantation avoided many of the snafus encountered in the previously highlighted communities, a noted instance of national debate emerged in the summer of 2020, mainly regarding the city's namesake.

Fresh off the massive protests occurring in the wake of the death of George Floyd, many places across the country began reexamining their ties to troublesome figures and uncomfortable periods of history. It was during this period that Haile Plantation's namesake came to light, as it was built over the site of an 1852 plantation owned by the Haile family.

While it's true that the site of the community does indeed stand on historic land once belonging to the Haile family, the fact that the word "plantation" was used to sell property rubbed some people the wrong way. This exploded in a very big way when an opinion piece published by Haile resident Yelena Moroz Alpert made its way online:

> Any other summer, this University of Florida college town would be buzzing with talk of whether the Gators will win the Southeastern Conference title. But with the revival of the Black Lives Matter movement, I can't ignore that the name of my predominantly White neighborhood invokes a dark history....
>
> It's easy to ask of someone like me: Well, if you don't like it, why are *you* living there? Yes, I could move to another neighborhood, but I also want to make this neighborhood, and neighborhoods like it, live up to their promise of true community.
>
> We cannot move forward and teach our kids about diversity and inclusion if we are pushed out by bullies who say things like, "Deal with it or move up North where all the riots are."[33]

After being picked up by CNN, the piece ignited a firestorm in the community and debate raged whether to change the name. Residents quickly turned on each other, with many espousing opposing views:

> "If you change the name, they might not know it was a plantation and be able to find the resources to learn that is where their ancestors were enslaved...."
>
> "It was really disheartening to see that people just didn't know history," Kirkman said. "There are people now who are disturbed by the word 'plantation' and I'm sitting there thinking 'When you closed on your house, you didn't notice the word and think about whether that was a real plantation?"[34]

By early fall, an exploratory committee was formed to see about changing the name. Some discussed scrapping it altogether, while others still talked about keeping it, and at the same time raising funds to build a monument to highlight the slaves who had worked the land. In the end, residents were polled resulting in the name remaining in place:

> The results included 708 responses out of a possible 1,567 homeowners. 61% (432) were not in favor of changing the name.... Based on the results of the survey, the Board voted (7-0) to not move forward with a ballot.[35]

While this controversy proved deeply polarizing for residents in the neighborhood, it would only be a harbinger of things to come for all of the Sunshine State, as it grappled with the final years of the 2010s.

New Communities Same Problems

There's no doubt that Florida has been a pioneer in the concept of New Urbanism, not only in the state, but across the country. What began as one man's dream to reacquaint himself with memories of his childhood vacation turned into a movement that has helped shape the development of hundreds of master-planned communities in nearly every state. While such communities have successfully attracted residents, many suffer from the very woes the developers sought to shield them from, with results ranging from the tragic to the utterly bizarre.

15

Demagoguery, Disease and Division
Florida in the Age of DeSantis

A funny thing happened in the years between 2000 and the present—Florida began to trend. Long the butt of retiree jokes—a mantle increasingly being taken over by the likes of Arizona—Florida began to come into its own in the decades to follow.

Emerging from the Great Recession bruised but not slain, it not only continued to attract newcomers to its shores, but actually became one of the fastest growing states in the country, so much so that by 2020, it surpassed New York to become the third-largest state in the country by population. This is incredible given the nearly 5 million person deficit these states had between them just 30 years prior in 1990!

As Florida's population boomed, so too did its influence. The outsized importance of the Sunshine State is now no longer a matter of regional influence, but one of national significance. Such prominence is slowly eclipsing the clout once enjoyed by older, more settled states like New York and Pennsylvania, resulting in an era where Florida not only drives the conversation of the country, but dictates it.

A Decade of Chaos

No one today refutes the enormity that the 2016 U.S. presidential election played on our national psyche. Coming off an already tumultuous twelve years, which saw the Iraq War, the Great Recession, Occupy Wall Street protests, race riots, and increased political infighting, polarization between the two parties had reached catastrophic levels. The campaign between Hillary Clinton and Donald Trump was unlike any other since 1860 and Americans for the first time began cutting each other off based purely on political preference. When Trump won on election night, carrying the State of Florida, along with the swing states of Michigan, Pennsylvania, and Wisconsin, many were shocked and pondered what the future would hold. Little did they know that the polarization, which had cemented so much during the previous two administrations, was about to get so much worse.

DeSantis Rising

During the 2018 midterms, America was at a crossroads. Having just come off two years of majority Republican rule, many were ready to try a divided government once again, handing Democrats in many states a path back to power. Florida, however, bucked this trend, choosing instead to elect a relatively unknown congressman to the office of governor.

After announcing his desire to compete for the top job in Tallahassee, Ron DeSantis, a native of Jacksonville, wasted no time declaring his loyalties to Trump. During the Republican primary, DeSantis emphasized his support for Trump by running an ad in which DeSantis taught his children how to "build the wall" and say "Make America Great Again" and dressed one of his children in a red "Make America

Elected in a nailbiter against Democratic challenger Andrew Gillum in 2018, Ron DeSantis has since risen to become one of the most influential politicians in Florida history. His bouts against other governors, and his foray into the nation's culture wars also set him up to run for president in 2024. Ultimately, he was unsuccessful in winning the Republican party's nomination in that contest [TW1](Official portrait, November 6, 2019, State of Florida).

Great Again" jumper.¹ Asked if he could name an issue where he disagreed with Trump, DeSantis did not identify a single one.

Defeating his primary opponents, DeSantis began to craft a platform that appealed directly to rural Floridians. His gubernatorial platform included support for legislation that would allow people with concealed weapons permits to carry firearms openly. He also supported a law mandating the use of E-Verify by businesses and a promise to place a state-level ban on sanctuary city protections for undocumented immigrants.

Running against Democrat Andrew Gillum, a former mayor of Tallahassee who was widely viewed as a Far Left Progressive, the race was pitted by many in the media to be a battle for the soul of Florida. While "election night tallies were close, decided by roughly 34,000 votes out of over 8 million cast,"² DeSantis walked away with the top job, sealing Florida's political fate.

Redefining Florida

DeSantis wasted no time setting himself apart from his predecessor, Rick Scott. In his first year, he reversed a lot of decisions from the former governor, taking a surprisingly active role on the environment. Among his accomplishments, DeSantis:

- Called for the resignations of, and later replaced, the entire South Florida Water Management District board….
- He OK'd $2.5 billion in spending for water quality and Everglades restoration work.
- He appointed two new environmental-related positions—a chief science officer and a chief resiliency officer.
- In one more environmentally friendly act, DeSantis created blue-green algae and red tide task forces.³

On issues of race, DeSantis even reached across the aisle on occasion, pardoning the Groveland Four, a group of Black men falsely accused of raping a 17-year-old and assaulting her husband in 1949. This was something previous governors, including Scott, were unwilling to take on. In addition, he agreed with lawmakers that felons should pay all fines and restitution before regaining voting rights. He also favored non-violent offenders serving on juries and being allowed to run for office.

While all of these things helped soften his image, DeSantis remained in lockstep with Trump on broader policy issues, angering many Democrats in the state. This was most noted in his appointment of new judges. During his first two weeks in office, "DeSantis appointed Barbara Lagoa, Robert J. Luck and Carlos G. Muñiz to fill three vacancies on the

Florida Supreme Court, shifting the court from a liberal to a conservative majority."[4]

While Florida had long been considered a purple state with neither a conservative nor liberal majority, it appeared by the end of his first year in office that changes were in the works. A Mason-Dixon poll released at the end of 2019 showed DeSantis received high marks even among Democrats:

> The poll showed that 65 percent of those surveyed approve of the job he's doing versus just 26 percent who disapprove. Brad Coker, managing director for Mason-Dixon Polling and Strategy, noted that the Republican governor is getting good marks across the state even in Democratic strongholds such as South Florida.[5]

By the start of 2020, things looked bright indeed for DeSantis, but just like the rest of the world, things were about turn upside down.

Along Came Covid

Few could predict in January 2020 the impact that Covid-19 would have on the world. Concerned more about potential conflict with Iran, rather than a disease that was causing cities to lockdown in China, many here didn't even think about it. Then, like a bolt from the blue, it arrived on our shores.

Detected first in California, the virus swept across the country, until becoming contracted by Patient Zero in New York City. The novel virus, for which the population had little to no natural immunity, spread quickly to all 50 states. By March 12, diagnosed cases had reached 1,000 and four days later the White House was advising everyone to avoid crowds of ten or more people. By mid–March, almost every state had enacted stay-at-home quarantines in a bid to quell the spread, grinding the country's economy to a halt—almost every state, that is, except Florida.

Waiting until April, Governor DeSantis reluctantly imposed a stay-at-home order, roughly two weeks after 42 other states had enacted some kind of ban on gatherings, leaving Florida, the most populous of the states left, the last to do so. As was reported April 1, 2020, in the *Washington Post*:

> Florida had been the only one not under a statewide "stay-at-home" order. DeSantis has until now urged people in Southeast Florida to remain at home and said this week he would issue a "safer at home" order codifying that advice.
>
> Even Tuesday, DeSantis said at a news conference that he had no plans to issue a statewide order because the White House had not told him to do so.[6]

15. Demagoguery, Disease and Division

Florida was an epicenter of Covid-19 early in the pandemic. Pictured here is a drive-thru vaccination site in The Villages, early 2021 (photograph by Whoisjohngalt, February 7, 2021, CC BY-SA 4.0, Wikimedia Commons).

DeSantis' approach to the pandemic won him derision across the board from other state executives, but earned him extensive praise from Donald Trump who called him a "great Governor."[7] Contradicting his own head of CDC, Trump praised the patchwork approach DeSantis had imposed in March, which allowed local hotspots the authority to contain the virus while ridiculing the harsher measures implemented by other states. Such measures, however, seemed to make the situation that much worse as cases spread rapidly:

> Weeks before Florida ordered people to stay at home, the coronavirus was well into its insidious spread in the state, infecting residents and visitors who days earlier had danced at beach parties and reveled in theme parks. Only now, as people have gotten sick and recovered from—or succumbed to—Covid-19, the disease caused by the coronavirus, has the costly toll of keeping Florida open during the spring break season started to become apparent.[8]

Just days after returning from parties such as the Winter Party Festival, which occurred in Fort Lauderdale on March 11, at a time when the largest states were imposing travel bans, people began spreading Covid-19 at unprecedented rates. Soon, fresh outbreaks directly attributed to the Winter Party Festival were popping up in places like Massachusetts and California, leading many to criticize Governor DeSantis for not taking action to clamp down on tourism.

> The first festivalgoer to die was Israel Carrera, a 40-year-old Lyft and Uber driver who spent several days in the hospital in Miami Beach before his death on March 26. His boyfriend, who also attended, got mildly sick and is now making plans to deliver Mr. Carrera's ashes to his surviving family in Cuba.
>
> Ron Rich, a 65-year-old festival volunteer, died over the weekend of March 28.[9]

By the end of March, Florida had surpassed every other state for coronavirus infections. This trend continued unabated in spite of restrictions enacted by Governor DeSantis the following month to screen those entering the state from New Orleans and New York for mandatory quarantines. As was reported in the *Tampa Bay Times* in December of 2020:

> Over the summer, Florida shattered national records when it recorded more than 15,000 cases in one day. Since then, only California and Texas have reported higher single-day increases.
> On Wednesday about 166,000 tests were processed, resulting in a daily positivity rate of 11.57 percent, according to state data which is updated and reported every 24 hours.
> "The number we're getting now is probably an underestimate of the disease," said Dr. Marissa Levine, a professor of public health and family medicine at the University of South Florida.[10]

By the end of 2020, Florida once again broke single day records with 17,500 new cases, cementing the fears that the state was becoming the epicenter of the virus.

DeSantis' Swedish Model

In spite of cases increasingly mounting, DeSantis stayed the course and quickly instigated a model based on one utilized by the Swedish government. In contrast to other nations which had instituted strict lockdowns and legal restrictions, the Swedish public was instead encouraged to follow a series of non-voluntary recommendations from the Public Health Agency of Sweden. These included working from home where possible, limiting travel within the country, social distancing, and for people above 70 and those with potential COVID-19 symptoms to self-isolate. Changes were also made to sick leave. Primary schools remained open throughout the pandemic, and face masks were not generally recommended for the public or in healthcare settings. While their model placed a strain on the healthcare system, "reaching 99% of intensive care bed occupancy by mid–December 2020,"[11] their mortality rate—while higher than surrounding Nordic countries—actually remained far below that of other nations imposing more reaching lockdowns. Furthermore, their economic contraction, while significant, paled in comparison to their neighbors.

Sensing the seemingly successful nature of Sweden's approach, DeSantis employed the system in the Sunshine State, officially reopening Florida's beaches, and the economy to the public on April 17, a mere two weeks after an imposed lockdown. The reopening triggered a wave of people visiting the shore, igniting fresh controversy. This controversy blew

15. Demagoguery, Disease and Division   231

up in a big way when Rebekah Jones was terminated from her role in the Florida Department of Health in May 2020. According to Jones, who was assigned to lead a group of scientists tracking Covid-19 data in the state, she was pressured by DeSantis to manipulate or change the data to support the Governor's position to keep the state open.

> In her email [to colleagues announcing her departure] … Jones said the management of the dashboard—which initially earned widespread praise for its transparency and accessibility, and has since been replicated by officials in other states—was now under a new team for "reasons beyond my division's control."[12]

Jones' statements were dismissed by DeSantis as an outright lie, but she continued to press her case with the media, appearing on CNN, CBS News, MSNBC, and other major networks sounding the alarm on what she said was really happening behind the scenes. Taking things further, in June Jones launched her own dashboard tracking cases to report the verified information. This last step ignited a surprise December 2020 raid into her home by Florida Department of Law Enforcement agents.

> State investigators were executing a search warrant that they had probable cause to believe Jones was behind an anonymous message sent last November [2020] to Jones' former colleagues at the health department using the emergency operations ReadyOps system.[13]

An NPR story at the time reported Jones' response to the raid:

> Florida law enforcement agents searched the home of former state data scientist Rebekah Jones on Monday [December 7, 2020], entering her house with weapons drawn as they carried out a warrant as part of an investigation into an unauthorized message that sent on a state communications system…
> "They took my phone and the computer I use every day to post the case numbers in Florida, and school cases for the entire country," she said via Twitter. "They took evidence of corruption at the state level. They claimed it was about a security breach. This was DeSantis. He sent the gestapo."[14]

Jones' 31-second clip of the raid quickly went viral, and her credibility began to be attacked in a public way with past legal troubles coming to light, particularly about a previous relationship she had with a college student during her doctoral studies:

> The incident was detailed in a more than 300-page document Jones wrote and posted online, which was submitted in her court case.
> Jones lost her graduate assistant teaching position at FSU over the affair, and her online post about the relationship resulted in the charge of stalking. When she was hired by the state health department in 2019, her hiring paperwork noted the pending charges, but she was cleared to be hired.[15]

Championed by Democrats in the State, Jones received official Whistleblower Status the following year, and her allegations were sent to the Office of Inspector General (OIG), but nothing came of it.

Jones issued a 70-page rebuttal to the findings disputing the 27-page report issued by the OIG point by point, presenting evidence from emails, texts and other communications from other workers at the Department who had expressed similar complaints about the State's manipulation. Now a resident of Navarre, Jones has continued to make headlines, attempting to secure political office, but ultimately losing to Matt Gaetz in the 2022 congressional elections. In December 2022, she signed a plea deal admitting guilt and agreeing to $20,000 for accessing a state computer without authorization. Most recently, Jones' 13-year-old son made headlines for threatening to shoot up Holley Navarre Middle School in April 2023. After his arrest, Jones took to Twitter:

> "My family is not safe," Rebekah Jones tweeted. "My son has been taken on the gov's orders and I've had to send my husband and daughter out of state for their safety THIS is the reality of living in DeSantis' Florida. There is no freedom here. Only retaliatory rule by a fascist who wishes to be king."

When Jones asked the officers who ordered the arrest, she says an officer told her "it was the state."[16]

DeSantis Shoves Florida into the Culture Wars

Early in his tenure, DeSantis had the opportunity to remodel the Florida courts by appointing three judges for unoccupied seats. While initially there were few changes that resulted from these appointments, this changed by the end of 2021 as national issues began to creep into the state.

Among the first of such topics to be addressed was Critical Race Theory (CRT)—an analytical framework originally developed by legal scholars examining how race and racism have become ingrained in American law and institutions since slavery and Jim Crow.

> The state's Republican governor—who gained a national following amid his battles over Covid restrictions—also want[ed] the GOP-controlled Legislature to help employees at private corporations that are subjected to what he called "harassment" by being forced to undergo sensitivity and racial awareness training.[17]

A hot button issue at school boards across the country, the DeSantis proposal would give parents the power to sue local school districts that teach lessons rooted in critical race theory. This part, which also allows parents to collect attorney fees, is similar to the bounties permitted under

Texas' controversial abortion law. Under that law, ordinary citizens can sue those who provide abortions and collect attorney fees.

Announcing the moves under a new "Stop WOKE Act" at a press conference held near The Villages, a bulwark of Republican support in central Florida, DeSantis went on to say: "Nobody wants this crap," DeSantis told the crowd. "This is an elite-driven phenomenon being driven by bureaucratic elites, elites in universities and elites in corporate America. And they're trying to shove it down the throats of the American people. You're not doing that in the state of Florida."[18] Arguing that CRT is nothing short of corporate sanctioned racism, he summarily pushed the bill through and signed it in April 2022. The bill drew quick condemnation from Florida Democrats and educators who felt that some of the language incorporated into the bill, particularly the section that prohibited educators from promoting lessons that would make students feel anguish, guilt, or distress about past events, proved too open for interpretation.

DeSantis Tackles Roe

Happening at the same time as the debate over Critical Race Theory was the Florida's Legislature's stint into a woman's right to choose.

Buoyed by the impending Supreme Court case of *Dobbs v. Jackson*, the Florida Legislature rushed to replace the previous provision that allowed women up to 24 weeks to seek out an abortion with a stricter 15-week ban. Unlike the previous law, this new 15-week ban did not make exceptions for cases of incest, rape or human trafficking. It did, however, allow an abortion if it would save the life of a pregnant person and made exceptions for fetal abnormalities past 15 weeks.

Almost immediately after its passage in April 2022, the new law was under assault from Planned Parenthood of America, the Center for Reproductive Rights and the American Civil Liberties Union which filed suit against the state to block the new law from going into effect. "We've entered a dangerous time for Floridians' reproductive freedom," said Planned Parenthood President Aleix McGill Johnson in a statement at the time. "In just a few months, thousands of pregnant people in Florida will no longer be able to access the care they need without leaving their state."[19]

Arguing that the bill was in violation of the right to privacy enshrined in the Florida constitution, urgency surrounding the case grew after the overturning of Roe v. Wade in June 2022. Temporarily blocked from going into effect by one state judge, the ban was restored by another a few days later. In a prepared statement to the press at the time, Christina Pushaw, a spokeswoman for DeSantis, said: "The Florida constitution does not include—and has never included—a right to kill an innocent unborn child."[20] The Supreme Court of Florida agreed to hear the case in January 2023 but did not issue a ruling until April 2024. This ruling upheld the 15-week ban. In the meantime, a new bill passed the state legislature and was signed into law by DeSantis stating that abortion would be illegal (with a few exceptions) after six weeks. The state supreme court's ruling in April 2024 also upheld this ban and the law went into effect on May 1, 2024. These events in Florida no doubt served to embolden the numerous other states with current bans or limitations in place.

"Don't Say Gay"

While DeSantis' wading into Critical Race Theory and abortion proved controversial, it was nothing compared to his meddling in education on gay and transgender issues under what became known as the "Don't Say Gay" bill.

First filed among a list of bills by the Florida House of Representatives, the "Parental Rights in Education Act," went largely unnoticed until catching the eye of Democrat lawmakers in early 2022. The measure essentially prevented public primary teachers from engaging in classroom instruction related to sexual orientation or gender identity. Specifically, it targeted those educators from teaching on these subjects in grades K–3.

The text of the bill stated that "classroom instruction by school personnel or third parties on sexual orientation or gender identity may not occur in kindergarten through [third grade]" or "in a manner that is not age appropriate or developmentally appropriate for students in accordance with state standards" in other grades. It also stated that parents "may bring an action against a school district to obtain a declaratory judgment"[21] and a court may award damages and attorney's fees if it finds that a school violated the measure. It was this last provision that proved the most controversial. This was most demonstrated in a Q&A session following a special session for educators convened by the Orange County Public Schools after the law's passage:

> [N]either the state nor the district had offered formal guidance on what that new law would actually mean for their classrooms…. *Could staff wear the rainbow articles of clothing—like the "Ally" lanyards the district had handed out? What about the "Safe Space" stickers teachers put on their classroom doors? Can teachers display photos of a same-sex partner and, if so, can they tell students who that person is?*
>
> When the seminar concluded, the district's teachers learned that the answer to all of those questions had been an emphatic "no."[22]

Rep. Carlos Guillermo Smith, a Democrat representing Orange County, summed up frustrations surrounding the bill when he stated:

> When we talk about the culture of fear that this bill has created and the chilling effect, we're talking about the fact that educators and school districts are scared to approach anything related to LGBTQ people or issues out of fear of lawsuits and professional ruin.... The real enforcement mechanism for this law is not oversight from the state department of education... It's litigation.[23]

DeSantis vs Disney

After the Parental Rights in Education Act was passed by the Florida Legislature, the Walt Disney Co., under CEO Bob Chapek's orders, remained silent.

> Chapek reportedly said that Disney leaders were opposed to the bill "from the outset," but chose to work quietly behind the scenes, "engaging directly with lawmakers." He said he called DeSantis the morning of the shareholders meeting "to express our disappointment and concern that if the legislation becomes law, it could be used to unfairly target gay, lesbian, nonbinary and transgender kids and families."[24]

His explanation did little to quell some of his more outraged employees, however, and after a mea culpa with his shareholders, Chapek finally took a hardline stance, stating publicly on March 28: "Our goal as a company is for this law to be repealed by the legislature or struck down in the courts, and we remain committed to supporting the national and state organizations working to achieve that."[25] While Chapek's statements were lauded in the press, his comments set off a firestorm of controversy between Disney and the State of Florida, with DeSantis declaring all-out war on the company.

Working openly with legislators, DeSantis whipped up a new law that would effectively strip the company of its 55-year-old grip on a 40 square mile piece of land straddling Orange and Osceola counties known as the Reedy Creek Improvement District. This district allotted special tax and governing privileges to Disney and was supported so that Disney could have more control over the development of its theme park projects. "The bill was passed after only two days of discussions and without a fiscal impact analysis. This led to debates about the bill's effects on taxes and bond debt."[26]

Set to take effect in 2023, the bill was challenged on multiple fronts, with some Florida taxpayers filing suit arguing that the dissolution meant that they would acquire more than $1 billion in debt and that DeSantis had acted out of retaliation. The suit was thrown out by a federal judge, however, who found that the plaintiffs did not effectively prove that their personal First Amendment rights were violated nor that they suffered any concrete injury as a result of the dissolution.

In 2023 when DeSantis' hand-appointed board took the reins over from Disney to nullify the district, the latter retaliated by launching a lawsuit against the State. From a CNN report on the lawsuit at the time of its filing:

> The lawsuit characterizes Wednesday's vote [April 26, 2023] as the "latest strike" in "a targeted campaign of government retaliation—orchestrated at every step by Governor DeSantis as punishment for Disney's protected speech."
>
> It says DeSantis' retaliation "now threatens Disney's business operations, jeopardizes its economic future in the region, and violates its constitutional rights."
>
> "Disney finds itself in this regrettable position because it expressed a viewpoint the Governor and his allies did not like. Disney wishes that things could have been resolved a different way," the lawsuit says. "But Disney also knows that it is fortunate to have the resources to take a stand against the State's retaliation—a stand smaller businesses and individuals might not be able to take when the State comes after them for expressing their own views. In America, the government cannot punish you for speaking your mind."[27]

While an opinion poll published shortly after this spat showed the public roughly split in sympathies between DeSantis and Disney, "with Disney slightly edging out DeSantis 33% to 28%,"[28] it nevertheless helped rally the Republican base behind DeSantis, granting him more national prominence.

Ultimately, on January 31, 2024, Disney's lawsuit against DeSantis was thrown out in federal court by Judge Allen Winsor, who argues that "Disney lacked standing and jurisdiction in arguing that actions pushed by DeSantis were retaliatory and violated the First Amendment right of the company."[29]

DeSantis vs. Newsom

For whatever reason, Floridians and Californians have never gotten along. Instinctively, they just view the world differently. While on paper, both states share warm climates, beautiful beaches and large Hispanic populations, in practicality they are about as far apart on things as Mercury and Pluto. These differences are accentuated in a huge way when it comes to politics. As modern-day bastions of conservatism and liberalism, both are looked on by each party as political standard bearers. As goes

15. Demagoguery, Disease and Division

California, so goes the direction of the Democratic Party, and vice versa with Florida and the Republican Party. Thus, it is fitting that these differences have boiled over between the two executives of each state, who have increasingly attacked each other, while attempting to poach residents.

The rivalry began innocuously enough on July 4, 2022, when California Governor Gavin Newsom took a dig at DeSantis' conservative policies in a 30-second ad.

> "Freedom is under attack in your state," Newsom says in the ad, which ran in Florida. "Republican leaders, they're banning books. Making it harder to vote, restricting speech in classrooms, even criminalizing women and doctors," Newsom said. "I urge all of you living in Florida to join the fight or join us in California, where we still believe in freedom.... Don't let them take your freedom."[30]

While Newsom received heavy praise from the ad, particularly from people within the press who were quick to applaud his brazenness with regards to confronting a rising star in the GOP (DeSantis), the realities of the ad proved the opposite. In writing for the *City Journal*, Dave Seminara criticized the ad for holding little truth. Picking apart Newsom's arguments, Seminara stated that contrary to Newsom's accusations, DeSantis' Florida actually remains more free than Newsom's California, citing several examples: Florida kept schools open; navigated Covid better; and kept the economy moving at a time when millions lost their jobs. He also cites Florida's substantial gains at a time when California has lost population for the first time in its history. He concluded stating:

> Many of the millions who have come here [Florida] sought to escape the sort of "nightmarish future" they believe is unfolding in blue states. Newsom's attacks on Florida overlook this reality—and obscure basic facts.[31]

Responding in kind at a press conference five days later, DeSantis ripped apart Newsom's arguments highlighting that Californians rarely visit Florida and vice versa.

He then brought up Newsom's infamous unmasked dinner at the French Laundry during the height of the pandemic in November 2020 before moving on to California's dismal school performance, its rising crime rate, its out-of-control homeless problems, its sharp decline in economy and tourism, and its hypocrisy when it came to enforcing Covid rules on state residents.

> "Let's just be clear, California is driving people away with their terrible governance," DeSantis said. He said that California had never lost population until Newsom came to office, "and now they're hemorrhaging population." "It's almost hard to drive people out of a place like California given all their natural advantages, and yet they're finding a way to do it," DeSantis said.[32]

A Proxy War for the Soul of the Nation

The squabbling between DeSantis and Newsom is hardly surprising given the rising profiles of each executive. In an interesting July 2022 article from *USA Today*, the writer describes their spat as a reflection of the current political environment as DeSantis and Newsom seemed to be jockeying ahead of both their party's current heads, perhaps reflecting their presidential ambitions:

> Now, as Newsom and DeSantis face reelection this fall with easy wins expected, the pair all but certainly have presidential ambitions, as they continue to grab their parties'—and the nation's—attention....
> DeSantis' path forward, however, may possess fewer hurdles. In his reelection campaign for governor, DeSantis has been clear that he doesn't need Trump, bucking an endorsement perhaps in an attempt to launch a presidential bid. But even with a massive pool of donations, which could possibly be diverted from seeking gubernatorial reelection to a run for the White House, he continues to say he's focused on Florida, even as some straw polls project him beating out Trump.[33]

This jockeying was exacerbated greatly with DeSantis' resounding victory during the 2022 midterms—one of the few highlights Republicans had that evening—where he won almost 60 percent of the vote, including in heavily Democratic counties like Miami-Dade and Broward. Such a victory put him in instant front-runner status for the 2024 GOP nomination, earning him the ire of not only Newsom, but Trump as well, who declared his intentions to run just days after DeSantis' stunning victory.

Publicly dubbing him "DeSanctimonious," Trump and DeSantis' once close relationship was in tatters as DeSantis was forced to fight a two-pronged war not only against Democrats like Newsom, but also against Republicans like Trump and Nikki Haley. While DeSantis may have hoped such political posturing against Newsom would lead towards a presidential path, his open feuding with former president Donald Trump, along with his less than stellar performance in the 2024 GOP presidential primary, failed to materialize any real electoral support. His disappointing second place finish in the Iowa Caucuses eventually led to his dropping out of the race altogether. Although he has patched up relations with Trump, and was even included on his shortlist for vice president, it's unclear what path he may take following the conclusion of his second term.

Florida: A State Transformed

Love him or hate him, there is no denying the monumental impact that Ron DeSantis has had while governor of Florida. A transformative rather than transitional political figure, DeSantis has taken Florida from a reliably purple state into a solidly red bastion. Between thumbing his nose at federal Covid regulations, wading into controversial topics, and battling with politicians on a national scale, there is no one that can deny that Florida has become a local battlefield in a war for the nation's soul.

Conclusion
A Trip Through the Darkness and Back

Among many, there's a misconception that Florida is just beaches and hotels, with little else to offer other than retirement villages and theme parks. This couldn't be further from the truth; for Florida's greatest export is in fact its history.

Think about it.

By the time the Pilgrims had first set foot in Massachusetts in 1620, Florida had already been navigated and explored for over 100 years and settled for over a half a century. Its shores had already witnessed two international conflicts, and its mission system was well established. It was on these shores that the first Thanksgiving took place and that the legend of Pocahontas was born. In a nutshell, Florida history is American history: warts and all.

While not all experienced in the Sunshine State was pretty, with Native suppressions, slavery, environmental degradation, and much more playing out under its skies, it was nevertheless significant. For without these things, it wouldn't be the state it is today.

As *Weird Florida* author Eliot Kleinberg once said: "Any time you jam descendants of slaves, rednecks, Indians, con artists, carpetbaggers, drug smugglers, fugitives, UFO abductees, strippers, alligators, and political refugees into a flat peninsula surrounded by water but with hardly a drop to drink anymore, you get a pretty weird place."

Chapter Notes

Chapter 1

1. Peck. p. 40.
2. *Ibid.*
3. "European Contact." *Jupiter Inlet Lighthouse and Museum.* 2022. https://www.jupiterlighthouse.org/explore/history/european-contact/. Retrieved February 2, 2023.
4. Peck. p. 56.
5. *Ibid.*, p. 57.
6. *Ibid.*
7. *Ibid.*, p. 58.
8. Gannon. p. 41.
9. Milanich and Hudson. p. 35.
10. Weitzel. p. 99.
11. "The Calusa Domain." *Florida Museum.* 2018. https://www.floridamuseum.ufl.edu/sflarch/research/calusa-domain/. Retrieved July 4, 2022.
12. *Ibid.*
13. *Ibid.*
14. Morris. p. 57.
15. Peck. p. 57.
16. Milanich and Hudson. p. 164.
17. Weitzel. p. 49.
18. "Timucua Religion." *Access Genealogy.* https://accessgenealogy.com/florida/timucua-religion.htm. Retrieved August 17, 2022.
19. "John Cabot's Voyage of 1498." *Heritage Newfoundland and Labrador.* 2023. https://www.heritage.nf.ca/articles/exploration/cabot-1498.php. Retrieved February 5, 2023.
20. Williams. "Ponce Not the First to Pounce." *Naples Florida Weekly.* April 2, 2020. https://naples.floridaweekly.com/articles/ponce-not-the-first-to-pounce/. Retrieved December 21, 2020.
21. "Peter Martyr's Account." *Original Sources.com.* 2022. https://www.originalsources.com/Document.aspx?DocID=3NYVYDD51WRKL6T. Retrieved September 5, 2022.
22. "Brutal Journey." *Sarasota Magazine.* 2006. https://www.sarasotamagazine.com/news-and-profiles/2006/12/brutal-journey. Retrieved May 15, 2022.
23. *Ibid.*
24. Fleming. "The Story of Juan Ortiz and Uleleh." *Florida Historical Quarterly* V. 1. 1908. https://stars.library.ucf.edu/cgi/viewcontent.cgi?article=1390&context=fhq. Retrieved February 12, 2023.
25. *Ibid.*
26. "Brutal Journey." *Sarasota Magazine.* 2006. Retrieved May 15, 2022.
27. *Ibid.*
28. *Ibid.*
29. *Ibid.*
30. *Ibid.*
31. Fleming. "The Story of Juan Ortiz and Uleleh." *Florida Historical Quarterly* V. 1. 1908. https://stars.library.ucf.edu/cgi/viewcontent.cgi?article=1390&context=fhq. Retrieved February 12, 2023.
32. *Ibid.*
33. *Ibid.*
34. Holloway. "Uncovering the Luna Colony, a Lost Remnant of Spanish Florida." *The New Yorker.* 2016. https://www.newyorker.com/news/news-desk/uncovering-the-luna-colony-a-lost-remnant-of-spanish-florida/amp. Retrieved June 19, 2022.
35. *Ibid.*
36. "Second Voyage Commanded by René Goulaine De Laudonniére." *Access Genealogy.* 2023. https://accessgenealogy.com/south-carolina/second-voyage-commanded-by-rene-goulaine-de-

laudonniere.htm. Retrieved January 2, 2023.
   37. Davis. *History of Jacksonville*. p. 12.
   38. *Ibid.*, p. 13.
   39. *Ibid.*, p. 14.
   40. *Ibid.*, p. 16.
   41. *Ibid.*
   42. "De Gourgues, Dominique." *A History of Florida*. 1904. https://fcit.usf.edu/florida/docs/d/degour.htm. Retrieved August 29, 2022.
   43. *Ibid.*
   44. Daniels. "De Gourgues Florida Expedition 1567." *The New World*. 2014. https://thenewworld.us/de-gourges-florida-expedition-in-1567/. Retrieved August 29, 2022.
   45. "Murder and Martyrdom in Spanish Florida: The True Story Behind the Guale Uprising." *Secrets of the Dead: PBS*. 2017. https://www.pbs.org/wnet/secrets/secrets-spanish-florida-murder-martyrdom-spanish-florida-true-story-behind-guale-uprising/3702/. Retrieved February 12, 2023.
   46. *Ibid.*
   47. Johnson. "The Yamassee Revolt of 1597 and the Destruction of the Georgia Missions." https://penelope.uchicago.edu/Thayer/E/Gazetteer/Places/America/United_States/Georgia/_Texts/GaHQ/7/1/Yamassee_Revolt_of_1597*.html#ref5. Retrieved September 5, 2022.
   48. *Ibid.*

Chapter 2

   1. Cummins. p. 273.
   2. Fagan. "Sir Francis Drake Was in Cartagena, Colombia." *World's Best Golf Destinations*. 2019. https://www.worldsbestgoltdestinations.com/sir-francis-drake-was-in-cartagena-colombia/. Retrieved September 26, 2022.
   3. McCarthy. p. 21.
   4. *Ibid.*
   5. *Ibid.*, p. 24.
   6. *Ibid.*
   7. *Ibid.*
   8. Tebeau. p. 57.
   9. "Piratical Life in St. Augustine: Then and Now." *Florida Historic Coast*. 2022. https://www.floridashistoriccoast.com/blog/piratical-life-in-st-augustine-then-now/. Retrieved June 10, 2022.
   10. McCarthy. p. 36.
   11. Dillon. "St. Augustine, FL History: A Pirate Execution." *Doug Dillon*. 2012. https://dougdillon.com/2012/04/21/st-augustine-history-pirate-execution/. Retrieved February 2, 2023.
   12. *Ibid.*
   13. McCarthy. p. 36.
   14. *Ibid.*, p. 53.
   15. Blumetti. "The First Floridians." *Bitter Southerner*. 2020. https://bittersoutherner.com/the-first-floridians-fort-mose-st-augustine. Retrieved September 26, 2022.
   16. "Captain Francisco Menéndez Helped Found the First Free Black Settlement in the U.S." *aaron-gustafson.com*. 2022. https://www.aaron-gustafson.com/notebook/captain-francisco-menndez-helped-found-the-first-free-black-settlement-in-the-us/. Retrieved June 30, 2022.
   17. Wilson. "The 1715 Plate Fleet and the Rise of the Pirates." *History Today*. 2015. https://www.historytoday.com/1715-plate-fleet-and-rise-pirates. Retrieved April 22, 2023.
   18. *Ibid.*
   19. *Ibid.*
   20. "Henry Jennings." *pirates.hegewisch.net*. 2022. https://pirates.hegewisch.net/whosjennings.html. Retrieved May 29, 2022.
   21. *Ibid.*
   22. *Ibid.*
   23. Dimri. "Was the Legendary Spanish Pirate Jose Gaspar Real?" *Historic Mysteries*. 2022. https://www.historicmysteries.com/jose-gaspar/. Retrieved February 10, 2023.
   24. McCarthy. p. 56.
   25. Dimri. "Was the Legendary Spanish Pirate Jose Gaspar Real?" *Historic Mysteries*. 2022. https://www.historicmysteries.com/jose-gaspar/. Retrieved February 10, 2023.
   26. McCarthy. p. 57.
   27. "Ye Mystic Crew of Gasparilla." *Ymkg.com*. 2023. https://ymkg.com/. Retrieved February 5, 2023.

Chapter 3

   1. "War of 1812." *Exploring Florida*. 2022. https://fcit.usf.edu/florida/docs/w/war1812.htm. Retrieved February 2, 2023.
   2. *Ibid.*

3. "Lighthouse History Pre–1874." *St. Augustine Lighthouse and Museum.* 2014. https://www.staugustinelighthouse.org/2014/11/18/lighthouse-history-pre-1874/. Retrieved December 14, 2023.
4. Davis. "MacGregor's Invasion of Florida." *Florida Historical Quarterly V.7-1*. 1928. https://stars.library.ucf.edu/cgi/viewcontent.cgi?article=1768&context=fhq. Retrieved October 10, 2022.
5. McCarthy. p. 65.
6. "Florida's Oldest Surviving Plantation House." *Florida Irish Heritage Center.* 2010. https://floridairishheritagecenter.wordpress.com/2010/06/29/floridas-oldest-surviving-plantation-house/. Retrieved June 1, 2022.
7. O'Riordan. p. 46.
8. *Ibid.*, p. 10.
9. *Ibid.*, p. 12.
10. *Ibid.*, p. 15.
11. "Siege of Pensacola." *American Battlefield Trust.* 2022. https://www.battlefields.org/learn/revolutionary-war/battles/siege-pensacola. Retrieved June 1, 2022.
12. *Ibid.*
13. *Ibid.*
14. Heidler and Heidler. *Old Hickory's War: Andrew Jackson and the Quest for Empire.* p. 174.
15. Cox. "The West Florida Controversy, 1798–1813; A Study in American Diplomacy." *Archive.org.* 1918. https://archive.org/details/westfloridacontr00coxi. Retrieved June 1, 2022.
16. Arthur. *The Story of the West Florida Rebellion.* St. Francisville, LA: St. Francisville Democrat. 1935. Retrieved September 11, 2022.
17. *Ibid.*
18. "The 'Negro Fort' Massacre." *Libcom.org.* 2022. https://libcom.org/article/negro-fort-massacre. Retrieved February 2, 2023.
19. Mahon. p. 23.
20. Aptheker. p. 26.
21. "The 'Negro Fort' Massacre." *Libcom.org.* 2022. https://libcom.org/article/negro-fort-massacre. Retrieved February 2, 2023.
22. *Ibid.*
23. *Ibid.*
24. "The Battle of Fowltown." *Exploresouthernhistory.com.* 2015. https://www.exploresouthernhistory.com/fowltown.html. Retrieved June 2, 2022.
25. Parton. p. 430.
26. *Ibid.*, p. 431.
27. *Ibid.*
28. Missall and Missall. p. 40.
29. *Ibid.*, p. 42.
30. Parton. p. 632.
31. Fuller. p. 349.
32. DeBolt. "How Andrew Jackson Set up a 'Good Government' for Pensacola and Florida." *Pensacola News Journal.* 2021. https://www.pnj.com/story/news/2021/03/07/andrew-jackson-set-up-good-government-pensacola-and-florida/4579079001/. Retrieved June 1, 2022.
33. Zinn. p. 129.

Chapter 4

1. Mahon. p. 183.
2. Tebeau. p. 154.
3. *Ibid.*
4. Tebeau. p. 155.
5. *Ibid.*, 154.
6. "The Struggle for the Southern Frontier: The Seminole Wars of Florida." *Floridahistory.org.* 2022. http://floridahistory.org/seminoles.htm. Retrieved June 12, 2022.
7. Meltzer. p. 76.
8. Tebeau. p. 154.
9. Biggs. "The Second Seminole War." *Issuu.com.* 2020. https://issuu.com/oghmacreative/docs/saddlebag_winter_2020_final/s/11539584. Retrieved April 22, 2023.
10. "The Struggle for the Southern Frontier: The Seminole Wars of Florida." *Floridahistory.org.* 2022. http://floridahistory.org/seminoles.htm. Retrieved June 12, 2022.
11. Hitchcock and Foreman, ed. p. 125.
12. McIver, S. "Massacre: The Day an Island Died. Indian Key Was Once the Capital of Dade County. Then, on an August Morning in 1840, the Indians Came Ashore. The Lucky Ones Escaped." *South Florida Sun Sentinel.* 1985. https://www.sun-sentinel.com/news/fl-xpm-1985-08-11-8502020480-story.html. Retrieved June 8, 2022.
13. *Ibid.*
14. "Indian Key." *Ghosttowns.com.* http://www.ghosttowns.com/states/fl/indiankey.html. Retrieved July 1, 2022.
15. *Ibid.*

16. Missall and Missall. p. 105.
17. Mahon. p. 148.
18. Missall and Missall. pp. 128–129.
19. *Ibid.*, pp. 131–132.
20. Gannon. pp. 195.
21. *Ibid.*
22. Hatch. p. 19.
23. "Seminole History." *Florida Department of State.* 2022. https://dos.myflorida.com/florida-facts/florida-history/seminole-history/. Retrieved October 25, 2022.
24. Missall and Missall. p. 138.
25. *Ibid.*, p. 142.
26. *Ibid.*
27. *Ibid.*
28. *Ibid.*
29. *Ibid.*, p. 143.
30. *Ibid.*
31. "Distribution of Population 1830–1840. *Maps Etc.* 2007. http://fcit.usf.edu/florida/maps/pages/2400/f2447/f2447.htm. Retrieved June 4, 2022.
32. Missall and Missall. p. 132.
33. Mahon. p. 316.
34. *Ibid.*, p. 317.
35. *Ibid.*, pp. 317–318.
36. *Ibid.*, p. 323.
37. *Ibid.*, p. 323.
38. Scallet. "This Inglorious War: The Second Seminole War, the Ad Hoc Origins of American Imperialism, and the Silence of Slavery." *Dissertation, Washington University in St Louis.* 2011. https://openscholarship.wustl.edu/cgi/viewcontent.cgi?article=1637&context=etd. Retrieved June 3, 2022.

Chapter 5

1. Francis, Mormino, and Sanderson. "Slavery Took Hold in Florida Under the Spanish in the 'Forgotten Century' of 1492–1619." *Tampa Bay Times.* 2019. https://www.tampabay.com/opinion/2019/08/29/before-1619-africans-and-the-early-history-of-spanish-colonial-florida-and-america-column/. Retrieved June 1, 2022.
2. "The Spanish Colonial and Slavery Eras in Florida." *Florida Humanities.* 2020. https://floridahumanities.org/the-spanish-colonial-and-slavery-eras-in-florida/. Retrieved December 14, 2023.
3. *Ibid.*
4. "Fort Mose Site Florida." *NPS.gov.* 2022. https://www.nps.gov/nr/travel/american_latino_heritage/fort_mose.html#:~:text=Slavery%20existed%20in%20Spain%2C%20but,together%2C%20and%20purchase%20their%20freedom. Retrieved February 5, 2023.
5. *Ibid.*
6. Stowell. p. 30.
7. *Ibid.*
8. "1833 Alabama Slave Code." *Sensagent.* 2022. http://dictionary.sensagent.com/Slave%20codes/en-en/. Retrieved June 15, 2022.
9. Schafer. p. 24.
10. *Ibid.*, pp. 32–33.
11. *Ibid.*, p. 43.
12. *Ibid.*, p. 50.
13. "Anna Madgigine Jai Kingsley." *Florida Department of State.* 2022. https://dos.myflorida.com/offices/historical-museums/united-connections/women-in-history/anna-madgigine-jai-kingsley/. Retrieved February 10, 2023.
14. Schafer. p. 75.
15. Conrad. "The Cracker Prince." *Tallahassee Magazine.* 2012. https://www.tallahasseemagazine.com/the-cracker-prince/. Retrieved October 25, 2022.
16. *Ibid.*
17. *Ibid.*
18. *Ibid.*
19. MacCartney and Dorrance., p. 137.
20. *Ibid.*, p. 145.
21. "Mack Mullen: Florida Slave Narratives 1936–1938." *Exploring Florida.* 2022. http://fcit.usf.edu/florida/docs/s/slave/slave28.htm. Retrieved July 5, 2022.
22. *Ibid.*
23. "Douglas Dorsey: Ex-Slave Narratives from the Federal Writers' Project 1936–1938." *Exploring Florida.* 2005. http://fcit.usf.edu/florida/docs/s/slave.htm#slave02. Retrieved July 1, 2022.
24. "Mack Mullen: Florida Slave Narratives 1936–1938." *Exploring Florida.* 2022. http://fcit.usf.edu/florida/docs/s/slave/slave28.htm. Retrieved July 5, 2022.
25. "Douglas Dorsey: Ex-Slave Narratives from the Federal Writers' Project 1936–1938." *Exploring Florida.* 2005. http://fcit.usf.edu/florida/docs/s/slave.htm#slave02. Retrieved July 5, 2022.
26. Allen and Jewett. p. 69.
27. *Ibid.*
28. *Ibid.*, p. 70.
29. Gannon. p. 231.
30. "Links to Online Census Records

Duval Co., Florida." 2022. *Census Online*. http://www.census-online.com/links/FL/Duval/. Retrieved October 25, 2022.

31. Davis. *History of Jacksonville*. p. 86.

32. "House Divided: In Tallahassee, the Florida Secession Convention Votes by 62-7 to Leave the United States" *Dickinson College*. 2023. https://hd.housedivided.dickinson.edu/node/35300. Retrieved February 11, 2023.

33. Davis. *History of Jacksonville*. p. 119.

34. Tebeau. p. 202.

35. Latner, "Fort Pickens." *Tulane.edu*. 1996. https://www2.tulane.edu/~sumter/Pickens.html. Retrieved October 25, 2022.

36. Nelson. "Back Off SC! Fla. Claims First Shot of Civil War." *NBCNews*. 2011. https://www.nbcnews.com/id/wbna42569813. Retrieved September 19, 2011.

37. Weitz. "Defending the Old South: The Myth of the Lost Cause and Political Immorality in Florida, 1865–1968." *The Historian*. 2009. https://onlinelibrary.wiley.com/doi/full/10.1111/j.1540-6563.2008.00232.x. Retrieved October 25, 2022.

38. Cash. "Taylor County History and Civil War Deserters." *Florida Historical Quarterly* V. 27, N. 1. 1948. https://www.jstor.org/stable/30138660. Retrieved October 25, 2022.

39. "The Battle of Olustee Florida." *Battle of Olustee*. http://battleofolustee.org/battle.html. Retrieved June 10, 2022.

40. *Ibid*.

41. "Excerpt from the Reminiscences of William Fredrick Penniman." *Battle of Olustee*. 2022. https://battleofolustee.org/letters/penniman.htm. Retrieved October 25, 2022.

42. "From Soldiers to 'Fugitives.'" *Civil War Era NC*. https://cwnc.omeka.chass.ncsu.edu/exhibits/show/35th-usct/olustee/fugitives. Retrieved June 25, 2022.

43. *Ibid*.

44. *Ibid*.

45. Ensley. "Battle of Natural Bridge Myths Endure." *Tallahassee Democrat*. 2017. https://www.tallahassee.com/story/news/2017/03/01/battle-natural-bridge-myths-endure/98525912/. Retrieved June 30, 2022.

46. Cash. "Taylor County History and Civil War Deserters." *Florida Historical Quarterly* V. 27, N. 1. 1948. https://www.jstor.org/stable/30138660. Retrieved October 25, 2022.

47. "Douglas Dorsey: Ex-Slave Narratives from the Federal Writers' Project 1936–1938." *Exploring Florida*. 2022. https://fcit.usf.edu/florida/docs/s/slave/slave02.htm. Retrieved July 1, 2022.

48. *Ibid*.

Chapter 6

1. Tebeau. p. 309.

2. *Ibid*.

3. Gonzalez. "Cables from Cuba: Cross-Strait Solidarity and Politics in Ybor City 1898–1961." *Undergraduate History Honors Thesis, University of Florda*. 2021. https://ufdcimages.uflib.ufl.edu/AA/00/08/24/42/00001/Gonzalez_Arturo_Thesis.pdf. Retrieved July 1, 2022.

4. Schoultz. p. 58.

5. Bemis. p. 314.

6. *Ibid*., p. 320.

7. "Ostend Manifesto." *Wikisource*. 2022. http://en.wikisource.org/wiki/Ostend_Manifesto. Retrieved October 25, 2022.

8. Potter. p. 190.

9. "What Thomas Jefferson Said About Annexing Cuba." *San Francisco Call*, V. 83 N. 13, April 10, 1898. *UCR California Digital Newspaper Collection*. https://cdnc.ucr.edu/cgi-bin/cdnc?a=d&d=SFC18980410.2.132.26&e=-------en--20-1--txt-txIN--------. Retrieved February 10, 2023.

10. Jordan. "In the 1850s, Narciso López Launched Illegal Cuban Invasions from New Orleans." *The Historic New Orleans Collection*. 2021. Retrieved February 8, 2022.

11. "López, Narciso." *Encyclopedia.com*. 2022. https://www.encyclopedia.com/humanities/encyclopedias-almanacs-transcripts-and-maps/lopez-narciso-1797-1851. Retrieved February 9, 2022.

12. "Narciso López." *HistoryofCuba.com*. 2022. http://www.historyofcuba.com/history/funfacts/narciso.htm. Retrieved October 24, 2022.

13. Sierra. "Captain Joseph Fry." *History of cuba.com*. http://www.historyofcuba.com/history/matanzas/Joseph-Fry.htm. Retrieved October 25, 2022.

14. Ault. "The Virginius Incident."

Centennial Website. 1996. https://www.spanamwar.com/virginius.htm. Retrieved July 1, 2022.
 15. *Ibid*.
 16. *Ibid*.
 17. *Ibid*.
 18. Martí. "Our America, March 5, 1892." *Historyofcuba.com*. http://www.historyofcuba.com/history/marti/America.htm. Retrieved October 30, 2011.
 19. Martí. "A Sincere Man Am I." *AllPoetry.com*. http://allpoetry.com/poem/8531743-A_Sincere_Man_Am_I___Verse_I_-by-Jose_Marti. Retrieved October 13, 2011.
 20. England. "José Martí and the Fernandina Plan." *Amelia Museum*. 2020. https://ameliamuseum.org/jose-marti-and-the-fernandina-plan/. Retrieved July 1, 2022.
 21. *Ibid*.
 22. *Ibid*.
 23. *Ibid*.
 24. *Ibid*.

Chapter 7

 1. McIver, *Death in the* Everglades. p. 139.
 2. Reilly. "The Most Dangerous Job: The Murder of America's First Bird Warden." *Mental Floss*. 2018. https://www.mentalfloss.com/article/559363/most-dangerous-job-murder-americas-first-bird-warden. Retrieved June 1, 2022.
 3. McIver. *Death in the Everglades*. p. 156.
 4. Wilbanks. p. 93.
 5. Knetsch. "Hamilton Disston and the Development of Florida." *University of South Florida*. 1998. https://digitalcommons.usf.edu/cgi/viewcontent.cgi?article=1308&context=sunlandtribune. Retrieved August 18, 2022.
 6. *Ibid*.
 7. *Ibid*.
 8. "Distinguish Jacksonville: The Silent Film Industry." *Metro Jacksonville*. 2007. http://www.metrojacksonville.com/article/2007-feb-distinguish-jacksonville-the-silent-film-industry. Retrieved July 10, 2022.
 9. *Ibid*.
 10. *Ibid*.
 11. *Ibid*.
 12. "The Flying Ace." *Norman Studios*. 2023. http://normanstudios.org/films-stars/norman-films/the-flying-ace/. Retrieved January 3, 2023.
 13. Douglas. p. 312.
 14. Carter. p. 78.
 15. Dovell. "The Everglades Before Reclamation." *Florida Historical Quarterly*, V. 26, N. 1. 1947. p. 26.
 16. McCally. p. 96.
 17. *Ibid*., p. 101.
 18. *Ibid*., pp. 111–112.
 19. *Ibid*., pp. 93–94.
 20. *Ibid*.
 21. Davis, T.F. *History of Jacksonville*. p. 410.
 22. "Herman Glogowski–21st, 23rd, 25th and 27th Mayor of Tampa." *Tampa.gov*. 2023. https://www.tampa.gov/cityclerk/info/previous-mayors/glogowski-herman. Retrieved February 11, 2023.
 23. Davis, T.F. *History of Jacksonville*. p. 410.
 24. *Ibid*.
 25. "Restrictive Pacts Bar Jews from Purchasing Property in Miami Area." *Jewish Telegraphic Agency*. 1960. https://www.jta.org/archive/restrictive-pacts-bar-jews-from-purchasing-property-in-miami-area. Retrieved July 12, 2022.
 26. *Ibid*.
 27. "Encyclopedia of Southern Jewish Communities–St Petersburg, Florida." *Goldring/Woldenberg Institute of Southern Jewish Life*. 2022. https://www.isjl.org/florida-st-petersburg-encyclopedia.html. Retrieved July 20, 2022.
 28. *Ibid*.
 29. "Florida Governor Sidney J. Catts: The Polarizing Populist." 2017. *The U.S. Caribbean and Florida Digital Newspaper Project*. 2017. https://ufndnp.domains.uflib.ufl.edu/florida-governor-sidney-j-catts-the-polarizing-populist-ufndnp/. Retrieved October 19, 2022.
 30. *Ibid*.
 31. Krishnaiyer. "The Racist, Anti-Catholic Populism of Sidney Catts, and Woodrow Wilson-Era Florida Racist Politics." *The Florida Squeeze*. 2019. https://thefloridasqueeze.com/2019/11/10/the-racist-anti-catholic-populism-of-sidney-catts-and-woodrow-wilson-era-florida-racist-politics/. Retrieved July 20, 2022.
 32. *Ibid*.
 33. "Fr. John Francis Conoley." *Saint Augustine Church and Catholic Student*

Center. 2022. https://catholicgators.org/our-founder. Retrieved July 15, 2022.
34. *Ibid*.
35. *Ibid*.
36. Perry. "The Great Miami Hurricane of 1926. *Faith. Hope. Love*. http://faithhopelove.net/autobiography miamihurricane.htm. Retrieved October 18, 2022.
37. Tebeau. p. 388.
38. *Ibid*., p. 388.
39. "Hurricanes in History." *National Hurricane Center and Central Pacific Hurricane Centernational Oceanic And Atmospheric Administration*. 2022. https://www.nhc.noaa.gov/outreach/history/?text. Retrieved October 19, 2022.
40. "Hurricane of 1928 Mass Burial Site." *Waymarking.com*. 2022. https://www.waymarking.com/waymarks/wm7HMQ_Hurricane_of_1928_Mass_Burial_Site. Retrieved October 19, 2022.
41. *Ibid*.
42. *Ibid*.
43. *Ibid*.

Chapter 8

1. "Ybor City Historic District." *National Park Service*. 2021. https://www.nps.gov/nr/travel/american_latino_heritage/ybor_city_historic_district.html. Retrieved July 15, 2022.
2. Guzzo. "Bolita, Tampa's Illegal Lottery Was Deadly and Lucrative." *Tampa Bay Times*. 2021. https://www.tampabay.com/life-culture/history/2021/09/28/bolita-tampas-illegal-lottery-was-deadly-and-lucrative/. Retrieved July 15, 2022.
3. *Ibid*.
4. Guzzo. "Meet Charlie Wall, the Dean of Tampa's Early Underworld." *Tampa Bay Times*. 2020. https://www.tampabay.com/arts-entertainment/2020/06/11/meet-charlie-wall-the-dean-of-tampas-early-underworld/. Retrieved July 15, 2022.
5. *Ibid*.
6. *Ibid*.
7. *Ibid*.
8. Guzzo. "Bolita, Tampa's Illegal Lottery Was Deadly and Lucrative." *Tampa Bay Times*. 2021. https://www.tampabay.com/life-culture/history/2021/09/28/bolita-tampas-illegal-lottery-was-deadly-and-lucrative/. Retrieved July 15, 2022.

9. *Ibid*.
10. Deitche. "The Tampa Mob." *Americanmafia.com*.1999. https://www.americanmafia.com/Cities/Tampa.html. Retrieved July 15, 2022.
11. Guzzo. "Why Was Charlie Wall, Dean of Tampa's Underworld, Murdered?" *Tampa Bay Times*. 2021. https://www.tampabay.com/life-culture/history/2021/12/08/why-was-charlie-wall-dean-of-tampas-early-underworld-murdered/. Retrieved July 15, 2022.
12. *Ibid*.
13. *Ibid*.
14. McIver, S.B. *Murder in Tropics*. p. 66.
15. Guzzo. "Why Was Charlie Wall, Dean of Tampa's Underworld, Murdered?" *Tampa Bay Times*. 2021. https://www.tampabay.com/life-culture/history/2021/12/08/why-was-charlie-wall-dean-of-tampas-early-underworld-murdered/. Retrieved July 15, 2022.
16. *Ibid*.
17. *Ibid*.
18. Worrall. "When the Mob Owned Cuba." *Smithsonian Magazine*. 2016. https://www.smithsonianmag.com/travel/mob-havana-cuba-culture-music-book-tj-english-cultural-travel-180960610/. Retrieved July 20, 2022.
19. "Frank Ragano." *Spartacus Educational*. 2020. https://spartacus-educational.com/JFKraganoF.htm. Retrieved December 1, 2023.
20. Ecker. "Hell in Miami." *Ronaldecker.com*. 2004. Retrieved May 1, 2023.
21. Lardner. "Gangland Figure Refuses to Answer." *Washington Post*. March 17, 1977. Retrieved July 20, 2022.
22. *Ibid*.
23. Colloff and Hall. "Married to the Mob." *Texas Monthly*. 1998. https://www.texasmonthly.com/news-politics/married-to-the-mob/. Retrieved October 25, 2022.
24. Chardy and Yanez. "Fidel Castro Once Used Miami as Haven, Revolutionary Springboard." *Miami Herald*. 2008. http://www.latinamericanstudies.org/fidel/miami.htm. Retrieved July 1, 2022.
25. "The Murder of John Fitzgerald Kennedy: There Never Was a Camelot." *Angelfire.com*. 2000. http://www.angelfire.com/nh/hca/jfk.html. Retrieved July 1, 2022.
26. "Operation Mongoose." *PBS American Experience*. 2022. https://www.pbs.

org/wgbh/americanexperience/features/rfk-operation-mongoose/. Retrieved July 10, 2022.

27. "Attempted Assassination of FDR in Bayfront Park in 1933." *Miami-History.com*. 2022. http://miami-history.com/attempted-assassination-of-fdr-in-bayfront-park/. Retrieved August 1, 2022

28. *Ibid.*

29. "FDR Escapes Assassination Attempt in Miami." *History.com*. 2021. https://www.history.com/this-day-in-history/fdr-escapes-assassination-in-miami. Retrieved July 12, 2022.

30. Dwyer, ed. "An Assassin's Bullets for FDR." *Strange Stories, Amazing Facts of America's Past.* p. 14.

31. Luckhardt. "Was Gangster Al Capone a Stuart Visitor and Property Owner?" *TCPalm.com*, June 2, 2016. Retrieved May 12, 2024.

32. "Al Capone." *PBS*. 2022. https://www.pbs.org/wgbh/americanexperience/features/miami-al-capone/. Retrieved July 12, 2022.

33. Feldberg. "Jewish Gangsters in America." *Jewish Virtual Library*. 1998. https://www.jewishvirtuallibrary.org/jewish-gangsters-in-america. Retrieved October 19, 2022.

34. Duryea. "Three Indicted in Key Bank Fraud Case." *Tampa Bay* Times. November 7, 1992.

35. *Ibid.*
36. *Ibid.*
37. *Ibid.*

Chapter 9

1. Ashton. "Camp Blanding: The War Years." *Indianamilitary.org*. 1996. http://www.indianamilitary.org/30TH/FT-SITE/CampBlandingWarYears/CampBlanding.htm. Retrieved November 20, 2011.

2. *Ibid.*

3. "Florida on the Home Front: German Submarine Threat Off the Florida Coast." *Florida Department of State*. 2022. https://www.museumoffloridahistory.com/explore/exhibits/permanent-exhibits/world-war-ii/florida-remembers-world-war-ii/florida-on-the-home-front-the-german-submarine-threat-off-floridas-coast/. Retrieved July 1, 2022.

4. *Ibid.*
5. *Ibid.*

6. Hickman. "World War II: Operation Pistorius." *Thought.co.* 2017. http://militaryhistory.about.com/od/socialeffectsofwar/p/pastorius.htm. Retrieved July 8, 2022.

7. *Ibid.*
8. *Ibid.*
9. *Ibid.*
10. *Ibid.*

11. "The Enemy Presence: German U-Boats." *Palm Beach County History Online*. 2009. https://pbchistory.org/educational-articles. Retrieved July 5, 2022.

12. *Ibid.*

13. Nieman. "Promises to Keep: African Americans and the Constitutional Order, 1776 to the Present." *Oxford Academic*. 2020. https://academic.oup.com/book/33633. Retrieved July 10, 2022.

14. Ortiz. "Remembering One of the Bloodiest Elections in U.S. History." *The Gainesville Sun.* 2019. https://www.gainesville.com/story/opinion/columns/more-voices/2019/02/07/paul-ortiz-remembering-one-of-bloodiest-elections-in-us-history/6069757007/. Retrieved July 10, 2022.

15. *Ibid.*
16. *Ibid.*
17. *Ibid.*

18. Stephens. "The Truth Laid Bare." *University of Central Florida.* 2020. https://www.ucf.edu/pegasus/the-truth-laid-bare/. Retrieved July 10, 2022.

19. *Ibid.*
20. *Ibid.*

21. "Rosewood Massacre." *History.com.* 2022. https://www.history.com/topics/early-20th-century-us/rosewood-massacre. Retrieved February 5, 2023.

22. "Rosewood Massacre." *Penny Liberty, The First African American Encyclopedia of African American and Cultural History.* 2012. https://pennylibertygbow.wordpress.com/2012/02/24/rosewood-massacre/. Retrieved October 19, 2022.

23. "'Ax Handle Saturday,' A Story." *AAREG.* 2022. https://aaregistry.org/story/ax-handle-saturday-a-brief-story/. Retrieved October 25, 2022.

24. *Ibid.*

25. Justice. "Nat Glover Credits His Strength as a Leader to Moment of Fear on Ax Handle Saturday." *News4Jax.com.* 2020. https://www.news4jax.com/features/2020/08/25/nat-glover-credits-

his-strength-as-a-leader-to-moment-of-fear-on-ax-handle-saturday/. Retrieved February 3, 2023.
26. Weathersbee. "The Story of a White Man Who Joined the '60s Sit-ins." *Florida Times-Union*. February 4, 2008.
27. "An American Beach." *Anamericanbeach.com*. 2007. http://www.anamericanbeach.com/. Retrieved July 12, 2022.
28. "Dr. Robert B. Hayling—'Father of the Civil Rights Act of 1964.'" *Accord Freedom Trail*. 2011. https://accordfreedomtrail.org/hayling.html. Retrieved February 5, 2023.
29. Ibid.
30. "Remembering a Civil Rights Swim-in. It Was a Milestone." *NPR*. 2014. https://www.npr.org/2014/06/13/321380585/remembering-a-civil-rights-swim-in-it-was-a-milestone. Retrieved February 5, 2023.
31. "Arrest of Dr. Martin Luther King, Jr." *Historic City News*. 2011. https://historiccity.com/2011/staugustine/news/arrest-dr-martin-luther-king-jr-14561. Retrieved February 8, 2023.
32. Huse. "USF History 101—The Witch Hunt Comes to USF." *The Oracle*. 2003. https://www.usforacle.com/2003/09/24/usf-history-101-the-witch-hunt-comes-to-usf/. Retrieved November 30, 2011.
33. "Exhibits." *Florida Memory*. 2021. http://www.floridamemory.com/exhibits/floridahighlights/investigation/. Retrieved July 19, 2022.
34. Ibid.
35. Coppleston. "My Experiences During the Inquisition" from Beutke, "Behind Closed Doors." M.A. Project, Documentary Institute, University of Florida. 2000.
36. Call. "The Time Has Come: Florida Lawmakers Want Apology for 'Lives Ruined' by Johns Committee." *Tallahassee Democrat*. 2019. https://www.tallahassee.com/story/news/2019/03/22/florida-lawmakers-push-apology-lives-ruined-johns-committee/3244097002/. Retrieved October 19, 2022.
37. "The Johns Committee at USF." *Digital Exhibits*. 2022. https://usflibexhibits.omeka.net/exhibits/show/witchhunt/flic-at-usf. Retrieved October 25, 2022.
38. Ibid.
39. "War of Words." *Digital Exhibits*. https://usflibexhibits.omeka.net/exhibits/show/witchhunt/war-of-words. Retrieved December 14, 2023.
40. "The Johns Committee at USF." *Digital Exhibits*. 2022. https://usflibexhibits.omeka.net/exhibits/show/witchhunt/flic-at-usf. Retrieved October 25, 2022.
41. Ibid.
42. Fehler. "The Purple Pamphlet: A Shadowy History in the Sunshine State." *Medium*. 2020. https://medium.com/@bfehler/the-purple-pamphlet-a-shadowy-history-in-the-sunshine-state-123a16f6724d. Retrieved July 30, 2022.
43. "Homosexuality and Citizenship in Florida: A Report of the Florida Legislative Investigation Committee." *University of Florida Digital Collections*. January 1964. https://ufdcimages.uflib.ufl.edu/UF/00/00/48/05/00001/Binder1.pdf. Retrieved February 8, 2023.
44. Ibid.
45. Munzenreider. "Florida Legislature Once Published Anti-Gay Pamphlet Full of Softcore Porn." *Miami New Times*. 2015. https://www.miaminewtimes.com/news/florida-legislature-once-published-anti-gay-pamphlet-full-of-softcore-porn-7707547. Retrieved February 11, 2023.
46. Ibid.
47. Adkins. "These People Are Frightened to Death: Congressional Delegations and the Lavender Scare." *National Archives*. 2016. https://www.archives.gov/publications/prologue/2016/summer/lavender.html. Retrieved February 5, 2023.

Chapter 10

1. Hamacher. "Dadeland Mall Massacre: Thursday Marks 40th Anniversary of Infamous 'Cocaine Cowboys' Shootout." *NBC 6*. 2019. https://www.nbcmiami.com/news/local/dadeland-mall-massacre-thursday-marks-40th-anniversary-of-cocaine-cowboys-shootout/127956/. Retrieved July 19, 2022.
2. Ibid.
3. Ibid.
4. Ibid.
5. "Bullets Once Flew at Dadeland Mall in a Deadly Shootout. The Cocaine Cowboys Were Here." *Miami Herald*. 2019. https://www.miamiherald.com/news/local/community/miami-dade/kendall/article231644003.html. Retrieved July 20, 2022.

6. "JFK Jr.'s Would-Be Kidnapper Griselda Blanco Was 'The Most Feared' Female Killer in History." *National Enquirer.* February 26, 2020. https://www.nationalenquirer.com/true-crime/jfk-jrs-would-be-kidnapper-griselda-blanco-was-feared-female-killer/.
7. Tikkanen. "Griselda Blanco: Colombian Cocaine Trafficker." *Britannica.* 2003.
8. *Ibid.*
9. *Ibid.*
10. Culliford. "Black Widow: I dated husband-murdering drug lord Blanco—She was a great kisser and showered me with gifts ... then she tried to kill me." *The Sun.* January 28, 2024. https://www.the-sun.com/news/10218421/dated-murdering-drug-lord-griselda-blanco-charles-cosby/.
11. "JFK Jr.'s Would-be Kidnapper Griselda Blanco Was 'the Most Feared' Female Killer in History." *OK! News.* 2020. https://okmagazine.com/news/jfk-jr-s-would-be-kidnapper-griselda-blanco-was-feared-female-killer/. Retrieved October 19, 2022.
12. *Ibid.*
13. *Ibid.*
14. *Ibid.*
15. *Ibid.*
16. *Ibid.*
17. Alvarado. "Former Marijuana Smuggler Robert Platshorn Pitches Pot to Seniors." *Miami New Times.* 2019. https://www.miaminewtimes.com/marijuana/the-black-tuna-gangs-robert-platshorn-post-smuggler-pitches-medical-marijuana-to-seniors-11147955. Retrieved February 8, 2023.
18. "Life in the Drug Trade." *Time,* November 23, 1981. https://content.time.com/time/subscriber/article/0,33009,922695,00.html. Retrieved July 29, 2022.
19. *Ibid.*
20. *Ibid.*
21. *Ibid.*
22. Cavanaugh. "Key West Declared a Faux War on the United States in 1982." *Medium.* 2015. https://medium.com/war-is-boring/key-west-declared-a-faux-war-on-the-united-states-in-1982-f2c40b429e75. Retrieved February 12, 2013.
23. Flank. "Key West and the Conch Republic: We Seceded Where Others Failed." *Daily Kos.* 2014. https://www.dailykos.com/stories/2014/7/2/1301623/-Key-West-and-the-Conch-Republic-We-Seceded-Where-Others-Failed. Retrieved February 23, 2023.
24. *Ibid.*
25. "Conch Republic Independence Celebration." *Rent Key West Vacations.* 2022. https://www.rentkeywest.com/key-west-events/conch-republic-independence-celebration-42nd-annual-2024/. Retrieved July 30, 2022.
26. Vitagliano. "Behind the Song Lyrics: That Smell by Lynyrd Skynyrd." *American Songwriter.* 2022. https://americansongwriter.com/that-smell-lynyrd-skynyrd-behind-song-lyrics-meaning/ Retrieved August 8, 2022.
27. *Ibid.*
28. Ambrus and Contreras. "Fighting the New Drug Lords." *Media Awareness Project.* 2000. http://www.mapinc.org/drugnews/v00/n218/a12.html?3110. Retrieved July 30, 2022.
29. de Vise. "Columbian Drug Cartel Suspect Lands in S. Florida." *Miami Herald.* 2001. http://www.latinamericanstudies.org/drugs/bernal.htm. Retrieved July 30, 2022.
30. "Florida Crime Rates 1960–2019." *Thedisastercenter.com.* https://www.disastercenter.com/crime/flcrime.htm. Retrieved July 30, 2022.

Chapter 11

1. Michaud and Aynesworth. p. 319.
2. Grimes and Paris. "Disturbing Facts About Serial Killer Ted Bundy." *Grunge.* 2019. https://www.grunge.com/145187/the-untold-truth-of-ted-bundy/. Retrieved February 5, 2022.
3. Rule. p. 527.
4. Michaud and Aynesworth. p. 91.
5. *Ibid.*, p. 143.
6. *Ibid.*, p. 92.
7. Rule. pp. 122–133.
8. *Ibid.*, p. 486.
9. *Ibid.*, p. 7.
10. *Ibid.*, p. 332.
11. Foreman. p. 34.
12. Rule. pp. 278–279.
13. Miller and Buchanan. "A 'Cool' Bundy: Friends of Two Murdered Sorority Sisters Testify as Pace of Trial Picks Up." *The Evening Independent.* 1979. http://news.google.com/newspapers?nid=950&

dat=19790710&id=JAEMAAAAIBAJ&sj id=2VgDAAAAIBAJ&pg=6424,1831474. Retrieved July 29, 2022.
14. "Ted Bundy's Sorority House Attack." *Timothy Hughes Rare and Early Newspapers*. 1978. https://www.rarenewspapers.com/view/673263. Retrieved October 25, 2022.
15. *Ibid.*
16. Norton. "Bundy's Last Stop: Recounting a Serial Killer's Arrest 40 Years Later." *ABC*. 2018. https://weartv.com/news/local/bundys-last-stop-recounting-a-serial-killers-arrest-40-years-later. Retrieved July 15, 2022.
17. Nelson. p. 257.
18. Howard and Smith. p. 332.
19. Margaritoff. "What Happened to Tyria Moore, the Girlfriend of Serial Killer Aileen Wuornos?" *ATI*. May 23, 2023. https://allthatsinteresting.com/tyria-moore.
20. Randall. *Murder in St. Augustine: The Mysterious Death of Athalia Ponsell Lindsley*, excerpt. *Florida Writers Association*. 2016. https://floridawriters.blog/wp-content/uploads/2018/05/Murder-in-Stexcerpt.pdf. Retrieved February 8, 2023.
21. Bergara and Madej. "The Shocking Florida Machete Murder." *BuzzFeed Unsolved: True Crime*. 2019. https://buzzfeed-unsolved.fandom.com/wiki/The_Shocking_Florida_Machete_Murder.
22. Randall. *Murder in St. Augustine: The Mysterious Death of Athalia Ponsell Lindsley*, excerpt. *Florida Writers Association*. 2016. https://floridawriters.blog/wp-content/uploads/2018/05/Murder-in-Stexcerpt.pdf. Retrieved February 8, 2023.
23. *Ibid.*
24. *Ibid.*
25. *Ibid.*
26. Seibert. "Only One Man with a Bullhorn and a Couple...." *UPI Archives*. 1981. https://www.upi.com/Archives/1981/02/07/Only-one-man-with-a-bullhorn-and-a-couple/1870350370000/. Retrieved December 30, 2022.
27. "Acts of Repudiation from Mariel 1980 Through International Human Rights Day 2009: Government Run and Organized Operations." *Cuban Exile Quarter*. 2009. http://cubanexilequarter.blogspot.com/2009/12/acts-of-repudiation-mariel-1980-and.html. Retrieved July 30, 2022.
28. "Castro Speech Database." *Latin American Network Information Center: Castro Speech Database*. 2022. http://lanic.utexas.edu/project/castro/db/1980/19800729.html. Retrieved October 15, 2023.
29. Fernández. "Race, Gender, and Class in the Persistence of the Mariel Stigma Twenty Years After the Exodus from Cuba." *ASCE*. 2004. https://ascecubadatabase.org/asce_proceedings/race-gender-and-class-in-the-persistence-of-the-mariel-stigma-twenty-years-after-the-exodus-from-cuba/. Retrieved July 15, 2022.
30. "Cubans Riot at Center in Arkansas." *The Washington Post*. 1980. https://www.washingtonpost.com/archive/politics/1980/06/02/cubans-riot-at-center-in-arkansas/1c050d85-ae99-4e7f-9ae3-d09c67aba3c5/. Retrieved July 30, 2022.
31. Card. "The Impact of the Mariel Boatlift on the Miami Labor Market." *JSTOR*. 1990. http://davidcard.berkeley.edu/papers/mariel-impact.pdf. Retrieved July 12, 2022.
32. *Ibid.*

Chapter 12

1. McTague. "Remember the '90s, Don't Long for a Return." *The Atlantic*. 2020. https://www.theatlantic.com/international/archive/2020/08/brexit-trump-china-90s-golden-era/615406/. Retrieved July 30, 2022.
2. Pleming. "Cuban Boy Draws Picture of Shipwreck Drama." *Wayback Machine Cubanet.org*. 2000. https://web.archive.org/web/20090112215621/http:/www.cubanet.org/CNews/y00/mar00/27e4.htm. Retrieved October 6, 2018.
3. Swanson and Garcia. "Why the Elián Gonzalez Saga Resonates 20 Years Later." *The Highlight By Vox*. 2019. https://www.vox.com/the-highlight/2019/11/4/20938885/miami-cuba-elian-gonzalez-castro. Retrieved October 25, 2022.
4. Payson-Denney. "So, Who Really Won? What the Bush v. Gore Studies Showed." *CNN*. 2015. https://www.cnn.com/2015/10/31/politics/bush-gore-2000-election-results-studies/index.html. Retrieved February 2, 2023.

5. "Bush Claims Victory." *ABC News*. 2000. https://abcnews.go.com/US/story?id=94895&page=1. Retrieved February 5, 2023.
6. Kettle. "Florida 'Recounts' Make Gore Winner." *The Guardian*. 2001. https://www.theguardian.com/world/2001/jan/29/uselections2000.usa. Retrieved July 19, 2022.
7. *Ibid.*
8. Palast. "Florida's Flawed 'Voter-Cleansing' Program." *Salon*. 2000. https://www.salon.com/2000/12/04/voter_file/. Retrieved October 19, 2022.
9. *Ibid.*
10. *Ibid.*
11. *Ibid.*
12. *Ibid.*
13. Cook. "The Mysterious Saudi Family That Vanished Two Weeks Before 9/11." *Gawker*. 2011. https://www.gawker.com/5838498/the-mysterious-saudi-family-that-vanished-two-weeks-before-911. Retrieved July 15, 2022.
14. *Ibid.*
15. *Ibid.*
16. Cox. "Florida Repeals Smart Growth Law." *New Geography*. 2011. http://www.newgeography.com/content/002471-florida-repeals-smart-growth-law. Retrieved June 30, 2022.
17. Smith and Stanley. "Great Recession, 10 Years Later: Foreclosure Crisis Cut Deeply; The Stings Is Still Felt." *News-Press*. 2018. https://www.news-press.com/story/news/local/2018/02/17/great-recession-10-years-later-foreclosure-crisis-cut-deeply-sting-still-felt/1079686001/. Retrieved June 18, 2022.

Chapter 13

1. Elfrink. "Latin American Dictators Love South Florida." *Miami New Times*. 2010. https://www.miaminewtimes.com/news/latin-american-dictators-love-south-florida-6377948?storyPage=3. Retrieved July 16, 2022.
2. "Judge Overturns Unanimous Jury Verdict That Found Former Bolivian President and Defense Minister Responsible for Massacre of Indigenous People." *Center for Constitutional Rights*. 2018. https://ccrjustice.org/home/press-center/press-releases/judge-overturns-unanimous-jury-verdict-found-former-bolivian. Retrieved June 30, 2022.
3. "CJA: Case Summary." *The Center for Justice and Accountability*. 2008. https://cja.org/wp-content/uploads/downloads/Rondon_P_Memo_in_Opposition_to_D_MTD_4.pdf. 2016. Retrieved October 25, 2022.
4. Zeitlin. "Butcher of the Andes." *Miami New Times*. 2007. https://www.miaminewtimes.com/news/butcher-of-the-andes-6333621. Retrieved June 2, 2022.
5. Elfrink. "Latin American Dictators Love South Florida." *Miami New Times*. 2010. https://www.miaminewtimes.com/news/latin-american-dictators-love-south-florida-6377948?storyPage=3. Retrieved July 16, 2022.
6. Constantine. "Torture at CIA Battalion 316." *Constantine Report*. 2009. https://constantinereport.com/torture-at-cia-battalion-316/. Retrieved December 14, 2023.
7. *Ibid.*
8. Miller and Farley. "Timing of Envoy's Departure Raises Questions." *LA Times*. May 7, 2001. https://www.latimes.com/archives/la-xpm-2001-may-07-mn-60375-story.html. Retrieved June 15, 2022.
9. "Former Guatemalan Special Forces Soldier Sentenced to 10 Years in Prison for Making False Statements on Naturalization Forms Regarding 1982 Massacre of Guatemalan Villagers." *Department of Justice*. 2010. https://www.justice.gov/opa/pr/former-guatemalan-special-forces-soldier-sentenced-10-years-prison-making-false-statements. Retrieved February 12, 2023.
10. *Ibid.*
11. *Ibid.*
12. "ICE Removes Former Member of Guatemalan Army Linked to 1982 Massacre." *Immigration and Customs Enforcement*. March 3, 2020. https://www.ice.gov/news/releases/ice-removes-former-member-guatemalan-army-linked-1982-massacre. Retrieved June 28, 2022.
13. Sierra. "Gerardo Machado." *Historyofcuba.com*. http://www.historyofcuba.com/history/machado.htm. Retrieved June 30, 2022.
14. *Ibid.*
15. "4 Are Killed in Cuban Outbreak; Bulletin Havana, Sept. 27." *Daily Illini*. September 28, 1932. *Illinois Digital Newspaper Collections*. https://idnc.library.illinois.edu/cgi-bin/illinois?a=d&d=DIL

19320928.2.77&e=------en-20—1—imgtxIN----------. Retrieved February 7, 2023.
16. Elfrink. "Latin American Dictators Love South Florida." *Miami New Times.* 2010. https://www.miaminewtimes.com/news/latin-american-dictators-love-south-florida-6377948?storyPage=3. Retrieved July 16, 2022.
17. "Fulgencio Batista." *Britannica.* 2019. https://www.britannica.com/biography/Fulgencio-Batista. Retrieved July 1, 2022.
18. *Ibid.*
19. Crowell. p. 17.
20. "The American Comandante in the Cuban Revolutionary Forces: William Morgan." *TheCubanHistory.com.* 2019. https://www.thecubanhistory.com/2012/05/william-morgan-a-rebel-americano-in-cuba/. Retrieved July 2, 2022.
21. O'Meilia. "Widow of Cuban Dictator Batista Dies in WPB." *Palm Beach Post.* October 4, 2006. https://freerepublic.com/focus/fr/1713569/posts.
22. "Cuban Foundation Museum." *MOAS.* 2022. https://www.moas.org/Cuban-Foundation-Museum-6-184.html. Retrieved July 1, 2022.
23. "Company of U.S.–Backed Somoza Dictatorship Sucked Nicaraguan Blood—Literally." *Telesur.* 2016. https://www.telesurenglish.net/news/Company-of-US-backed-Somoza-Sucked-Nicaraguan-Blood—Literally-20160719-0022.html. Retrieved July 21, 2022.
24. Kunzle. p. 4.
25. Pilger. p. 498.
26. Elfrink. "Latin American Dictators Love South Florida." *Miami New Times.* 2010. https://www.miaminewtimes.com/news/latin-american-dictators-love-south-florida-6377948?storyPage=3. Retrieved July 16, 2022.
27. *Ibid.*
28. "Prosper Avril." *Military-History.* 2010. https://military-history.fandom.com/wiki/Prosper_Avril. Retrieved July 14, 2022.
29. Galván. p. 85.
30. "Panamanian Dictator Manuel Noriega Surrenders to U.S." *History.com.* 2023. https://www.history.com/this-day-in-history/noriega-surrenders-to-u-s. Retrieved February 5, 2023.
31. *Ibid.*
32. Ramos, Lyons and Merzer. "He Was U.S. Prisoner #41586. How Noriega Landed in a Miami Jail After Invasion." *Miami Herald.* 2017. https://amp.miamiherald.com/news/nation-world/world/americas/article153300559.html. Retrieved July 14, 2022.

Chapter 14

1. "The Story of Seaside, Florida." *SoWal.* 2022. https://sowal.com/story/the-story-of-seaside-florida. July 12, 2022.
2. *Ibid.*
3. "Seaside." *Congress for the New Urbanism.* https://www.cnu.org/what-we-do/build-great-places/seaside. December 10, 2023.
4. Bente. "Spring Breakers Stir Up Trouble in Seaside." *News 4.* 2022. https://www.wtvy.com/2022/03/19/spring-breakers-stir-up-trouble-seaside/. Retrieved October 19, 2022.
5. "Walt Disney's Plan for EPCOT." *YouTube.* 2007. https://www.youtube.com/watch?v=u9M3pKsrcc8. Retrieved July 14, 2022.
6. "The Original EPCOT." *The Original EPCOT.com.* 2023. https://sites.google.com/site/theoriginalepcot/overview/the-florida-project?pli=1. Retrieved April 30, 2023.
7. Pilkington. "How the Disney Dream Died in Celebration." *The Guardian.* 2010. https://www.theguardian.com/world/2010/dec/13/celebration-death-of-a-dream. Retrieved July 12, 2022.
8. Blair, Jayson. "Failed Disney Vision: Integrated City." *The New York Times.* September 23, 2001. https://www.nytimes.com/2001/09/23/us/failed-disney-vision-integrated-city.html. Retrieved July 5, 2020.
9. *Ibid.*
10. "Disney's Celebration, Florida Crime Rate." *WFTV 9.* 2018. https://www.wftv.com/station/search/disneys-celebration-florida-crime-rate/703712802/. Retrieved December 14, 2023.
11. Pilkington. "How the Disney Dream Died in Celebration." *The Guardian.* 2010. https://www.theguardian.com/world/2010/dec/13/celebration-death-of-a-dream. Retrieved July 12, 2022.
12. *Ibid.*
13. Hitt. "Celebration, Florida: How Disney's 'Community of Tomorrow'

Became a Total Nightmare." *The Daily Beast.* 2019. https://www.thedailybeast.com/celebration-florida-how-disneys-community-of-tomorrow-became-a-total-nightmare. Retrieved July 14, 2022.

14. Prieto and Jacobson. "Homeless Man Accused in Hatchet Killing, the First Homicide in Disney Built Town of Celebration." *Palm Beach Post.* 2012. https://www.palmbeachpost.com/story/news/crime/2012/04/07/homeless-man-accused-in-hatchet/7842776007/. Retrieved February 2, 2023.

15. *Ibid.*

16. Spindel and Fernandez. "Murder in Celebration, Florida: The Victim's Secret Life." *Daily Beast.* 2017. https://www.thedailybeast.com/murder-in-celebration-florida-the-victims-secret-life. Retrieved February 12, 2023.

17. Baker. "Anthony Todt Convicted of Killing Wife, 3 Children and Family Dog in Celebration, Fla., Home." *People.com.* 2022. https://people.com/crime/anthony-todt-celebration-florida-father-convicted-killing-family/. Retrieved July 14, 2022.

18. *Ibid.*

19. *Ibid.*

20. Pilkington. "How the Disney Dream Died in Celebration." *The Guardian.* 2010. https://www.theguardian.com/world/2010/dec/13/celebration-death-of-a-dream. Retrieved July 12, 2022.

21. Hitt. "Celebration, Florida: How Disney's 'Community of Tomorrow' Became a Total Nightmare." *The Daily Beast.* 2019. https://www.thedailybeast.com/celebration-florida-how-disneys-community-of-tomorrow-became-a-total-nightmare. Retrieved July 14, 2022.

22. *Ibid.*

23. Kusisto. "Leaks and Mold Are Ruining the Disney Magic in Celebration, Florida." *The Wall Street Journal.* 2016. https://condomadness.info/decline-Celebration.html. Retrieved July 12, 2022.

24. *Ibid.*

25. "History of Ave Maria." *The Ave Herald.* 2012. https://www.aveherald.com/visiting-ave-maria/history-of-ave-maria.html. Retrieved July 14, 2022.

26. Brook. "Inside the Isolated Catholic Town Built by the Founder of Domino's." *Wired.* 2014. https://www.wired.com/2014/04/rawfile-0404-ave-maria/. Retrieved December 10, 2023.

27. "Ave Maria University's Strangle-Hold on Women Goes Way Beyond Suing Obamacare." *Daily Kos.* 2014. https://www.dailykos.com/stories/2014/9/30/1332354/-Ave-Maria-University-s-Strangle-Hold-on-Women-Goes-Way-Beyond-Suing-Obamacare. Retrieved December 14, 2023.

28. Miller. "Ave Maria University: A Catholic Project Gone Wrong." *Miami New Times.* 2011. https://www.miaminewtimes.com/news/ave-maria-university-a-catholic-project-gone-wrong-6384870?storyPage=2. Retrieved July 10, 2022.

29. *Ibid.*

30. *Ibid.*

31. *Ibid.*

32. Borns. "Ave Maria Diversifies as Home Sales Soar." *News-Press.* 2015. https://www.news-press.com/story/news/2015/11/04/ave-maria-diversifies-home-sales-soar/74430350/. 2015. Retrieved July 20, 2022.

33. Alpert. "What My Nextdoor Neighbors Don't Get About the Word 'Plantation.'" *CNN.* 2020. https://www.cnn.com/2020/08/01/opinions/black-lives-matter-renaming-plantations-alpert-opinion/index.html. Retrieved August 1, 2022.

34. Swirko. "Haile Plantation Residents Debate Name Change." *Gainesville Sun.* 2020. Retrieved July 20, 2020.

35. "Survey Results." *Haile Plantation West.* 2020. https://mailchi.mp/aa28bd9271f0/haile-plantation-west-survey-results?e=%5bUNIQID%5d. Retrieved July 15, 2022.

Chapter 15

1. Mahoney. "New Lighthearted Ron DeSantis Ad Features His Family, Trump Jokes." *Tampa Bay Times.* 2018. https://www.tampabay.com/florida-politics/buzz/2018/07/30/new-lighthearted-ron-desantis-ad-features-his-family-trump-jokes/. Retrieved July 28, 2022.

2. Wilson. "Florida Governor Election Results: Andrew Gillum Versus Ron DeSantis." *Tampa Bay Times.* 2018. https://www.tampabay.com/florida-politics/buzz/2018/11/06/florida-governor-election-results-andrew-gillum-versus-ron-desantis/. Retrieved July 30, 2022.

3. Walters. "Ron DeSantis Wraps-up

Notes—Chapter 15

His First Year as Governor of Florida. See What He's Accomplished." *Florida Today*. 2020. https://www.floridatoday.com/story/news/2020/01/08/ron-desantis-florida-governor-accomplishments-first-year/2806449001/. Retrieved August 2, 2022.

4. Ibid.

5. Fineout and Dixon. "Saying Goodbye to 2019—Gov. Ron DeSantis Ends Year on Top—Florida Voters Will Decide Whether to Boost Minimum Wage—House Speaker Wants to Investigate Moffitt Ties to China." *Politico*. 2019. https://www.politico.com/newsletters/florida-playbook/2019/12/20/saying-goodbye-to-2019-gov-ron-desantis-ends-year-on-top-florida-voters-will-decide-whether-to-boost-minimum-wage-house-speaker-wants-to-investigate-moffitt-ties-to-china-487954. Retrieved August 3, 2022.

6. Barbash and Horton. "Florida Governor Issues Stay-At-Home Order After Heavy Criticism." *The Washington Post*. 2020. https://www.washingtonpost.com/nation/2020/04/01/coronavirus-florida-desantis/. Retrieved August 2, 2022.

7. Ibid.

8. "The Costly Toll of Not Shutting Down Spring Break Earlier." *New York Times*. 2020. https://www.nytimes.com/2020/04/11/us/florida-spring-break-coronavirus.html. Retrieved August 2, 2022.

9. Ibid.

10. Ellenbogen and Kumar. "Florida Breaks Record with 17,000+ Coronavirus Cases In One Day." *Tampa Bay Times*. 2020. https://www.tampabay.com/news/health/2020/12/31/florida-breaks-record-with-more-than-17000-coronavirus-cases-reported-in-one-day/. Retrieved August 2, 2022.

11. Kennedy. "Sweden Tells Citizens to Wear Masks on Public Transport as It Struggles with Covid-19 Resurgence." *EuroNews.com*. 2020. https://www.euronews.com/my-europe/2020/12/18/sweden-tells-citizens-to-wear-masks-on-public-transport-as-it-struggles-with-covid-19-resu. Retrieved June 20, 2022.

12. Fang. "Ousted Designer of Florida's Covid-19 Dashboard Says She Was Asked to Censor Data." *Huffpost*. 2020. https://www.huffpost.com/entry/florida-covid-19-data-censorship_n_5ec3f4a0 c5b63814cd6bdb80. Retrieved July 10, 2022.

13. Bustos and Kennedy. "State Investigators Dismiss Rebekah Jones' Claims of Florida Fudging Covid-19 Data." *Tallahassee Democrat*. 2022. https://www.tallahassee.com/story/news/2022/05/27/rebekkah-jones-report-fails-support-claims-florida-covid-19-data-doctored/9953780002/. Retrieved August 4, 2022.

14. Chapell. "Florida Agents Raid Home of Rebekah Jones, Former State Data Scientist." *NPR*. December 8, 2020.

15. Bustos and Kennedy. "State Investigators Dismiss Rebekah Jones' Claims of Florida Fudging Covid-19 Data."

16. Johnson. "Rebekah Jones' Teen Son Pleads No Contest to Threatening Navarre School Shooting, Stabbing." *Pensacola News Journal*. December 15, 2023.

17. Atterbury. "DeSantis Pushes Bill That Allows Parent to Sue Schools Over Critical Race Theory." *Politico*. 2021. https://www.politico.com/news/2021/12/16/desantis-bill-critical-race-theory-525118. Retrieved August 1, 2022.

18. Ibid.

19. Davis. "Florida Gov. Ron DeSantis Signs a Bill Banning Abortions After 15 Weeks." *NPR*. 2022. https://www.npr.org/2022/04/14/1084485963/florida-abortion-law-15-weeks. Retrieved June 20, 2022.

20. Contorno. "Judge Says Florida's 15-Week Abortion Law is Unconstitutional." *CNN*. July 1, 2022.

21. Woodward. "What Is Florida's 'Don't Say Gay' Bill?" *Independent*. 2022. https://www.independent.co.uk/news/world/americas/us-politics/dont-say-gay-bill-florida-desantis-b2074720.html. Retrieved July 30, 2022.

22. Voght. "Florida's Don't Say Gay Law Took Effect. Chaos Ensued." *Rolling Stone*. 2022. https://www.rollingstone.com/politics/politics-news/florida-dont-say-gay-law-edcuators-1377353/. Retrieved August 3, 2022.

23. Migdon. "Florida's 'Don't Say Gay' Bill Takes Effect Today. Its Impact Is Already Being Felt." *The Hill*. 2022. https://thehill.com/changing-america/respect/equality/3543536-floridas-dont-say-gay-law-takes-effect-today-its-impact-is-already-being-felt/. Retrieved August 1, 2022.

24. Gore. "DeSantis vs. Disney Q&A." *FactCheck.org* 2022. https://www.factcheck.org/2022/05/desantis-vs-disney-qa/. Retrieved August 2, 2022.

25. Whitten. "Disney Vows to Repeal Don't Say Gay Law." *CNBC*. 2022. https://www.cnbc.com/2022/03/28/disney-vows-to-help-repeal-dont-say-gay-law.html. Retrieved August 3, 2022.

26. Swisher and Gillespie. "Disney World's Reedy Creek: What Happens After the Special District Is Abolished?" *Orlando Sentinel*. 2022. https://web.archive.org/web/20220422120908/https://www.orlandosentinel.com/politics/os-ne-abolishing-reedy-creek-20220422-hvzxgcdxq5e43mzgwbmrrbwfmy-story.html. Retrieved August 3, 2022.

27. Bradner and Contorno. "Disney Sues DeSantis and Oversight Board After Vote to Nullify Agreement with Special Taxing District." *CNN*. 2023. https://www.cnn.com/2023/04/26/politics/disney-desantis-reedy-creek-power/index.html. Retrieved April 30, 2023.

28. Gancarski. "Disney Edges Out Ron DeSantis in Popularity Poll." *Florida Politics*. 2022. https://floridapolitics.com/archives/524972-disney-edges-out-ron-desantis-in-popularity-poll/. Retrieved October 25, 2022.

29. Fineout. "Federal Judge Throws Out Disney's Lawsuit Against DeSantis." *Politico*. January 31, 2024.

30. Seminara. "Newsom v. DeSantis." *City Journal*. 2022. https://www.city-journal.org/newsom-v-desantis. Retrieved August 4, 2022.

31. Ibid.

32. Sheeler. "Ron DeSantis Rips Newsom. In California, 'You Ain't Seeing Very Many Florida License Plates." *Sacramento Bee*. 2022. https://www.sacbee.com/news/politics-government/capitol-alert/article263287578.html. Retrieved August 4, 2022.

33. Hubbard. "Newsom, DeSantis Fight a 'Proxy War' for America's Future." *U.S. News*. 2022. https://www.usnews.com/news/politics/articles/2022-07-07/newsom-desantis-fight-a-proxy-war-for-americas-future. Retrieved August 4, 2022.

Bibliography

"Acts of Repudiation from Mariel 1980 Through International Human Rights Day 2009: Government Run and Organized Operations." *Cuban Exile Quarter.* 2009. http://cubanexilequarter.blogspot.com/2009/12/acts-of-repudiation-mariel-1980-and.html. Retrieved July 30, 2022.
Adkins, J. "These People Are Frightened to Death: Congressional Delegations and the Lavender Scare." *National Archives.* 2016. https://www.archives.gov/publications/prologue/2016/summer/lavender.html. Retrieved February 5, 2023.
"Al Capone." *PBS.* 2022. https://www.pbs.org/wgbh/americanexperience/features/miami-al-capone/. Retrieved July 12, 2022.
Allen, J., and C. Jewett. *Slavery in the South: A State-by-State History.* Westport, CT: Greenwood Press. 2004.
Alpert, Y.M. "What My Nextdoor Neighbors Don't Get About the Word 'Plantation.'" *CNN.* 2020. https://www.cnn.com/2020/08/01/opinions/black-lives-matter-renaming-plantations-alpert-opinion/index.html. Retrieved August 1, 2022.
Alvarado, F. "Former Marijuana Smuggler Robert Platshorn Pitches Pot to Seniors." *Miami New Times.* 2019. https://www.miaminewtimes.com/marijuana/the-black-tuna-gangs-robert-platshorn-post-smuggler-pitches-medical-marijuana-to-seniors-11147955. Retrieved February 8, 2023.
Ambrus, S., and J. Contreras. "Fighting the New Drug Lords." *Media Awareness Project.* 2000. http://www.mapinc.org/drugnews/v00/n218/a12.html?3110. Retrieved July 30, 2022.
"An American Beach." *Anamericanbeach.com.* 2007. http://www.anamericanbeach.com/. Retrieved July 12, 2022.
"The American Comandante in the Cuban Revolutionary Forces: William Morgan." *TheCubanHistory.com.* 2019. https://www.thecubanhistory.com/2012/05/william-morgan-a-rebel-americano-in-cuba/. Retrieved July 2, 2022.
"Anna Kingsley: A Free Woman." *National Park Service.* 2022. https://www.nps.gov/timu/learn/historyculture/kp_anna_freewoman.htm. Retrieved June 15, 2022.
"Anna Madgigine Jai Kingsley." *Florida Department of State.* 2022. https://dos.myflorida.com/offices/historical-museums/united-connections/women-in-history/anna-madgigine-jai-kingsley/. Retrieved February 10, 2023.
Aptheker, H. *American Negro Slave Revolts.* New York: International Publishers. 1974.
"Arrest of Dr. Martin Luther King, Jr." *Historic City News.* 2011. https://historiccity.com/2011/staugustine/news/arrest-dr-martin-luther-king-jr-14561. Retrieved February 8, 2023.
Arthur, S.C. *The Story of the West Florida Rebellion.* St. Francisville, LA: St. Francisville Democrat. 1935. Retrieved September 11, 2022.
Ashton, J. "Camp Blanding: The War Years." *Indianamilitary.org.* 1996. http://www.indianamilitary.org/30TH/FT-SITE/CampBlandingWarYears/CampBlanding.htm. Retrieved November 20, 2011.
"The Attack on the Fort at Prospect Bluff." *ExploreSouthernHistory.com.* http://www.exploresouthernhistory.com/fortgadsden3.html. Retrieved September 15, 2011.

Bibliography

"Attempted Assassination of FDR in Bayfront Park in 1933." *Miami-History.com.* 2022. http://miami-history.com/attempted-assassination-of-fdr-in-bayfront-park/. Retrieved August 1, 2022

Atterbury, A. "DeSantis Pushes Bill That Allows Parent to Sue Schools Over Critical Race Theory." *Politico.* 2021. https://www.politico.com/news/2021/12/16/desantis-bill-critical-race-theory-525118. Retrieved August 1, 2022.

Ault, J. "The Virginius Incident." *Centennial Website.* 1996. https://www.spanamwar.com/virginius. Retrieved July 1, 2022.

"Ave Maria University's Strangle-Hold on Women Goes Way Beyond Suing Obamacare." *Daily Kos.* 2014. https://www.dailykos.com/stories/2014/9/30/1332354/-Ave-Maria-University-s-Strangle-Hold-on-Women-Goes-Way-Beyond-Suing-Obamacare. Retrieved December 14, 2023.

"'Ax Handle Saturday,' A Story." *AAREG.* 2022. https://aaregistry.org/story/ax-handle-saturday-a-brief-story/. Retrieved October 25, 2022.

Baker, K.C. "Anthony Todt Convicted of Killing Wife, 3 Children and Family Dog in Celebration, Fla., Home." *People.com.* 2022. https://people.com/crime/anthony-todt-celebration-florida-father-convicted-killing-family/. Retrieved July 14, 2022.

Barbash, F., and A. Horton. "Florida Governor Issues Coronavirus Stay-at-Home Order After Heavy Criticism." *The Washington Post.* 2020. https://www.washingtonpost.com/nation/2020/04/01/coronavirus-florida-desantis/. Retrieved August 2, 2022.

"The Battle of Fowltown." *Exploresouthernhistory.com.* 2015. https://www.exploresouthernhistory.com/fowltown.html. Retrieved June 2, 2022.

"The Battle of Olustee Florida." *Battle of Olustee.* http://battleofolustee.org/battle.html. Retrieved June 10, 2022.

Bemis, S.F. *A Diplomatic History of the United States.* New York: Henry Holt. 1965.

Bente, K. "Spring Breakers Stir Up Trouble in Seaside." *News 4.* 2022. https://www.wtvy.com/2022/03/19/spring-breakers-stir-up-trouble-seaside/. Retrieved October 19, 2022.

Bergara, R., and S. Madej. "The Shocking Florida Machete Murder." *BuzzFeed Unsolved: True Crime.* 2019. https://buzzfeed-unsolved.fandom.com/wiki/The_Shocking_Florida_Machete_Murder.

Beutke, A.A. "Behind Closed Doors: The Dark Legacy of the Johns Committee." M.A. Project, Documentary Institute, University of Florida. 2000.

Biggs, J.T. "The Second Seminole War." *Issuu.com.* 2020. https://issuu.com/oghmacreative/docs/saddlebag_winter_2020_final/s/11539584. Retrieved April 22, 2023

Blair, J. "Failed Disney Vision: Integrated City." *The New York Times.* September 23, 2001. https://www.nytimes.com/2001/09/23/us/failed-disney-vision-integrated-city.html. Retrieved July 5, 2020.

Blumetti, J. "The First Floridians." *Bitter Southerner.* 2020. https://bittersoutherner.com/the-first-floridians-fort-mose-st-augustine. Retrieved September 26, 2022.

Borns, P. "Ave Maria Diversifies as Home Sales Soar." *News-Press.* 2015. https://www.news-press.com/story/news/2015/11/04/ave-maria-diversifies-home-sales-soar/74430350/. Retrieved July 20, 2022.

Bradner, E., and S. Contorno. "Disney Sues DeSantis and Oversight Board After Vote to Nullify Agreement with Special Taxing District." *CNN.* 2023. https://www.cnn.com/2023/04/26/politics/disney-desantis-reedy-creek-power/index.html. Retrieved April 30, 2023.

Brook, P. "Inside the Isolated Catholic Town Built by the Founder of Domino's." *Wired.* 2014. https://www.wired.com/2014/04/rawfile-0404-ave-maria/. Retrieved December 10, 2023.

"Brutal Journey." *Sarasota Magazine.* 2006. https://www.sarasotamagazine.com/news-and-profiles/2006/12/brutal-journey. Retrieved May 15, 2022.

"Bullets Once Flew at Dadeland Mall in a Deadly Shootout. The Cocaine Cowboys Were Here." *Miami Herald.* 2019. https://www.miamiherald.com/news/local/community/miami-dade/kendall/article231644003.html. Retrieved July 20, 2022.

Burnett, G. *Florida's Past: People and Events That Shaped the State V. 3.* Sarasota, FL: Pineapple Press. 1996.

"Bush Claims Victory." *ABC News.* 2000. https://abcnews.go.com/US/story?id=94895&page=1. Retrieved February 5, 2023.
Bustos, S., and J. Kennedy. "State Investigators Dismiss Rebekah Jones' Claims of Florida Fudging Covid-19 Data." *Tallahassee Democrat.* 2022. https://www.tallahassee.com/story/news/2022/05/27/rebekkah-jones-report-fails-support-claims-florida-covid-19-data-doctored/9953780002/. Retrieved August 4, 2022.
Call, J. "The Time Has Come: Florida Lawmakers Want Apology for 'Lives Ruined' by Johns Committee." *Tallahassee Democrat.* 2019. https://www.tallahassee.com/story/news/2019/03/22/florida-lawmakers-push-apology-lives-ruined-johns-committee/3244097002/. Retrieved October 19, 2022.
"The Calusa Domain." *Florida Museum.* 2018. https://www.floridamuseum.ufl.edu/sflarch/research/calusa-domain/. Retrieved July 4, 2022.
"Captain Francisco Menéndez Helped Found the First Free Black Settlement in the U.S." *aaron-gustafson.com.* 2022. https://www.aaron-gustafson.com/notebook/captain-francisco-menndez-helped-found-the-first-free-black-settlement-in-the-us/. Retrieved June 30, 2022.
Card, D. "The Impact of the Mariel Boatlift on the Miami Labor Market." *JSTOR.* 1990. http://davidcard.berkeley.edu/papers/mariel-impact.pdf. Retrieved July 12, 2022.
Carter, W.H. *Stolen Water: Saving the Everglades from Its Friends, Foes, and Florida.* New York: Atria Books. 2004.
Cash, W.T. "Taylor County History and Civil War Deserters." *Florida Historical Quarterly* V. 27, N. 1. 1948. https://www.jstor.org/stable/30138660. Retrieved October 25, 2022.
"Castro Speech Database." *Latin American Network Information Center: Castro Speech Database.* 2022. http://lanic.utexas.edu/project/castro/db/1980/19800729.html. Retrieved October 15, 2023.
Cavanaugh, D. "Key West Declared a Faux War on the United States in 1982." *Medium.* 2015. https://medium.com/war-is-boring/key-west-declared-a-faux-war-on-the-united-states-in-1982-f2c40b429e75. Retrieved February 12, 2013.
"Caveri [Canerio] World Map." *MyOldMaps.com.* 2015. http://www.myoldmaps.com/renaissance-maps-1490-1800/307-caveri-canerio-world/307-caveri.pdf. Retrieved June 15, 2022.
Chardy, A., and L. Yanez. "Fidel Castro Once Used Miami as Haven, Revolutionary Springboard." *Miami Herald.* 2008. http://www.latinamericanstudies.org/fidel/miami.htm. Retrieved September 30, 2011.
"A Chronology of the Elián Gonzalez Saga." *PBS Frontline.* 2014. https://www.pbs.org/wgbh/pages/frontline/shows/elian/etc/eliancron.html. Retrieved July 19, 2022.
"Church of the Immaculate Conception Steeple." *Waymarking.com.* 2008. http://www.waymarking.com/waymarks/WM4JMG_Church_of_the_Immaculate_Conception_Steeple_Jacksonville_FL. Retrieved October 6, 2011.
"CJA: Case Summary." *The Center for Justice and Accountability.* 2008. https://cja.org/wp-content/uploads/downloads/Rondon_P_Memo_in_Opposition_to_D_MTD_4.pdf. Retrieved October 25, 2022.
Clendinen, D., and A. Nagourney. *Out for Good: The Struggle to Build a Gay Rights Movement in America.* New York: Simon & Schuster. 1999.
Colloff, P., and M. Hall. "Married to the Mob." *Texas Monthly.* 1998. https://www.texasmonthly.com/news-politics/married-to-the-mob/. Retrieved October 25, 2022.
"Company of U.S.–Backed Somoza Dictatorship Sucked Nicaraguan Blood—Literally." *Telesur.* 2016. https://www.telesurenglish.net/news/Company-of-US-backed-Somoza-Sucked-Nicaraguan-Blood—Literally-20160719-0022.html. Retrieved July 21, 2022.
"Conch Republic Independence Celebration." *Rent Key West Vacations.* 2022. https://www.rentkeywest.com/key-west-events/conch-republic-independence-celebration-42nd-annual-2024/. Retrieved July 30, 2022.
"Conditions of Antebellum Slavery." *PBS Online.* http://www.pbs.org/wgbh/aia/part4/4p2956.html. Retrieved October 9, 2011.
Conrad, G. "The Cracker Prince." *Tallahassee Magazine.* 2012. https://www.tallahasseemagazine.com/the-cracker-prince/. Retrieved October 25, 2022.

Constantine, A. "Torture at CIA Battalion 316." *Constantine Report*. 2009. https://constantinereport.com/torture-at-cia-battalion-316/. Retrieved December 14, 2023.

Cook, J. "The Mysterious Saudi Family That Vanished Two Weeks Before 9/11." *Gawker*. 2011. https://www.gawker.com/5838498/the-mysterious-saudi-family-that-vanished-two-weeks-before-911. Retrieved July 15, 2022.

Coppleston, A. "My Experiences During the Inquisition." from A. Beutke, "Behind Closed Doors." Master's thesis, University of Florida. 2000.

"The Costly Toll of Not Shutting Down Spring Break Earlier." *New York Times*. 2020. https://www.nytimes.com/2020/04/11/us/florida-spring-break-coronavirus.html. Retrieved August 2, 2022.

Cox, I.J. "The West Florida Controversy, 1798–1813; A Study in American Diplomacy." *Archive.org*. 1918. https://archive.org/details/westfloridacontr00coxi. Retrieved June 1, 2022.

Cox, W. "Florida Repeals Smart Growth Law." *Newgeography*. 2011. http://www.newgeography.com/content/002471-florida-repeals-smart-growth-law. Retrieved June 30, 2022.

Crowell, D.D. *The Brink: Cuban Missile Crisis, 1962*. London: J.M. Dent & Sons. 1980.

"Cuban Foundation Museum." *MOAS*. 2022. https://www.moas.org/Cuban-Foundation-Museum-6-184.html. Retrieved July 1, 2022.

"Cubans Riot at Center in Arkansas." *The Washington Post*. 1980. https://www.washingtonpost.com/archive/politics/1980/06/02/cubans-riot-at-center-in-arkansas/1c050d85-ae99-4e7f-9ae3-d09c67aba3c5/. Retrieved July 30, 2022.

Cummins, J. *Francis Drake: The Lives of a Hero*. London: Palgrave Macmillan. 1996.

Daniels, G.C. "De Gourgues Florida Expedition 1567." *The New World*. 2014. https://thenewworld.us/de-gourges-florida-expedition-in-1567/. Retrieved August 29, 2022.

Davis, T.F. "MacGregor's Invasion of Florida." *Florida Historical Quarterly V.7–1*. 1928. https://stars.library.ucf.edu/cgi/viewcontent.cgi?article=1768&context=fhq. Retrieved October 10, 2022.

Davis, T.F. *History of Jacksonville, Florida and Vicinity, 1513 to 1924*. Gainesville: University of Florida Press. 1964.

Davis, W. "Florida Gov. Ron DeSantis Signs a Bill Banning Abortions After 15 Weeks." *NPR*. 2022. https://www.npr.org/2022/04/14/1084485963/florida-abortion-law-15-weeks. Retrieved June 20, 2022.

DeBolt, D. "How Andrew Jackson Set up a 'Good Government' for Pensacola and Florida." *Pensacola News Journal*. 2021. https://www.pnj.com/story/news/2021/03/07/andrew-jackson-set-up-good-government-pensacola-and-florida/4579079001/. Retrieved June 1, 2022.

"De Gourgues, Dominique." *A History of Florida*. 1904. http://fcit.usf.edu/florida/docs/d/degour.htm. Retrieved August 29, 2022.

de Vise, D. "Columbian Drug Cartel Suspect Lands in S. Florida." *Miami Herald*. 2001. http://www.latinamericanstudies.org/drugs/bernal.htm. Retrieved July 30, 2022.

Dietche, S. "Florida Mafia Boss Santo Trafficante Jr. Died 30 Years Ago March 17." *The Mob Museum*. 2018. https://themobmuseum.org/blog/trafficante-jr-death/. Retrieved July 10, 2022.

Deitche, S. "The Tampa Mob." *Americanmafia.com*. 1999. https://www.americanmafia.com/Cities/Tampa.html. Retrieved July 15, 2022.

Dillon, D. "St. Augustine, FL History: A Pirate Execution." *Doug Dillon*. 2012. https://dougdillon.com/2012/04/21/st-augustine-history-pirate-execution/. Retrieved February 2, 2023.

Dimri, B. "Was the Legendary Spanish Pirate Jose Gaspar Real?" *Historic Mysteries*. 2022. https://www.historicmysteries.com/jose-gaspar/. Retrieved February 10, 2023.

"Disney's Celebration, Florida Crime Rate." *WFTV 9*. 2018. https://www.wftv.com/station/search/disneys-celebration-florida-crime-rate/703712802/. Retrieved December 14, 2023.

"Distinguish Jacksonville: The Silent Film Industry." *Metro Jacksonville*. 2007. http://www.metrojacksonville.com/article/2007-feb-distinguish-jacksonville-the-silent-film-industry. Retrieved July 10, 2022.

Bibliography

"Distribution of Population, 1830–1840." *Maps Etc.* 2007. http://fcit.usf.edu/florida/maps/pages/2400/f2447/f2447.htm. Retrieved June 4, 2022.
"Dr. Robert B. Hayling—'Father of the Civil Rights Act of 1964.'" *Accord Freedom Trail.* 2011. https://accordfreedomtrail.org/hayling.html. Retrieved February 5, 2023.
Douglas, M. *The Everglades: River of Grass.* New York: H. Wolff. 1947.
"Douglas Dorsey: Ex-Slave Narratives from the Federal Writers' Project 1936–1938." *Exploring Florida.* 2005. https://fcit.usf.edu/florida/docs/s/slave/slave02.htm. Retrieved July 1, 2022.
Dovell, J.E. "The Everglades Before Reclamation." *Florida Historical Quarterly*, V. 26, N. 1. 1947. Retrieved December 14, 2023.
"Drug Enforcement Agency History." *DEA* 2022. https://www.dea.gov/sites/default/files/2021-04/1975-1980_p_39-49.pdf. Retrieved October 25, 2022.
Dwyer, J., ed. "An Assassin's Bullets for FDR." *Strange Stories, Amazing Facts of America's Past.* Pleasantville, NY: The Reader's Digest Association. 1989.
Ecker, R.L. "Hell in Miami." *Ronaldecker.com.* 2004. http://ronaldecker.com/hell.html. Retrieved May 1, 2023.
"1833 Alabama Slave Code." *Sensagent.* http://dictionary.sensagent.com/Slave%20codes/en-en/. 2022. Retrieved June 15, 2022.
Elfrink, T. "Latin American Dictators Love South Florida." *Miami New Times.* 2010. https://www.miaminewtimes.com/news/latin-american-dictators-love-south-florida-6377948?storyPage=3. Retrieved July 16, 2022.
Ellenbogen, R., and D. Kumar. "Florida Breaks Record with 17,000+ Coronavirus Cases in One Day." *Tampa Bay Times.* 2020. https://www.tampabay.com/news/health/2020/12/31/florida-breaks-record-with-more-than-17000-coronavirus-cases-reported-in-one-day/. Retrieved August 2, 2022.
"Encyclopedia of Southern Jewish Communities–St Petersburg, Florida." *Goldring/Woldenberg Institute of Southern Jewish Life.* 2022. https://www.isjl.org/florida-st-petersburg-encyclopedia.html. Retrived July 20, 2022.
"The Enemy Presence: German U-Boats." *Palm Beach County History Online.* 2009. https://pbchistory.org/educational-articles/. Retrieved July 5, 2022.
England, J. "José Martí and the Fernandina Plan." *Amelia Museum.* 2020. https://ameliamuseum.org/jose-marti-and-the-fernandina-plan/. Retrieved July 1, 2022.
Ensley, G. "Battle of Natural Bridge Myths Endure." *Tallahassee Democrat.* 2017. https://www.tallahassee.com/story/news/2017/03/01/battle-natural-bridge-myths-endure/98525912/. Retrieved June 30, 2022.
"European Contact." *Jupiter Inlet Lighthouse and Museum.* 2022. https://www.jupiterlighthouse.org/explore/history/european-contact/. Retrieved February 2, 2023.
"Excerpt from the Reminiscences of William Frederick Penniman." *Battle of Olustee.* 2022. https://battleofolustee.org/letters/penniman.htm. Retrieved October 25, 2022.
"Exhibits." *Florida Memory.* 2021. http://www.floridamemory.com/Exhibits/florida highlights/investigation/. Retrieved July 19, 2022.
Fagan, B. "Sir Francis Drake Was in Cartagena, Colombia." *World's Best Golf Destinations.* 2019. https://www.worldsbestgolfdestinations.org/sir-francis-drake-was-in-cartagena-colombia/. Retrieved September 26, 2022.
Fang, M. "Ousted Designer of Florida's Covid-19 Dashboard Says She Was Asked to Censor Data." *Huffpost.* 2020. https://www.huffpost.com/entry/florida-covid-19-data-censorship_n_5ec3f4a0c5b63814cd6bdb80. Retrieved July 10, 2022.
"FDR Escapes Assassination Attempt in Miami." *History.com.* 2021. https://www.history.com/this-day-in-history/fdr-escapes-assassination-in-miami. Retrieved July 12, 2022.
Fehler, B. "The Purple Pamphlet: A Shadowy History in the Sunshine State." *Medium.* 2020. https://medium.com/@bfehler/the-purple-pamphlet-a-shadowy-history-in-the-sunshine-state-123a16f6724d. Retrieved July 30, 2022.
Feldberg, M. "Jewish Gangsters in America." *Jewish Virtual Library.* 1998. https://www.jewishvirtuallibrary.org/jewish-gangsters-in-america. Retrieved October 19, 2022.
Fernández, G. "Race, Gender, and Class in the Persistence of the Mariel Stigma Twenty Years After the Exodus from Cuba." *ASCE.* 2004. https://ascecubadatabase.org/

asce_proceedings/race-gender-and-class-in-the-persistence-of-the-mariel-stigma-twenty-years-after-the-exodus-from-cuba/. Retrieved July 15, 2022.

Fineout, G., and M. Dixon. "Saying Goodbye to 2019—Gov. Ron DeSantis Ends Year on Top—Florida Voters Will Decide Whether to Boost Minimum Wage—House Speaker Wants to Investigate Moffitt Ties to China." *Politico*. 2019. https://www.politico.com/newsletters/florida-playbook/2019/12/20/saying-goodbye-to-2019-gov-ron-desantis-ends-year-on-top-florida-voters-will-decide-whether-to-boost-minimum-wage-house-speaker-wants-to-investigate-moffitt-ties-to-china-487954. Retrieved August 3, 2022.

Flank, L. "Key West and the Conch Republic: We Seceded Where Others Failed." *Daily Kos*. 2014. https://www.dailykos.com/stories/2014/7/2/1301623/-Key-West-and-the-Conch-Republic-We-Seceded-Where-Others-Failed. Retrieved February 23, 2023.

Fleming, F.P. "The Story of Juan Ortiz and Uleleh." *Florida Historical Quarterly V. 1*. 1908. https://stars.library.ucf.edu/cgi/viewcontent.cgi?article=1390&context=fhq. Retrieved February 12, 2023.

"Florida Crime Rates 1960–2019." *Thedisastercenter.com*. https://www.disastercenter.com/crime/flcrime.htm. Retrieved July 30, 2022.

"Florida Governor Sidney J. Catts: The Polarizing Populist." *The U.S. Caribbean and Florida Digital Newspaper Project*. 2017. https://ufndnp.domains.uflib.ufl.edu/florida-governor-sidney-j-catts-the-polarizing-populist-ufndnp/. Retrieved October 19, 2022.

"Florida on the Home Front: German Submarine Threat Off the Florida Coast." *Florida Department of State*. 2022. https://www.museumoffloridahistory.com/explore/exhibits/permanent-exhibits/world-war-ii/florida-remembers-world-war-ii/florida-on-the-home-front-the-german-submarine-threat-off-floridas-coast/. Retrieved July 1, 2022.

"Florida Was Right: The Federal Government Admits Governor DeSantis' Decision to Put Seniors First Was the Correct Approach to Vaccine Distribution." *Flgov.com*. 2021. https://www.flgov.com/2021/10/06/florida-was-right-the-federal-government-admits-governor-desantis-decision-to-put-seniors-first-was-the-correct-approach-to-vaccine-distribution/. Retrieved June 15, 2022.

"Florida's Oldest Surviving Plantation House." *Florida Irish Heritage Center*. 2010. https://floridairishheritagecenter.wordpress.com/2010/06/29/floridas-oldest-surviving-plantation-house/. Retrieved June 1, 2022.

"The Flying Ace." *Norman Studios*. 2023. http://normanstudios.org/films-stars/norman-films/the-flying-ace/. Retrieved January 3, 2023.

Foreman, L. *Serial Killers—True Crime*. Alexandria, VA: Time-Life Books. 1992.

"Former Guatemalan Special Forces Soldier Sentenced to 10 Years in Prison for Making False Statements on Naturalization Forms Regarding 1982 Massacre of Guatemalan Villagers." *Department of Justice*. 2010. https://www.justice.gov/opa/pr/former-guatemalan-special-forces-soldier-sentenced-10-years-prison-making-false-statements. Retrieved February 12, 2023.

"Fort Mose Site Florida." *NPS.gov*. 2022. https://www.nps.gov/nr/travel/american_latino_heritage/fort_mose.html#:~:text=Slavery%20existed%20in%20Spain%2C%20but,together%2C%20and%20purchase%20their%20freedom. Retrieved February 5, 2023.

"4 Are Killed in Cuban Outbreak: Bulletin Havana, Sept. 27." *Daily Illini*, September 28, 1932. *Illinois Digital Newspaper Collections*. https://idnc.library.illinois.edu/cgi-bin/illinois?a=d&d=DIL19320928.2.77&e=-------en-20--1--img-txIN_____. Retrieved February 7, 2023.

"4 Slain, 2 Wounded, by Cuban Assassins; Army Rules Havana." *New York Times*. September 28, 1932. https://www.nytimes.com/1932/09/28/archives/4-slain-2-wounded-by-cuban-assassins-army-rules-havana-senate.html. Retrieved January 20, 2016.

Francis, J.M., G. Mormino, and R. Sanderson. "Slavery Took Hold in Florida Under the Spanish in the 'Forgotten Century' of 1492–1619." *Tampa Bay Times*. 2019. https://www.tampabay.com/opinion/2019/08/29/before-1619-africans-and-the-early-history-of-spanish-colonial-florida-and-america-column/. Retrieved June 1, 2022.

"Frank Ragano." *Spartacus Educational*. 2020. https://spartacus-educational.com/JFKraganoF.htm. Retrieved December 1, 2023.

Bibliography

"Fr. John Francis Conoley." *Saint Augustine Church and Catholic Student Center*. 2022. https://catholicgators.org/our-founder. Retrieved July 15, 2022.

"From Soldiers to 'Fugitives.'" *Civil War Era NC*. https://cwnc.omeka.chass.ncsu.edu/exhibits/show/35th-usct/olustee/fugitives. Retrieved June 25, 2022.

"Fulgencio Batista." *Britannica*. 2019. https://www.britannica.com/biography/Fulgencio-Batista. Retrieved July 1, 2022.

Fuller, H.B. *The Purchase of Florida: Its History and Diplomacy*. Sheridan, WY: Franklin Classics, an imprint of Creative Media Partners. 2018.

Galván, J.A. *Latin American Dictators of the 20th Century: The Lives and Regimes of 15 Rulers*. Jefferson, NC: McFarland. 2012.

Gancarski, A.G. "Disney Edges Out Ron Desantis in Popularity Poll." *Florida Politics*. 2022. https://floridapolitics.com/archives/524972-disney-edges-out-ron-desantis-in-popularity-poll/. Retrieved October 25, 2022.

Gannon, M., ed. *The New History of Florida*. Gainesville: University Press of Florida. 1996.

Gonzalez, A.S. "Cables from Cuba: Cross-Strait Solidarity and Politics in Ybor City 1898–1961." *Undergraduate History Honors Thesis, University of Florida*. 2021. https://ufdcimages.uflib.ufl.edu/AA/00/08/24/42/00001/Gonzalez_Arturo_Thesis.pdf. Retrieved July 1, 2022.

Gore, D. "Desantis vs. Disney Q&A." *FactCheck.org*. 2022. https://www.factcheck.org/2022/05/desantis-vs-disney-qa/. Retrieved August 2, 2022.

Griffin, J. "King Was Arrested in St. Augustine." *St. Augustine Record*. 2011. https://www.staugustine.com/story/news/local/2011/01/17/king-was-arrested-st-augustine/16213930007. Retrieved November 22, 2011.

Grimes, A., and L. Paris. "Disturbing Facts About Serial Killer Ted Bundy." *Grunge*. 2019. https://www.grunge.com/145187/the-untold-truth-of-ted-bundy/. Retrieved February 5, 2023.

Guinta, P. "A Recurring Horror." *Wayback Machine Staugustine.com*. 2007. https://web.archive.org/web/20100715053521/http://www.staugustine.com/stories/012907/news_4366914.shtml. Retrieved November 16, 2011.

Guthrie, A. "Meet the Cocaine Queen." *Miami New Times*. 2008. https://www.miaminewtimes.com/news/meet-the-cocaine-queen-6378530. Retrieved July 20 2022.

Guzzo, P. "Bolita, Tampa's Illegal Lottery, Was Deadly and Lucrative." *Tampa Bay Times*. 2021. https://www.tampabay.com/life-culture/history/2021/09/28/bolita-tampas-illegal-lottery-was-deadly-and-lucrative/. Retrieved July 15, 2022.

Guzzo, P. "Meet Charlie Wall, the Dean of Tampa's Early Underworld." *Tampa Bay Times*. 2020. https://www.tampabay.com/arts-entertainment/2020/06/11/meet-charlie-wall-the-dean-of-tampas-early-underworld/. Retrieved July 15, 2022.

Guzzo, P. "Why Was Charlie Wall, Dean of Tampa's Underworld, Murdered?" *Tampa Bay Times*. 2021. https://www.tampabay.com/life-culture/history/2021/12/08/why-was-charlie-wall-dean-of-tampas-early-underworld-murdered/. Retrieved July 15, 2022.

Hamacher, B. "Dadeland Mall Massacre: Thursday Marks 40th Anniversary of Infamous 'Cocaine Cowboys' Shootout." *NBC 6*. 2019. https://www.nbcmiami.com/news/local/dadeland-mall-massacre-thursday-marks-40th-anniversary-of-cocaine-cowboys-shootout/127956/. Retrieved July 19, 2022.

Hargrove, B. "Black Tuna Gang Leader Gets Out of Jail." *Miami New Times*. 2008. https://www.miaminewtimes.com/news/black-tuna-gang-leader-gets-out-of-jail-6378737. Retrieved July 30, 2022.

Hatch, T. *Osceola and the Great Seminole War: A Struggle for Justice and Freedom*. New York: St. Martin's Press. 2012.

Haug, J. "Cuban Dictator's Legacy Lives on in Daytona Art Collection." *Naples News*. 2015. http://archive.naplesnews.com/entertainment/arts-and-culture/cuban-dictators-legacy-lives-on-in-daytona-art-collection-ep-1090206048-334638941.html. Retrived October 22, 2022.

Heidler, D., and J.T. Heidler. *Encyclopedia of the War of 1812*. Santa Barbara, CA: ABC-CLIO. 1997.

Heidler, D., and J.T. Heidler. *Old Hickory's War: Andrew Jackson and the Quest for Empire*. Baton Rouge, LA: LSU Press. 1996.

"Henry Jennings." *pirates.hegewisch.net*. 2022. https://pirates.hegewisch.net/whos jennings.html. Retrieved May 29, 2022

"Herman Glogowski—21st, 23rd, 25th and 27th Mayor of Tampa." *Tampa.gov*. 2023. https://www.tampa.gov/city-clerk/info/previous-mayors/glogowski-herman. Retrieved February 11, 2023.

Hickman, K. "World War II: Operation Pastorius." *ThoughtCo*. 2017. https://www.thoughtco.com/world-war-ii-operation-pastorius-2361251. Retrieved July 8, 2022.

"History of Ave Maria." *The Ave Herald*. 2012. https://www.aveherald.com/visiting-ave-maria/history-of-ave-maria.html. Retrieved July 14, 2022.

Hitchcock, E.A., and G. Foreman, ed. *A Traveler in Indian Territory: The Journal of Ethan Allen Hitchcock, Late Major-General in the United States Army*. Cedar Rapids, IA: Torch. 1930.

Hitt, T. "Celebration, Florida: How Disney's 'Community of Tomorrow' Became a Total Nightmare." *Daily Beast*. 2019. https://www.thedailybeast.com/celebration-florida-how-disneys-community-of-tomorrow-became-a-total-nightmare. Retrieved July 14, 2022.

Holloway, M. "Uncovering the Luna Colony, a Lost Remnant of Spanish Florida." *The New Yorker*. 2016. https://www.newyorker.com/news/news-desk/uncovering-the-luna-colony-a-lost-remnant-of-spanish-florida/amp. Retrieved June 19, 2022.

"Homosexuality and Citizenship in Florida: A Report of the Florida Legislative Investigation Committee." *University of Florida Digital Collections*. January 1964. https://ufdcimages.uflib.ufl.edu/UF/00/00/48/05/00001/Binder1.pdf. Retrieved February 8, 2023.

"House Divided: In Tallahassee, the Florida Secession Convention Votes by 62–7 to Leave the United States." *Dickinson College*. 2023. https://hd.housedivided.dickinson.edu/node/35300. Retrieved February 11, 2023.

Howard, A., and M. Smith. *River of Blood: Serial Killers and Their Victims*. Irvine, CA: Universal-Publishers. 2004.

Hubbard, K. "Newsom, DeSantis Fight a 'Proxy War' for America's Future." *U.S. News*. 2022. https://www.usnews.com/news/politics/articles/2022-07-07/newsom-desantis-fight-a-proxy-war-for-americas-future. Retrieved August 4, 2022.

"Hurricane of 1928 Mass Burial Site." *Waymarking.com*. 2022. https://www.waymarking.com/waymarks/wm7HMQ_Hurricane_of_1928_Mass_Burial_Site. Retrieved October 19, 2022.

"Hurricanes in History." *National Hurricane Center and Central Pacific Hurricane Center national Oceanic And Atmospheric Administration*. 2022. https://www.nhc.noaa.gov/outreach/history/?text. Retrieved October 19, 2022.

Huse, A. "USF History 101—The Witch Hunt Comes to USF." *The Oracle*. 2003. https://www.usforacle.com/2003/09/24/usf-history-101-the-witch-hunt-comes-to-usf/. Retrieved November 30, 2011.

"ICE Removes Former Member of Guatemalan Army Linked to 1982 Massacre." *Immigration and Customs Enforcement*. March 3, 2020. https://www.ice.gov/news/releases/ice-removes-former-member-guatemalan-army-linked-1982-massacre. Retrieved June 28, 2022.

"Indian Key." *Ghosttowns.com*. http://www.ghosttowns.com/states/fl/indiankey.html. Retrieved July 1, 2022.

"The Inflation Calculator." *Morgan Friedman*. 2022. https://westegg.com/inflation/. Retrieved June 4, 2022.

Jahr, C. "Anita Bryant's Startling Reversal." *Ladies Home Journal*. December 1980, pp. 62–68.

"JFK Jr.'s Would-be Kidnapper Griselda Blanco Was 'the Most Feared' Female Killer in History." *OK! News*. 2020. https://okmagazine.com/news/jfk-jr-s-would-be-kidnapper-griselda-blanco-was-feared-female-killer/. Retrieved October 19, 2022.

"John Cabot's Voyage of 1498." *Heritage Newfoundland and Labrador*. 2023. https://www.heritage.nf.ca/articles/exploration/cabot-1498.php. Retrieved February 5, 2023.

"The Johns Committee at USF." *Digital Exhibits*. 2022. https://usflibexhibits.omeka.net/exhibits/show/witchhunt/flic-at-usf. Retrieved October 25, 2022.

Johnson, J.G. "The Yamassee Revolt of 1597 and the Destruction of the Georgia Missions." https://penelope.uchicago.edu/Thayer/E/Gazetteer/Places/America/United_States/Georgia/_Texts/GaHQ/7/1/Yamassee_Revolt_of_1597*.html#ref5. Retrieved September 5, 2022.
Jordan, D. "In the 1850s, Narciso López Launched Illegal Cuban Invasions from New Orleans." *The Historic New Orleans Collection*. 2021. https://www.hnoc.org/publications/first-draft/1850s-narciso-lopez-and-fellow-filibusters-launched-cuban-invasions-new. Retrieved February 8, 2022.
"Judge Overturns Unanimous Jury Verdict That Found Former Bolivian President and Defense Minister Responsible for Massacre of Indigenous People." *Center for Constitutional Rights*. 2018. https://ccrjustice.org/home/press-center/press-releases/judge-overturns-unanimous-jury-verdict-found-former-bolivian. Retrieved June 30, 2022.
Justice, K. "Nat Glover Credits His Strength as a Leader to Moment of Fear on Ax Handle Saturday." *News4Jax.com*. 2020. https://www.news4jax.com/features/2020/08/25/nat-glover-credits-his-strength-as-a-leader-to-moment-of-fear-on-ax-handle-saturday/. Retrieved February 3, 2023.
Kaufelt, D. "The Chosen in Paradise." *SunSentinel.com*. 1987. https://www.sun-sentinel.com/1987/05/17/the-chosen-in-paradise/. Retrieved September 30, 2011.
Kennedy, R. "Sweden Tells Citizens to Wear Masks on Public Transport as It Struggles with Covid-19 Resurgence." *euronews.com*. 2020. https://www.euronews.com/my-europe/2020/12/18/sweden-tells-citizens-to-wear-masks-on-public-transport-as-it-struggles-with-covid-19-resu. Retrieved June 20, 2022.
Kettle, M. "Florida 'Recounts' Make Gore Winner." *The Guardian*. 2001. https://www.theguardian.com/world/2001/jan/29/uselections2000.usa. Retrieved July 19, 2022.
"Kingsley Treatise Excerpt Text." *National Park Service*. 2009. http://www.nps.gov/timu/photosmultimedia/kp_zk_treatise_text.htm. Retrieved September 29, 2011.
Knetsch, J. "Hamilton Disston and the Development of Florida." *University of South Florida*. 1998. https://digitalcommons.usf.edu/cgi/viewcontent.cgi?article=1308&context=sunlandtribune. Retrieved August 18, 2022.
Krishnaiyer, K. "The Racist, Anti-Catholic Populism of Sidney Catts, and Woodrow Wilson-Era Florida Racist Politics." *The Florida Squeeze*. 2019. https://thefloridasqueeze.com/2019/11/10/the-racist-anti-catholic-populism-of-sidney-catts-and-woodrow-wilson-era-florida-racist-politics/. Retrieved July 20, 2022.
Kunzle, D. *The Murals of Revolutionary Nicaragua, 1979–1992*. Berkeley: University of California Press. 1995.
Kusisto, L. "Leaks and Mold Are Ruining the Disney Magic in Celebration, Florida." *The Wall Street Journal*. 2016. https://condomadness.info/decline-Celebration.html. Retrieved July 12, 2022.
Lardner, G., Jr. "Gangland Figure Refuses to Answer." *Washington Post*. March 17, 1977. Retrieved July 20, 2022.
Latner, R.B. "Fort Pickens." *Tulane University*. 1996. https://www2.tulane.edu/~sumter/Pickens.html. Retrieved October 25, 2022.
"Life in the Drug Trade." *Time*. November 23, 1981. https://content.time.com/time/subscriber/article/0,33009,922695,00.html. Retrieved July 29, 2022
"Lighthouse History Pre–1874." *St. Augustine Lighthouse and Maritime Museum*. 2014. https://www.staugustinelighthouse.org/2014/11/18/lighthouse-history-pre-1874/. Retrieved December 14, 2023.
"Links to Online Census Records Duval Co., Florida." 2022. *Census Online*. http://www.census-online.com/links/FL/Duval/. Retrieved October 25, 2022.
"López, Narciso." *Encyclopedia.com*. 2022. https://www.encyclopedia.com/humanities/encyclopedias-almanacs-transcripts-and-maps/lopez-narciso-1797-1851. Retrieved February 9, 2022.
MacCartney, C.E., and G. Dorrance. *The Bonapartes in America*. Philadelphia: Dorrance and Company. 1939.
"Mack Mullen: Florida Slave Narratives 1936–1938." *Exploring Florida*. 2022. http://fcit.usf.edu/florida/docs/s/slave/slave28.htm. Retrieved July 5, 2022.

Mahon, J.K. *History of the Second Seminole War. 2nd Revised Edition*. Gainesville: University of Florida Press. 1985.
Mahoney, E.L. "New Lighthearted Ron DeSantis Ad Features His Family, Trump Jokes." *Tampa Bay Times*. 2018. https://www.tampabay.com/florida-politics/buzz/2018/07/30/new-lighthearted-ron-desantis-ad-features-his-family-trump-jokes/. Retrieved July 28, 2022.
Margaritoff, M. "What Happened to Tyria Moore, the Girlfriend of Serial Killer Aileen Wuornos?" *ATI*. May 23, 2023. https://allthatsinteresting.com/tyria-moore.
Markowicz, K. "The Country Needs a Dose of Florida Gov. Ron DeSantis to Battle Covid-19." *New York Post*. 2021. https://nypost.com/2021/10/28/florida-gov-ron-desantis-has-shown-how-to-handle-covid-19/. Retrieved June 29, 2022.
Martí, J. "Our America, March 5, 1892." *Historyofcuba.com*. http://www.historyofcuba.com/history/marti/America.htm. Retrieved October 30, 2011.
Martí, J. "A Sincere Man Am I." *Allpoetry.com*. http://allpoetry.com/poem/8531743-A_Sincere_Man_Am_I___Verse_I_-by-Jose_Marti. Retrieved October 13, 2011.
Matthews, T., T. Fuller, and H. Camp. "Battle Over Gay Rights." *Newsweek*. June 6, 1977. pp. 16–26.
McCally, D. *The Everglades: An Environmental History*. Gainesville: University Press of Florida. 1999.
McCarthy, K. *Twenty Florida Pirates*. Sarasota, FL: Pineapple Press. 1994.
McIver, S. "Massacre the Day an Island Died Indian Key Was Once the Capital of Dade County. Then, on an August Morning in 1840, the Indians Came Ashore. The Lucky Ones Escaped." *South Florida Sun Sentinel*. 1985. https://www.sun-sentinel.com/news/fl-xpm-1985-08-11-8502020480-story.html. Retrieved June 8, 2022.
McIver, S.B. *Death in the Everglades: The Murder of Guy Bradley, America's First Martyr to Environmentalism*. Gainesville: University Press of Florida. 2003.
McIver, S.B. *Murder in the Tropics*. Sarasota, FL: Pineapple Press. 1995.
McTague, T. "Remember the '90s, Don't Long for a Return." *The Atlantic*. 2020. https://www.theatlantic.com/international/archive/2020/08/brexit-trump-china-90s-golden-era/615406/. Retrieved July 30, 2022.
Meltzer, M. *Hunted Like a Wolf: The Story of the Seminole War*. Sarasota, FL: Pineapple Press. 1972.
Michaud, S., and H. Aynesworth. *The Only Living Witness: The True Story of Serial Sex Killer Ted Bundy*. Irving, TX: Authorlink Press. 1999.
Migdon, B. "Florida's 'Don't Say Gay' Bill Takes Effect Today. Its Impact Is Already Being Felt." *The Hill*. 2022. https://thehill.com/changing-america/respect/equality/3543536-floridas-dont-say-gay-law-takes-effect-today-its-impact-is-already-being-felt/. Retrieved August 1, 2022.
Milanich, J.T. *The Timucua*. New Jersey: Blackwell Publishers. 1996
Milanich, J.T., and C. Hudson. *Hernando de Soto and the Indians of Florida*. Gainesville: University Press of Florida. 1993.
Miller, C., and M. Farley. "Timing of Envoy's Departure Raises Questions." *LA Times*. May 7, 2001. https://www.latimes.com/archives/la-xpm-2001-may-07-mn-60375-story.html. Retrieved June 15, 2022.
Miller, G., and J. Buchanan. "A 'Cool' Bundy: Friends of Two Murdered Sorority Sisters Testify as Pace of Trial Picks Up." *The Evening Independent*. 1979. http://news.google.com/newspapers?nid=950&dat=19790710&id=JAEMAAAAIBAJ&sjid=2VgDAAAAIBAJ&pg=6424,1831474. Retrieved July 29, 2022.
Miller, M.E. "Ave Maria University: A Catholic Project Gone Wrong." *Miami New Times*. 2011. https://www.miaminewtimes.com/news/ave-maria-university-a-catholic-project-gone-wrong-6384870?storyPage=2. Retrieved July 10, 2022.
"The Misadventures of Pánfilo de Narváez and Nuñez de Cabeza de Vaca." *Exploring Florida*. 2002. http://fcit.usf.edu/florida/lessons/narvaez/narvaez1.htm. Retrieved June 30, 2022.
Missall, J., and M.L. Missall. *The Seminole Wars: America's Longest Indian Conflict*. Gainesville: University Press of Florida. 2004.
Morris, T. *Florida's Lost Tribes*. Gainesville: University Press of Florida. 2004.
Munzenreider, K. "Florida Legislature Once Published Anti-Gay Pamphlet Full of

Softcore Porn." *Miami New Times*. 2015. https://www.miaminewtimes.com/news/florida-legislature-once-published-anti-gay-pamphlet-full-of-softcore-porn-7707547. Retrieved February 11, 2023.

"Murder and Martyrdom in Spanish Florida: The True Story Behind the Guale Uprising." *Secrets of the Dead: PBS*. 2017. https://www.pbs.org/wnet/secrets/secrets-spanish-florida-murder-martyrdom-spanish-florida-true-story-behind-guale-uprising/3702/. Retrieved February 12, 2023.

"The Murder of John Fitzgerald Kennedy: There Never Was a Camelot." *Angelfire.com*. 2000. http://www.angelfire.com/nh/hca/jfk.html. Retrieved July 1, 2022.

Nelson, M. "Back Off SC! Fla. Claims First Shot of Civil War." *NBCNews*. 2011. https://www.nbcnews.com/id/wbna42569813. Retrieved September 19, 2011.

Nelson, P. *Defending the Devil: My Story as Ted Bundy's Last Lawyer*. New York: William Morrow. 1994.

Nieman, D. "Promises to Keep: African Americans and the Constitutional Order, 1776 to the Present." *Oxford Academic*. 2020. https://academic.oup.com/book/33633. Retrieved July 10, 2022.

"Narciso López." *Historyofcuba.com*. 2022. http://www.historyofcuba.com/history/funfacts/narciso.htm. Retrieved October 24, 2022.

"The 'Negro Fort' Massacre." *Libcom.org*. 2022. https://libcom.org/article/negro-fort-massacre. Retrieved February 2, 2023.

Norton, A. "Bundy's Last Stop: Recounting a Serial Killer's Arrest 40 Years Later." *ABC*. 2018. https://weartv.com/news/local/bundys-last-stop-recounting-a-serial-killers-arrest-40-years-later. Retrieved July 15, 2022.

O'Meilia, T. "Widow of Cuban Dictator Batista Dies in WPB." *Palm Beach Post*. October 4, 2006. https://freerepublic.com/focus/fr/1713569/posts.

"Operation Mongoose." *PBS American Experience*. 2022. https://www.pbs.org/wgbh/americanexperience/features/rfk-operation-mongoose/. Retrieved July 10, 2022.

"The Original EPCOT." *The Original EPCOT.com*. 2023. https://sites.google.com/site/theoriginalepcot/overview/the-florida-project?pli=1. Retrieved April 30, 2023.

O'Riordan, C. "The 1795 Rebellion in East Florida." Jacksonville: University of North Florida. 1995. *UNF Graduate Theses and Dissertations*. https://digitalcommons.unf.edu/cgi/viewcontent.cgi?article=1098&context=etd.

Ortiz, P. "Remembering One of the Bloodiest Elections in U.S. History." *The Gainesville Sun*. 2019. https://www.gainesville.com/story/opinion/columns/more-voices/2019/02/07/paul-ortiz-remembering-one-of-bloodiest-elections-in-us-history/6069757007/. Retrieved July 10, 2022.

"Ostend Manifesto." *Wikisource*. 2022. http://en.wikisource.org/wiki/Ostend_Manifesto. Retrieved October 25, 2022.

"Our America." *Historyofcuba.com*. http://www.historyofcuba.com/history/marti/America.htm. Retrieved July 1, 2022.

Palast, G. "Florida's Flawed 'Voter-Cleansing' Program." *Salon*. 2000. https://www.salon.com/2000/12/04/voter_file/. Retrieved October 19, 2022.

"Panamanian Dictator Manuel Noriega Surrenders to U.S." *History.com*. 2023. https://www.history.com/this-day-in-history/noriega-surrenders-to-u-s. Retrieved February 5, 2023.

Parton, J. *Life of Andrew Jackson Vol. 2*. Whitefish, MT: Kessinger Publishing. 2006.

Patrick, R., and A. Morris. *Florida Under Five Flags*. Gainesville: University Press of Florida. 1967.

Payson-Denney, W. "So, Who Really Won? What the Bush v. Gore Studies Showed." *CNN*. 2015. https://www.cnn.com/2015/10/31/politics/bush-gore-2000-election-results-studies/index.html. Retrieved February 2, 2023.

Peck, D.T. *Ponce de Léon and the Discovery of Florida*. St. Paul, MN: Pogo Press. 1993.

Pemberton, J. "Focus on: Nat Glover." *Wayback Machine Florida Times-Union*. February 22, 1998. https://web.archive.org/web/20170701062553/http://jacksonville.com/tu-online/stories/022298/met_glover.html#.WVdAdRDP32c.

Perry, M. "The Great Miami Hurricane of 1926." *Faith, Hope, Love*. http://faithhopelove.net/autobiographymiamihurricane.htm. Retrieved October 18, 2022.

"Peter Martyr's Account." *Original Sources.com*. 2022. https://www.originalsources.com/Document.aspx?DocID=3NYVYDD51WRKL6T. Retrieved September 5, 2022.
Pilger, J. *Heroes*. London: Vintage Press. 2001.
Pilkington, E. "How the Disney Dream Died in Celebration." *The Guardian*. 2010. https://www.theguardian.com/world/2010/dec/13/celebration-death-of-a-dream. Retrieved July 12, 2022.
"Piratical Life in St. Augustine: Then and Now." *Florida Historic Coast*. 2022. https://www.floridashistoriccoast.com/blog/piratical-life-in-st-augustine-then-now/. Retrieved June 10, 2022.
Pleming, S. "Cuban Boy Draws Picture of Shipwreck Drama." *Wayback Machine Cubanet.org*. 2000. https://web.archive.org/web/20090112215621/http://www.cubanet.org/CNews/y00/mar00/27e4.htm. Retrieved October 6, 2018.
Potter, D.M. *The Impending Crisis 1848–1861*. New York: Harper & Row. 1996.
Prieto, B., and S. Jacobson. "Homeless Man Accused in Hatchet Killing, the First Homicide in Disney-Built Town of Celebration." *Palm Beach Post*. 2012. https://www.palmbeachpost.com/story/news/crime/2012/04/07/homeless-man-accused-in-hatchet/7842776007/. Retrieved February 2, 2023.
"Prosper Avril." *Military-History*. 2010. https://military-history.fandom.com/wiki/Prosper_Avril. Retrieved July 14, 2022.
Purcell, A.D. "Plumb Lines, Politics and Projections: The Florida Everglades and the Wright Report Controversy." *Florida Historical Quarterly*. 2001. https://stars.library.ucf.edu/cgi/viewcontent.cgi?article=4301&context=fhq. Retrieved July 10, 2022.
"Quotes About Spanish American War." *Morefamousquotes.com*. 2022. https://www.morefamousquotes.com/topics/quotes-about-spanish-american-war/. Retrieved June 1, 2022.
Raab, S. *Five Families: The Rise, Decline, and Resurgence of America's Most Powerful Mafia Empires*. New York: St. Martin's Press. 2005.
Ramos, R., D. Lyons, and M. Merzer. "He Was U.S. Prisoner #41586. How Noriega Landed in a Miami Jail After Invasion." *Miami Herald*. 2017. https://amp.miamiherald.com/news/nation-world/world/americas/article153300559.html. Retrieved July 14, 2022.
Randall, E. *Murder in St. Augustine: The Mysterious Death of Athalia Ponsell Lindsley*, excerpt. *Florida Writers Association*. 2016. https://floridawriters.blog/wp-content/uploads/2018/05/Murder-in-Stexcerpt.pdf. Retrieved February 8, 2023.
Reilly, L. "The Most Dangerous Job: The Murder of America's First Bird Warden." *Mental Floss*. 2018. https://www.mentalfloss.com/article/559363/most-dangerous-job-murder-americas-first-bird-warden. Retrieved June 1, 2022.
"Remembering a Civil Rights Swim-in: It Was a Milestone." *NPR*. 2014. https://www.npr.org/2014/06/13/321380585/remembering-a-civil-rights-swim-in-it-was-a-milestone. Retrieved February 5, 2023.
"Reports of Investigators on Meetings of the Southern Christian Leadership Conference and the Ku Klux Klan." *Florida Memory*. http://www.floridamemory.com/exhibits/floridahighlights/investigation/. Retrieved October 12, 2011.
"Restrictive Pacts Bar Jews from Purchasing Property in Miami Area." *Jewish Telegraphic Agency*. 1960. https://www.jta.org/archive/restrictive-pacts-bar-jews-from-purchasing-property-in-miami-area. Retrieved July 12, 2022.
Rich, R., and L. Arguelles. *Homosexuality, Homophobia, and Revolution: Notes Toward an Understanding of the Cuban Lesbian and Gay Male Experience, Part II*. Chicago: University of Chicago Press. 1985.
"Rosewood Massacre." *History.com*. 2022. https://www.history.com/topics/early-20th-century-us/rosewood-massacre. Retrieved February 5, 2023.
"Rosewood Massacre." *Penny Liberty, The First African American Encyclopedia of African American and Cultural History*. 2012. https://pennylibertygbow.wordpress.com/2012/02/24/rosewood-massacre/. Retrieved October 19, 2022.
Rule, A. *The Stranger Beside Me*. New York: Signet. 2000.
"Santo Trafficante, Jr." *WN.com*. http://wn.com/Santo_Trafficante,_Jr. Retrieved November 30, 2011.

Scallet, D. "This Inglorious War: The Second Seminole War, the Ad Hoc Origins of American Imperialism, and the Silence of Slavery." *Dissertation, Washington University in St Louis.* 2011. https://openscholarship.wustl.edu/cgi/viewcontent.cgi?article=1637&context=etd. Retrieved June 3, 2022.

Schafer, D.L. *Anna Madgigine Jai Kingsley: African Princess, Florida Slave, Plantation Slaveowner.* Gainesville: University Press of Florida. 2003.

Schoultz, L. *That Little Infernal Cuban Republic: The United States and the Cuban Revolution.* Chapel Hill: University of North Carolina Press. 2009.

"Seaside." *Congress for the New Urbanism.* https://www.cnu.org/what-we-do/build-great-places/seaside. December 10, 2023.

"Second Voyage Commanded by René Goulaine De Laudonniére." *Access Genealogy.* 2023. https://accessgenealogy.com/south-carolina/second-voyage-commanded-by-rene-goulaine-de-laudonniere.htm. Retrieved January 2, 2023.

Seibert, B. "Only One Man with a Bullhorn and a Couple..." *UPI Archives.* 1981. https://www.upi.com/Archives/1981/02/07/Only-one-man-with-a-bullhorn-and-a-couple/1870350370000/. Retrieved December 30, 2022.

Seminara, D. "Newsom v. DeSantis." *City Journal.* 2022. https://www.city-journal.org/newsom-v-desantis. Retrieved August 4, 2022.

"Seminole." *Merriam-Webster.* http://www.merriam-webster.com/dictionary/Seminole. Retrieved June 30, 2022.

"Seminole History." *Florida Department of State.* 2022. https://dos.myflorida.com/florida-facts/florida-history/seminole-history/. Retrieved October 25, 2022.

Shearer, V. *It Happened in the Florida Keys.* Guilford, CT: Globe Pequot Press. 2008.

Sheeler, A. "Ron DeSantis rips Newsom. In California, 'You Ain't Seeing Very Many Florida License Plates." *Sacramento Bee.* 2022. https://www.sacbee.com/news/politics-government/capitol-alert/article263287578.html. Retrieved August 4, 2022.

"Siege of Pensacola." *American Battlefield Trust.* 2022. https://www.battlefields.org/learn/revolutionary-war/battles/siege-pensacola. Retrieved June 1, 2022.

Sierra, J. "Captain Joseph Fry." *HistoryofCuba.com.* http://www.historyofcuba.com/history/matanzas/Joseph-Fry.htm. Retrieved October 25, 2022.

Sierra, J. "Gerardo Machado." *Historyofcuba.com.* http://www.historyofcuba.com/history/machado.htm. Retrieved June 30, 2022.

Sloane, A. *Hoffa.* Cambridge, MA: MIT. 1991.

Smith, B., and G. Stanley. "Great Recession, 10 Years Later: Foreclosure Crisis Cut Deeply; The Stings Is Still Felt." *News-Press.* 2018. https://www.news-press.com/story/news/local/2018/02/17/great-recession-10-years-later-foreclosure-crisis-cut-deeply-sting-still-felt/1079686001/. Retrieved June 18, 2022.

"The Spanish Colonial and Slavery Eras in Florida." *Florida Humanities.* 2020. https://floridahumanities.org/the-spanish-colonial-and-slavery-eras-in-florida/. Retrieved December 14, 2023.

Spindel, B., and M. Fernandez. "Murder in Celebration, Florida: The Victim's Secret Life." *Daily Beast.* 2017. https://www.thedailybeast.com/murder-in-celebration-florida-the-victims-secret-life. Retrieved February 12, 2023.

Stephens, R. "The Truth Laid Bare." *University of Central Florida.* 2020. https://www.ucf.edu/pegasus/the-truth-laid-bare/. Retrieved July 10, 2022.

"The Story of Seaside, Florida." *SoWal.* 2022. https://sowal.com/story/the-story-of-seaside-florida. Retrieved July 12, 2022.

Stowell, D., ed. *Balancing Evils Judiciously: The Proslavery Writings of Zephaniah Kingsley.* Gainesville: University Press of Florida. 2000.

"The Struggle for the Southern Frontier: The Seminole Wars of Florida." *Floridahistory.org.* 2022. http://floridahistory.org/seminoles.htm. Retrieved June 12, 2022.

"Survey Results." *Haile Plantation West.* 2020. https://mailchi.mp/aa28bd9271f0/haile-plantation-west-survey-results?e=%5bUNIQID%5d. Retrieved July 15, 2022.

Swanson, J., and A. Garcia. "Why the Elián Gonzalez Saga Resonates 20 Years Later." *The Highlight By Vox.* 2019. https://www.vox.com/the-highlight/2019/11/4/20938885/miami-cuba-elian-gonzalez-castro. Retrieved October 30, 2022.

Swirko, C. "Haile Plantation Residents Debate Name Change." *Gainesville Sun.*

2020. https://www.gainesville.com/story/news/local/2020/06/17/haile-plantation-residents-debate-name-change/42111881/. Retrieved July 20, 2020.
Swisher, S., and R. Gillespie. "Disney World's Reedy Creek: What Happens After the Special District Is Abolished?" *Orlando Sentinel*. 2022. https://www.orlandosentinel.com/politics/os-ne-abolishing-reedy-creek-20220422-hvzxgcdxq5e43mzgwbmrrbwfmy-story.html. Retrieved August 3, 2022.
Tebeau, C.W. *A History of Florida*. Miami: University of Miami Press. 1971.
"Ted Bundy's Sorority House Attack." *Timothy Hughes Rare and Early Newspapers*. 1978. https://www.rarenewspapers.com/view/673263. Retrieved October 25, 2022.
"Telmo Hurtado Testifies to Cover-up Accomarca Massacre in Peruvian Court." *The Center for Justice and Accountability*. 2012. https://cja.org/what-we-do/litigation/accomarca-massacre/related-resources/telmo-hurtado-testifies-to-cover-up-of-accomarca-massacre-in-peruvian-court/. Retrieved July 1, 2022.
"35 Incredible Facts About Disney's EPCOT Theme Park." *ABC13 News*. 2017. https://abc13.com/happy-birthday-epcot-disney-theme-park-turns-35/2475648/. Retrieved July 10, 2017.
"This Week in St. Johns County History: King Jailed in St. Augustine." *St. Augustine Record*. 2022. https://www.staugustine.com/story/news/history/2022/06/04/week-st-johns-county-history-king-jailed-st-augustine-1964/7458135001/. Retrieved February 5, 2022.
Tikkanen, A. "Griselda Blanco: Colombian Cocaine Trafficker." *Britannica*. 2023. https://www.britannica.com/science/cocaine. Retrieved February 8, 2023.
"Timucua Religion." *Access Genealogy*. https://accessgenealogy.com/florida/timucua-religion.htm. Retrieved August 17, 2022.
"Upcoming Events." *Dade Battlefield Society*. 2022. http://www.dadebattlefield.com/. Retrieved June 3, 2022.
Vitagliano, J. "Behind the Song Lyrics: That Smell by Lynyrd Skynyrd." *American Songwriter*. 2022. https://americansongwriter.com/that-smell-lynyrd-skynyrd-behind-song-lyrics-meaning/. Retrieved August 8, 2022.
Voght, K. "Florida's Don't Say Gay Law Took Effect. Chaos Ensued." *Rolling Stone*. 2022. https://www.rollingstone.com/politics/politics-news/florida-dont-say-gay-law-edcuators-1377353/. Retrieved August 3, 2022.
"Walt Disney's Plan for EPCOT." *YouTube*. 2007. https://www.youtube.com/watch?v=u9M3pKsrcc8. Retrieved July 14, 2022.
Walters, T. "Ron DeSantis Wraps-up His First Year as Governor of Florida. See What He's Accomplished." *Florida Today*. 2020. https://www.floridatoday.com/story/news/2020/01/08/ron-desantis-florida-governor-accomplishments-first-year/2806449001/. Retrieved August 2, 2022.
"War of 1812." *Exploring Florida*. 2022. https://fcit.usf.edu/florida/docs/w/war1812.htm. Retrieved February 2, 2023.
"War of Words." *Digital Exhibits*. https://usflibexhibits.omeka.net/exhibits/show/witchhunt/war-of-words. Retrieved December 14, 2023.
Weathersbee, T. "The Story of a White Man Who Joined the '60s Sit-ins." *Florida Times-Union*. February 4, 2008.
Weitz, S. "Defending the Old South: The Myth of the Lost Cause and Political Immorality in Florida, 1865–1968." *The Historian*. 2009. https://onlinelibrary.wiley.com/doi/full/10.1111/j.1540-6563.2008.00232.x. Retrieved October 25, 2022.
Weitzel, K.G. *Journeys with Florida's Indians*. Gainesville: University Press of Florida. 2002.
"What Thomas Jefferson Said About Annexing Cuba." *San Francisco Call*, V. 83 N. 13, April 10, 1898. *UCR California Digital Newspaper Collection*. https://cdnc.ucr.edu/cgi-bin/cdnc?a=d&d=SFC18980410.2.132.26&e=-------en--20--1--txt-txIN_____. Retrieved February 10, 2023.
White, G. *Historical Collections of Georgia*. New York: Pudney & Russell. 1855.
Whitten, S. "Disney Vows to Repeal Don't Say Gay Law." *CNBC*. 2022. https://www.cnbc.com/2022/03/28/disney-vows-to-help-repeal-dont-say-gay-law.html. Retrieved August 3, 2022.

Bibliography

Wilbanks, W. *Forgotten Heroes: Police Officers Killed in Early Florida, 1840–1925.* Paducah, KY: Turner Publishing Company. 1998.
Williams, R. "Ponce Not the First to Pounce." *Naples Florida Weekly.* April 2, 2020. https://naples.floridaweekly.com/articles/ponce-not-the-first-to-pounce/. Retrieved December 21, 2020.
Wilson, D. "The 1715 Plate Fleet and the Rise of the Pirates." *History Today.* 2015. https://www.historytoday.com/1715-plate-fleet-and-rise-pirates. Retrieved April 22, 2023.
Wilson, K. "Florida Governor Election Results: Andrew Gillum Versus Ron DeSantis." *Tampa Bay Times.* 2018. https://www.tampabay.com/florida-politics/buzz/2018/11/06/florida-governor-election-results-andrew-gillum-versus-ron-desantis/. Retrieved July 30, 2022.
Woodward, A. "What Is Florida's 'Don't Say Gay' Bill?" *Independent.* 2022. https://www.independent.co.uk/news/world/americas/us-politics/dont-say-gay-bill-florida-desantis-b2074720.html. Retrieved July 30, 2022.
Worrall, S. "When the Mob Owned Cuba." *Smithsonian Magazine.* 2016. https://www.smithsonianmag.com/travel/mob-havana-cuba-culture-music-book-tj-english-cultural-travel-180960610/. Retrieved July 20, 2022.
"Ybor City Historic District." *National Park Service. 2021.* https://www.nps.gov/nr/travel/american_latino_heritage/ybor_city_historic_district.html. Retrieved July 15, 2022.
"Ye Mystic Crew of Gasparilla." *Ymkg.com.* 2023. https://ymkg.com/. Retrieved February 5, 2023.
Zeitlin, J. "Butcher of the Andes." *Miami New Times.* 2007. https://www.miaminewtimes.com/news/butcher-of-the-andes-6333621. Retrieved June 2, 2022.
Zinn, H. *A People's History of the United States.* New York: HarperCollins. 2005.

Index

Adams Onis, Treaty of 52, 71
al Hijji, Abdulaziz 192
al Hijji, Anoud 192, 194
Amelia Island 38-39
American Beach 149-150
Apalachee 8, 12
Apalachen 12
Aury, Louis-Michel 40
Ave Maria 219-222
Avril, Prosper 208
Ax Handle Saturday 147-149

Batista, Fulgencio 137, 205-206
Bersheba 33
Berzain, Carlos Sánchez 198-199
Bethune, Mary McLeod 144, 145
Black Tuna Gang 163-164, 165
Blanco, Griselda 161-163
Bolita 125-127
Bradley, Guy 103-105
Broward, Napoleon Bonaparte 110-112
Bundy, Ted 172-176

Cabot, John 9, 11, 26
Callava, Jose 51-52, 90
Calusa 6-7, 16
Camp Blanding 139-140
Capone, Al 134-135
Carlos 6
Cassadaga 212
Castro, Fidel 131-133, 136
Catts, Sidney J. 116-117
Caucasian Clause 113-114, 143
Celebration 214, 216-219
Charlotte Harbor 6
Chi Omega Murders 174-175
Cocaine Cowboys 160-161, 166
Conch Republic 166-168
Conoley, John 117-118
Coral Gables 115

Covid-19 228-232, 239
Critical Race Theory 232-233, 234

Dade Massacre 56-57
Dadeland Mall Massacre 159-160, 166, 182
Davis, Daryl 213, 214
Davis, Robert 213, 214
Daytona 176-177, 205-206
Debayle, Anastasio Somoza 206-207
de Galvez, Don Bernardo 43
de Gourgues, Dominique 18-20, 21, 24
de Laudonnière, Rene Goulaine 10, 16
de León, Ponce 5-9, 12, 15, 23, 112
Delray Beach 203
de Narváez, Pánfilo 11-14
DeSantis, Ron 226-239
de Soto, Hernando 14
Disney, Walt 214-215, 217
Disney Development Corporation 216, 217, 218, 219, 235-236
Disston, Hamilton 106-108
Don't Say Gay 234-235
Drake, Francis 25
Duvalier, Francois 207
Duvalier, Jean-Claude 207-208

East Florida 43, 46
EPCOT 198, 214-215

Fernandina 38, 100
Fernandina Plan 100-102
First Seminole War 46
Fisher, Carl 114-115
Flagler, Henry 106, 114, 115
Flying Ace 110, 111
Floridablanca 34
Fort Barrancas 51, 81-82
Fort Caroline 8, 16-18, 24
Fort Chaffee Riots 184-185
Fort George Island 41

273

Fort Mose 31–32
Fort Pierce 32
Fort Scott Massacre 49
Fowltown, Battle of 48
Fry, Joseph 95–97, 99

Gaines 59
Garcon 46–48
Gaspar, Jose 33–34
Gasparilla 34–35
Gillum, Andrew 226, 227
Giovanditto, Matteo Patrick 217
Glover, Nat 148
González, Elián 187–188
Great Recession 195–196, 217, 225
Guale Rebellion 22–23

Haile Plantation 222–224
Harris, Katharine 189–190
Hirrihigua 12–13
Housman, Jacob 58–59
Hurtado, Telmo Ricardo 199–201

Indian Key Massacre 58–59

Jackson, Andrew 43–44, 47, 50, 51–52
Jacksonville 15, 37, 80–81, 106, 108–110, 116, 143, 147–149, 169
Jekyll Island 23
Jennings, Henry 32–33
Jesup, Thomas Sidney 60–61
Johns Committee 154–158
Jones, Rebekah 231–232
Jones, Sam 60–61, 63
Jordan, Gilberto 202–203
Juanillo 22

Key Bank Scandal 136–138
Key West 58, 80, 94, 99, 124, 132, 166–168
King, Martin Luther, Jr. 148, 151–152, 153
Kingsley, Anna 71–74
Kingsley Zephaniah 72–73, 77
Kingsley Plantation 41, 72–74

Lake City 174
Lansky, Meyer 135–136
Lara, Juan Hernández 201–202
Lavender Scare 154–158
Le Moyne, Jacques 9
Liberty City Riots 181–182
Lindsley, Athalia Ponsell 177–180
López, Narciso 92–94
Lummus Brothers 115
Lynyrd Skynyrd 169

MacGregor, Gregor 39–40
Machado, Gerardo 203–205

Madrigal, Alejandro Bernal 169–171
Marielitos 182–185
Martí, José 97–102
Martyr, Peter 11
Matanzas Massacre 18
McDuffie, Arthur 180–182
McIntosh, John 38, 41–42
McQueen, Don Juan 40–42
Melbourne 5
Menéndez, Francisco 31–32
Menéndez, Pedro 16–20, 112
Miami 113–115, 116, 119–120, 122, 123, 129, 131–132, 134–135, 143, 144, 159–161, 162, 171, 182, 187, 200, 205, 207, 208, 209
Miami Beach 114–115, 136, 205
micanopy 54
Monaghan, Tom 220–222
Moultrie Creek, Treaty of 53–54
Murat, Achille 75–77
Murillo, David-Israel Zenon 217

Natural Bridge, Battle of 86–87
Negrin, Metin 218–219
Negro Fort 46–48
Newsom, Gavin 236–238
9/11 192–194
1926 Hurricane 119–120
Noriega, Manuel 208–210
Norman, Mose 144–145
Norman Studios 109–110, 111

Ocoee Massacre 144–146
Okeechobee Hurricane, 120–122
Olustee, Battle of 84–86
Operation Pastroius 141–142
Ortiz, Juan 13–14
Osceola 54–56, 57, 60–63
Ostend Manifesto 90–92

Palatka 106
Palm Beach 115
Payne's Landing, Treaty of 54
Pensacola 14, 37, 43–44, 50–52
Pinecrest 199
Purple Pamphlet 156–158

Ranson, Andrew 30
Republic of West Florida 45–46
Ribault, Jean 15, 17–18
Rosewood Massacre 146–147

St. Augustine 17–18, 23, 25, 27–32, 37, 43, 75, 106, 150–152, 177–180
St. Johns River 15, 18, 94
St. Petersburg 115
San Mateo 18–19, 21
Sanibel Island 6

Scott Massacre 49-50
Searle, Robert 27-28
Seaside 212-214
Seminole 37, 44, 46, 47, 50, 51-56, 59-65
Siete Partidas 69
Stanford, Alan Griffin, Jr. 178-180
Steinberg, Donald 165

Taino 5, 8
Tallahassee 76, 77, 79, 80, 84, 86-87, 174, 226, 227
Tampa 95, 97, 99, 113, 123-125, 127, 128, 129, 132, 134, 137, 138, 181
Taylor, Fannie 146-147
Taylor, Zachary 63-64
Taylor County 82-84, 88
Tequesta 7
Timucua 7-10, 16, 19-22, 24, 26
Todt, Antony 217-218
Tornado 96
Trafficante, Santo, Jr. 127, 128-131, 137
Trafficante, Santo, Sr. 127
Trafficante, Santo III 137-138
Tuttle, Julia 113-114
2000 U.S. Presidential Election & Recount 188-191, 192

Ulele 13-14
Utina 10

Van Zant, Ronnie 169
Virginius 95-97, 99

Wall, Charlie 125-127
Wellington 201-202
West Florida 43-44, 50-51, 53
Wuornos, Aileen 176-177

Ybor City 100, 124-127, 128
Yulee, David Levy 90-92, 112-113

Zangara, Giuseppe 133-134

www.ingramcontent.com/pod-product-compliance
Lightning Source LLC
Chambersburg PA
CBHW032033300426
44117CB00009B/1048